The Psychic Hold of Slavery

D1596219

DISCARD

The Psychic Hold of Slavery

Legacies in American Expressive Culture

EDITED BY

SOYICA DIGGS COLBERT

ROBERT J. PATTERSON

AND AIDA LEVY-HUSSEN

RUTGERS UNIVERSITY PRESS

NEW BRUNSWICK, NEW JERSEY, AND LONDON

LIBRARY OF CONGRESS CATALOGING-IN-PUBLICATION DATA

Names: Colbert, Soyica Diggs, 1979– editor. | Patterson, Robert J., editor. |
Levy-Hussen, Aida, 1981– editor.
Title: The psychic hold of slavery : legacies in American expressive culture /
edited by Soyica Diggs Colbert, Robert J. Patterson, and Aida Levy-Hussen.
Description: New Brunswick, NJ : Rutgers University Press, 2016. | Includes
bibliographical references and index.
Identifiers: LCCN 2015041072 (print) | LCCN 2015048371 (ebook) | ISBN 9780813583969
(hardback) | ISBN 9780813583952 (pbk.) | ISBN 9780813583976 (e-book (ePub)) |
ISBN 9780813583983 (e-book (Web PDF))
Subjects: LCSH: African Americans—Study and teaching—United States. | American
literature—African American authors—History and criticism. | African Americans in
literature. | BISAC: SOCIAL SCIENCE / Slavery. | LITERARY CRITICISM / American /
African American. | PSYCHOLOGY / Social Psychology. | SOCIAL SCIENCE /
Black Studies (Global). | HISTORY / United States / Civil War Period (1850–1877).
Classification: LCC E184.7 .P79 2016 (print) | LCC E184.7 (ebook) |
DDC 810.9/896073—dc23
LC record available at http://lccn.loc.gov/2015041072

A British Cataloging-in-Publication record for this book is available
from the British Library.

Excerpts from *the new black* © 2011 by Evie Shockley. Reprinted with
permission of Wesleyan University Press.

Visit our website: http://rutgerspress.rutgers.edu

Manufactured in the United States of America

Soyica Diggs Colbert
to Rodger

Robert J. Patterson
to the Spirit

CONTENTS

ACKNOWLEDGMENTS

What ultimately has become *The Psychic Hold of Slavery: Legacies in American Expressive Culture* began as a conversation between Soyica Diggs Colbert and her former colleague Donald Pease. In the spring of 2013, after the November 2011 publication of *The African American Theatrical Body: Reception, Performance, and the Stage*, the Leslie Center for the Humanities' Psychoanalysis Study Group at Dartmouth College invited Colbert to present some of her research on how racial melancholia and mourning function in James Baldwin's *Blues for Mister Charlie*. Following the presentation, Colbert explained that her current research project, "Black Movements: Performance and Politics," was less focused on the psychic dynamics of race and racism. Pease encouraged her to continue to consider how psychoanalysis animates racial dynamics. So, after some thought, Colbert invited Robert J. Patterson and Aida Levy-Hussen to collaborate on the project that became this book.

Patterson's *Exodus Politics: Civil Rights and Leadership in African American Literature and Culture* was published in the fall of 2013. It challenges a growing trend in African American studies of situating current political striving in a post–civil rights context. Patterson's book delineates the paradoxical aims of the civil rights movement, not only to demonstrate what limited artists and activists from achieving their aims during the classic phase of the movement but also to reveal how African American literature written in the late twentieth century offers a future for the freedom dreams conjured in the 1950s and 1960s.

Given Patterson's interest in black cultural production after the classical phase of the civil rights movement, he and Colbert discussed curating a volume that would examine the spate of late twentieth- and early twenty-first century cultural productions about slavery. Aware that Aida Levy-Hussen was in the midst of drafting *How to Read African American Literature: Post–Civil Rights Fiction and the Task of Interpretation*, a forthcoming monograph that draws on psychoanalytic theory to account for African American literature's historical turn and its implications for hermeneutics, they asked her to join them as an editor of their proposed volume.

The editors are grateful for the support and assistance of many people and institutions. They thank New York University Press for permission to reprint chapter 10, "Trauma and the Historical Turn in Black Literary Discourse," which is a modified version of a chapter in Levy-Hussen's forthcoming monograph. In addition, the generosity of Chester Gillis, dean of Georgetown College, and G. William Rebeck, former interim dean of Georgetown University's Graduate School of Arts and Sciences, gave all three editors the opportunity to convene a symposium for workshopping papers that responded to the question "What desires, investments, or identitarian logics account for our inability—or unwillingness—to 'get over' slavery?" The purpose of this symposium was to foster dialogue and generate cohesive chapters engaging a question that currently lies at the heart of cross-disciplinary African Americanist study. The symposium enabled the contributors to begin a discussion that eventually informed the volume as a whole.

The editors would not have been able to carve out either the time or the psychic, emotional, and physical space to edit this volume without the support of family, friends, and colleagues. They thank the contributors for their willingness to participate in a true collaboration; Leslie Mitchner, their acquisitions editor at Rutgers University Press, for her careful stewardship of the volume through each stage of its development; and the reviewers for their helpful feedback, which guided the revision process. They also would like to thank the individuals who read portions of the manuscript before publication. Thank you to Michael Awkward, Erica Edwards, and Meta DuEwa Jones for useful comments and clear feedback. Finally, thank you to Linda Blair for compiling the bibliography.

The Psychic Hold of Slavery

INTRODUCTION

"Do You Want to Be Well?"

SOYICA DIGGS COLBERT

"Do you want to be well?" A question, seemingly so simple, only warrants an affirmative response. But what is wellness, and how do the social conditions that constitute the subject inform the individual's ability to be well? In a world of shifting power relations (according to Michel Foucault), how does the individual's decision to be well relate to the complex context of making decisions in general? And if all decisions are made within the context of the subject's relative and ever-changing relationship to power, then, as the chapters that follow suggest, wellness is a temporally bound state that requires examination of the relationship between trauma of the past and domination in the present.

This book builds on James Baldwin's depiction in *The Fire Next Time* of racism as a national illness that prevents the civic body from being well. It focuses, however, on how the national illness of racism affects black folks. Because we contend that black people exert a constitutive force on the nation-state, we believe that curing the national illness requires examining the effects of racism on black people. The question "Do you want to be well?" assumes that the individual actor has the agency and the ability to incorporate and work through the pasts that ail her.[1]

The original title of our book was *Do You Want to Be Well: The Psychic Hold of Slavery,* a reference to the first line of Toni Cade Bambara's novel *The Salt Eaters* (1980). The novel, which begins "Are you sure, sweetheart, that you want to be well?," features a main character, Velma Henry, who attempts to commit suicide after participating in the 1960s and 1970s civil and women's rights movements. Those events not only haunt Bambara's character but also shaped the work of late twentieth-century black women writers. As Cheryl Wall writes, "to a great extent, the urgent preoccupation with history in the writings of black women in the 1970s and 1980s registered alarm at the potential

1

loss of a history that had never been accurately recorded."[2] Beginning with the 1970 publications of *The Bluest Eye* (Toni Morrison) and *The Third Life of Grange Copeland* (Alice Walker), black women writers sought to recuperate partially documented histories.

Although a resurgent interest in the slave past can be traced to the late sixties, the 1987 publication of Morrison's *Beloved* established the spectral nature of the history of slavery as *the* primary political and epistemological feature of cross-disciplinary African American studies.[3] Morrison posited that exorcising the national ghost of slavery required working through painful histories with no promise of repair. Engaging with traumatic pasts signaled a realization of the psychic, not just juridical, hold of slavery. Morrison's novel, and the vast literature it inspired, presumed that the revelatory power of intellectual engagement would enable a fuller experience of citizenship. One could also understand engaging with the ghosts of history as a part of an ongoing abolitionist project.[4]

By considering the overlap of late twentieth-century projects that seek to understand the power relations that produce antiblackness, *The Psychic Hold of Slavery* animates a question at the heart of black studies today: how can we imagine a political future that responds to antiblack racism in the present as a feature of a long history of black domination? The intrusive force of the past informs the present and future in our formulation, suggesting that time works in a contrapuntal fashion rather than a linear one. In this view, understanding the time of abolition requires understanding abolition not just as a juridical fiat but also as a psychic and social process elaborated in time. In "Fugitive Justice," Stephen Best and Saidiya Hartman famously define *abolition* as an incomplete, future-oriented project. They contend that a justice project "on behalf of the slave (the stateless, the socially dead, and the disposable)" takes place "in the political present." They clarify that "in posing the question of slavery in terms of the incomplete nature of abolition, we are concerned neither with 'what happened then' nor with 'what is owed because of what happened then,' but rather with the contemporary predicament of freedom, with the melancholy recognition of foreseeable futures still tethered to this past."[5]

Critics (including me, as I demonstrate in chapter 7) read "Fugitive Justice" as an assertion of the ongoing impact of transatlantic slavery in the twenty-first century. But Hartman and Best do not confine the "past" in which "the contemporary predicament of freedom" remains tethered to transatlantic slavery but consider how political projects in the present may address contemporary manifestations of slavery. Certainly, as the authors understand, the words *slave* and *abolition* have long associations with transatlantic slavery. Nevertheless, the language of "Fugitive Justice" invites abolitionist projects that rethink what pasts structure the formation of contemporary experiences of statelessness, social death, and disposability. Implicitly, the structuring of the essay's argument also asks us to consider how holding onto certain pasts undercuts justice movements.

Beloved had a powerful impact in shaping the field of African American studies and establishing its ongoing work as an abolitionist project. Thus, it is no surprise that several chapters in *The Psychic Hold of Slavery* use Morrison's work as a touchstone.[6] The book, however, curiously avoids an extensive investigation of *haunting* or the *spectral,* terms that have been key to the recuperative project of late twentieth-century black women writers. Our contributors consider how temporality shapes the twenty-first-century subject's relationship to slavery, forgoing analysis of the ghostly quality of the historical past. (Although all the essays do not agree about the viability or conceivability of the black subject in the context of western domination, I use the formulation here as placeholder.)

In addition to shifting focus from history to temporality and the past, the book examines how and if slavery functions as the most extreme feature of a system of domination that informs and delimits the possibility for western subjects to be well, to be free of the toxicity of racism. It proposes that our inability—or unwillingness—to "get over" slavery emerges in relationship to contemporary philosophical debates about whether slavery serves as the distinguishing feature of black social life. To even begin to consider slavery as a feature of western domination rather than a singular manifestation of it dangerously rubs against the grain of some of the most important works in black studies, including Hortense Spillers's "Mama's Baby, Papa's Maybe." Yet by considering how twenty-first-century manifestations of antiblack violence, dehumanization, disposability, and social death emerge in relationship to pasts and presents, our contributors ask how the late twentieth-century orientation to understanding the impact of transatlantic slavery informs and opens an understanding of our current conjuncture. In other words, the book does not seek to diminish the irrecoverable impact of slavery.

The Psychic Hold of Slavery asks, What desires, investments, or identitarian logics account for our inability—or unwillingness—to get over slavery? The inquiry into the relationship between slavery and antiblack domination in general examines how the primary psychic rubric of loss becomes a discursive device that animates contemporary relationships with slavery as a traumatic historical object. To better understand how the primary loss associated with slavery manifests cultural production and criticism in the twenty-first century, the book takes up poetics, film, drama, the novel, and the cartoon. The compulsion to get over slavery also informs aesthetic practices that negotiate the possibility, or lack thereof, to represent slavery.

Post- and New Blacks

If one critical trend has been the turn toward the past, then another has been the inauguration of a new era in blackness marked by the formulation of post- and new blacks. Set in the wake of mid-twentieth-century freedom movements, Evie Shockley's book of poetry *the new black* meditates on twenty-first-century political and social formations of blackness and how they rethink relationships to the past. *The new black* affirms the saying "Everything old is new again." It participates in "post-black," "post-soul," and other "new black" artists' impulse to define blackness in ways that reflect current historical conditions. All new millennial identifications—post-black, post-soul, and new black—present aesthetic configurations that emerge in relationship to shifting political, social, and purportedly racial contexts. And all three terms attempt to define *blackness* after the classical phase of the civil rights movement.[7]

In the book *Freestyle* that accompanied the exhibition *Freestyle* at the Studio Museum in Harlem, New York, April 28–June 24, 2001, Thelma Golden explains that, as a child of the 1960s and 1970s who came of age during the multicultural movements of the 1980s, "I was intellectually formed by the artist Raymond Saunders' polemic 'Black Is a Color.'" The term *post-black*, which Golden says she developed with the visual artist Glenn Ligon, "characterized . . . artists who were adamant about not being labeled as 'black' artists, though their work was steeped, in fact deeply interested, in redefining complex notions of blackness. In the beginning, there were only a few marked instances of such an outlook, but at the end of the 1990s, it seemed that post-black had fully entered into the art world's consciousness. Post-black was the new black."[8] Golden explains the visual artists' desire to focus attention on their work rather than their identity in order to consider how blackness manifests itself through objects. Context may not be everything, but understanding the implications of post-black as a category depends on its initial use in the visual art world, in which black functions primarily as a color. Golden clarifies that the artists she identifies as post-black jettison the identity of black artist while actively participating in the project of constructing blackness because they believe visual media have the potential to provide new understandings of racial construction that expand upon rather than simply affirm existing political positions. She assigns an avant-garde quality to such activity as a function of its prevalence, not its novelty. In other words, the conjunction of disidentification with the assignation of black artist and participation in the "redefining complex notions of blackness" marked the distinctive combination of post-black artists' and their work.[9]

Moving along a similar line of demarcation, Mark Anthony Neal's *Soul Babies: Black Popular Culture and the Post-Soul Aesthetic* (2002) argues that music is an ideal form to explicate the generational shift in artistic production that emerged in relationship to the *"Regents of the University of California v. Bakke* challenge to affirmative action in 1978." In Neal's view, the post-soul aesthetic "ultimately renders many 'traditional' tropes of blackness dated and even meaningless; in its borrowing from black modern traditions, it is so consumed with its contemporary existential concerns that such traditions are not just called into question but obliterated." In its distinctive departure from tradition, the post-soul aesthetic attempts a "radical reimagining of the contemporary African American experience" in order to "liberate contemporary interpretations of the experience from sensibilities that were formalized and institutionalized during earlier social paradigms."[10] Similar to post-black art, post-soul aesthetics seeks to read contemporary cultural production in relationship to the political and cultural contexts that the production shapes and is shaped by rather than the calcified political and social conditions of a previous generation. Both terms assert that understanding late twentieth-century cultural production requires attending to the distinctive work of periodization after the classical phase of the civil rights movement. Proffering the reciprocal relationship between social formulations and aesthetics ones, the post-soul aesthetic suggests, importantly, that the sensibilities informing earlier aesthetic modes render the formulations themselves ill-fitted for late twentieth- and early twenty-first-century cultural production.

Although Shockley's collection, as evidenced by its title, participates in a reimagining of black aesthetics and politics, it also centers on early twentieth-century attempts (the New Negro Renaissance) to distinguish the work, identity, and political strivings of the Negro as "new."[11] Shockley's collection produces temporal confusion rather than generational distinction. *The new black* begins with "my last modernist poem, #4 (or, re-re-birth of a nation)," which, in the title, situates newness as cyclical process. The poem's first three stanzas read:

> a clean-cut man brings a brown blackness
> to a dream-carved, unprecedented
>   place. some see in this the end of race,
>
> like the end of a race that begins
>   with a gun: a finish(ed) line we might
> finally limp across. for others,
>
>   this miracle marks an end like year's
> end, the kind that whips around again
>   and again: an end that is chilling,
> with a lethal spring coiled in the snow.[12]

As the poem suggests, the civil rights dream of Martin Luther King Jr. expands the American dream to individuals on both sides of the color line. Given the implicit relationship between King's dream and state formation, one can see how the passing of civil rights legislation that ended de jure segregation might function as an early step in the fulfillment of his dream in the inauguration of "a clean-cut man" named Barack Obama to the presidency of the United States of America.[13] Such a rendering of King's dream, however, limits his prophetic vision to the operation of liberal individualism within state formation rather than an understanding of the full flourishing of the democratic state as one facet of the dream.

The poem's language calls attention to the circumscription of King's vision. For example, the description of "a clean-cut man" supports an investment in what Robert J. Patterson describes in chapter 1 as behaviorist modes of uplift that correlate freedom with individual striving. Obama enables an understanding of "brown blackness," a particular kind of blackness that is not as severe, offensive, or troubling as an unmodified blackness. Obama's entrance into the "dream-carved, unprecedented place," remembered today on the national mall by way of the towering statue of King, supports the speaker's claim in "my last modernist poem, #4" that some see in this "the end of race," or at least race as we know it.[14] Similar to the early twentieth century, which oversaw the shift from old to new Negroes, the twenty-first century welcomes the emergence of the new black referenced in the title of Shockley's collection, which denotes a temporal and social shift. The movement from the "clean-cut" "brown-blackness" in the poem to the dream-carved place moves us back in time and places us between two turning points, where we note how the patriarch's passing functions to establish a new orientation to black social life in the late twentieth- and early twenty-first centuries.

The Psychic Hold of Slavery emerges in response to two lines of thought that enable a reading of Obama's inauguration as the teleological unfolding of the civil rights project or "re-re-birth of a nation": the notion of the liberal subject's unfettered access to agency in a millennium unmarked by de jure segregation and a notion of slavery as *a* chapter rather than *the* chapter of black life in the western world. While many (but not all) of the chapters agree with the second line of thought, the volume in general calls into question a black subject's ability to exercise the liberal ideal of self-willed individualism.

The chapters consider how cultural objects (films, novels, poems, dramas), ostensibly about slavery, reveal the impossibility of representing slavery yet mark a temporal feature of domination that elaborates a unique order of subjectivity that may qualify as something else altogether. The ontological position of black people remains contested in black studies and is often deciphered in relationship to Frantz Fanon's assertion, in *Black Skin, White Masks*, that "the black man has no ontological resistance in the eyes of the white man."[15] Chapters 3, 6, and 7 offer distinctive positions about the viability of black subjectivity in a western context, ranging from asserting the being of blackness to making the case for its theoretical impossibility. Arguments from each perspective on black subjectivity draw a relationship between black people as enslaved and the movement toward black people as full citizens.

The movement toward citizenship includes juridical and economic shifts. Given the hundred-year-plus lapse from chattel to voter, property relations distinguish the black citizen-subject.[16] In the poem "improper(ty) behavior," Shockley's *the new black* demonstrates through a series of couplets how racism renders seemingly benign self-willed behaviors improper (from homeownership, to driving, to swimming) because of the actors' legacy as property. The final couplets read:

> post-katrina new orleans is open to anyone with the money to rebuild— except the 9th ward, which they're discouraged from reviving while black.

> it's all about belonging: even now, who belongs where is often based on who belonged to whom. i sometimes wonder how i get away with living while black.[17]

The poem calls to mind the limitations of behaviorist modes of self-actualization within an ongoing system of domination. In post-Katrina New Orleans, the seemingly benign subject position of a homebuyer transforms into an object position in the context of the Ninth Ward because the storm transformed residents into refugees and citizens into objects, ones not even worthy of rescue from a national disaster. As the voice in the final stanza expresses, "it's all about belonging," which suggests that the ongoing nature of domination informs who belongs based on who belonged to whom. Capturing a full sense of national belonging has eluded black diasporic subjects in part because, as Robin Kelley explains, "our entire political and legal foundations were built on an ideology of settler colonialism—an ideology in which the protection of white property rights was always sacrosanct; predators and threats to those privileges were almost always black, brown, and red; and where the very purpose of police power was to discipline, monitor, and contain populations rendered a threat to white property and privilege."[18] Kelley argues that understanding the contemporary operation of antiblack domination, including the murder of Trayvon Martin, requires exploring the deep investment in capital over black humans and seeing blacks as a type of expendable capital. Shockley's "my last modernist poem, #4 (or, re-re-birth of a nation)" makes references to the depiction of the violent policing and murder of black bodies during Reconstruction in D. W. Griffith's film *The Birth of a Nation*. In the renderings of Kelley and Shockley, the national order depends on securing property rights through the domination of black people.

The new black is not only an articulation of the persistent threat of death as a result of "living while black" but also the neoliberal exceptionalism that President Obama or hip hop artist Pharrell Williams experience. In an interview with *GQ* magazine, Williams defines the new black as exemplified in figures such as Oprah Winfrey: "That's the new black. She's a black billionaire" and "President Obama: He is a black American president. . . . That's the new black," as well as "LeBron James: the first black man ever shot on a *Vogue* cover, a black man." He includes himself within the twenty-first-century version of the New Negro: "Me: a guy that's written a song at 40! Nominated for an Oscar, four Grammy awards—at 40! That's the new black! . . . Black ain't a color: Black is a spirit, and it is ubiquitous. . . . We have nothing to be insecure about."[19]

Williams's assertions suggest that the accumulation of a certain amount of property in a certain amount time—by age forty—purchases a new configuration of blackness. His explanation of the term *new black* also invigorates the desire to forget the old black that equated blackness with slavery, loss, or domination, something "to be insecure about." But his attempt to belie an ongoing connection to the old only reinforces the psychic hold of slavery and its legacy because his designation of newness draws attention to a difference from the past that his act of articulation must establish. As Alain Locke did in his period-shaping anthology *The New Negro*, Williams highlights individuals who represent the great achievements within the race, an effort not to forgo blackness but to redefine it as a unique privilege uncoupled from the burdens of victimhood predicated on an alignment of blackness with slavery. As our book suggests, such a focus misreads as incommensurate an individual black person's accumulation of wealth and the ever-evolving practices that reinforce the perpetual state of antiblack domination in the western world. At the same time it points to a debate within our book about the temporal confusion that slavery produces. We consider how twenty-first-century subjects experience a discontinuity between the historical past of slavery and the antiblack domination of the present. The emergence of Williams's new black requires attenuating the hold of slavery while Shockley's *the new black* suggests the racial rebirth of a nation, a cyclical end "like year's end, the kind that whips around again." In Shockley's terms, the cycle produces the at times lethal sting of the whip that enables the specific type of individualization that Williams calls "the new black." The trajectory from chattel to citizen entails forward progression that does not account for the whip and whirl of black time experienced, for example, in the return of redlining in Chicago, which pulls twenty-first-century loan applicants back to the deferral of the mid-twentieth-century dream of homeownership.[20]

The Time of Slavery

The first stanza of Shockley's "my last modernist poem, #4 (or, re-re-birth of a nation)" puns on race as an identity category and an embodied activity. The idea of running a race emerges more fully in the second stanza to suggest the possibility of a finish line and triumph. The constitution of an identity through action, once again, calls into question the relationship between being and doing, black being and living, as blackness bounces from property to (im)-proper behavior. In the second stanza of "my last modernist poem, #4" race becomes something to be conquered or lost. This is the problem of the twenty-first century, the "finish(ed) line of race."[21] This is a line that the chapters in this volume trouble. Yet while all of them call into question the finitude of the racial project, the authors vary on the implication of how we demarcate the time of slavery. Douglas A. Jones Jr., for example, critiques the impulse to present "the present as affectively and ethically bound by the slave past," while GerShun Avilez, through a reading of the play *Unfinished Women*, argues that "halted time, suggesting the end of time, history, or life—arguably the realm of death," constitutes the positions of the characters in the play that live within the contexts of the social death that slavery sets into motion. The renderings of time in Jones's and Avilez's chapters situate the late twentieth century or early twenty-first century in relationship to the time of slavery, suggesting a correlation or stark distinction between the experience of then and now. Time signifies duration and temporality, the experience of the long or short duration, which differs from the constitution of a period through the writing of history. The assumption of temporal progression underpins the narration of history, but the two knowledge structures function not only in relationship to one another but also, as Avilez and I suggest, in opposition to one another when histories require temporal linearity.

Making the book's strongest statement about the foundational nature of temporality to understandings of slavery, Calvin Warren's chapter asserts:

> Our conceptions of slavery have overwhelmingly been historiographi-cal, and historiography traffics the metaphysical violence of temporality that engenders it. The event-horizon that structures modern thought and meaning is reduced to a mere scientific object with a beginning (supposedly 1619) and an end (supposedly 1865). It is this violence that determines the way in which we talk about slavery, that it is something we can get over, control, calculate, and dominate. . . . Slavery is pre-cisely a surplus that resists scientific capture, despite the indefatigable effort of metaphysics to dominate it. The "time of slavery," then, is a temporality outside of metaphysical time; it is time that fractures into an infinite array of absurdities, paradoxes, and contradictions. It is precisely this "time" outside of time that we must confront when we discuss slavery.

Warren makes the case that slavery constitutes a problem for metaphysics. As an event-horizon and not an object to be dominated, it structures mod-ern thought. Therefore, getting over slavery constitutes getting over modern thought. The impossibility of getting over the latter correlates with the former. As Tavia Nyong'o argues in *The Amalgamation Waltz: Race Performance and the Ruses*, "temporality is not simply the neutral medium within which structures like 'heritage' and 'race' appear but an effect that their deployment in thought and action produces."[22] To examine the time of slavery, then, engenders a different line of thought than analysis of the history of slavery because it emphasizes *how* instead of *what*.

Temporality informs the shape of history and, in the case of the Avilez chapter as well as mine, curves the "finish(ed) line" of race. Similarly, "my last modernist poem, #4 (or, re-re-birth of a nation)" in the title and final stanza produces repeated finality. The title suggests that the author has written her final modernist poem four times, resulting in two revisions of Griffith's influential text. The filmmaker's tale of Civil War and Reconstruction sutures together a national order with threads of racialized violence and subordination in order to reaffirm teleological uniformity. Instead of understanding Reconstruction as a brief detour from the racial order of things in the United States, Griffith's film positions it as enabling and requiring the progressive unfolding of antiblack violence.

Shockley's poem multiplies the title of Griffith's work to disrupt narrations of national cohesion predicated on affirmation of racial hierarchies or the promise, as Nyong'o investigates, of a national transcendence of race.[23] The poem ironically reconciles the newness of the nation through a resurrection. Similar to the biblical depiction of Lazarus, the poem likens endings to returns. Following a line that marks a break in an electronic document, the final stanza of the poem states:

> ask lazarus about miracles:
> the hard part comes afterwards. he stepped
>   into the reconstruction of his
> life, knowing what would come, but not how.

The breaks, repetition, and time stamps (that is, "last," "modernist," "end," and "reconstruction") situate temporality in the break, to borrow from the title of Fred Moten's important critical work.[24] As I have written elsewhere (borrowing from Thomas DeFrantz's theorization), the break creates space in the music for improvisational or choreographed dance; it operates in excess of the music structuring time outside of the time of the song.[25] The break disrupts the flow while being constitutive of the whole performance of bringing song in relationship to dance. The break in "my last modernist poem, #4" recalibrates the poem toward a somewhat unknown futurity. The poem's unfinished business provides room for the ongoing abolitionist project, moving forward with the knowledge that the limited gains of the classical phase of the civil rights movement were nothing short of miraculous.[26]

Domination As a Feature of American Life

By considering the nature of freedom as a feature of domination, the last sentence of Shockley's poem, "he stepped into the reconstruction of his life, knowing what would come, but not how," elaborates one of the central philosophical threads of our book. In chapter 1, Robert J. Patterson contends that slavery "is only a *manifestation* of the larger, more complicated problem that propels that plot [of *12 Years a Slave*]—a globalized antiblack racism." His claim boldly suspends the long-held belief that slavery functions as the primary historical feature of American social life and instead focuses on how "antiblack racism" constitutes national belonging. Patterson foregrounds the volume's overall concern with how to relate contemporary experiences of antiblack racism to past ones without collapsing the differences between then and now.

Our book is organized to introduce its central themes through analysis of (1) the time of slavery, (2) the possibility or impossibility of representing slavery, and (3) the operation of memory in nation building. Through an exploration of film, drama, fiction, performance art, and the graphic novel as modes of cultural production, the chapters examine how artists confront the push and pull of slavery, the "re-re-birth of a nation," in the context of twenty-first-century depictions of the slave past as at best usable and at worst baggage that weighs black folks down.[27] Working through different genres, each chapter takes up one or more of the aforementioned themes. In his examination of Steve McQueen's 2013 film *12 Years a Slave* (chapter 1), Patterson questions the ability to represent slavery in film. His chapter investigates "how representational strategies compel or foreclose a range of affective responses, such as shock, inspiration, guilt, or terror." In addition, it asks "how representations of slavery mediate messages about the nature of antiblack oppression and the modes of agency and resistance exercised by African Americans." Patterson argues that the film depends on "behaviorist discourses" to engender sympathy for its protagonist that ignore the structures that sustain black domination. Moreover, he interrogates what connects cultural production, representational politics, and political desires, examining if filmic representation has the ability to advance political strivings.

In chapter 2, Douglas A. Jones Jr. analyzes how Terrance Hayes's poem "The Avocado" uses the imagery of guacamole to represent the slave past as a historical mashup that generates a contemporary manifestation but critiques how we got from tit to tat. In Jones's words, "simply put, the world *has* changed; thus, the conditions for black political belonging and the attendant terms of critical inquiry and imaginative narration, if they are to be efficacious, must change along with it." Given the most recent spate of antiblack violence that has consumed national attention (involving Jordan Davis, Renisha McBride, Michael Brown, Eric Garner, Tamir Rice, Walter Scott, Freddie Gray, Sandra

Bland, and others), the stakes of considering how to develop an efficacious abolitionist movement for the present could not be higher.

Turning a critical eye toward new discourses of post-racialism, Calvin Warren (chapter 3) argues that the heart of the compulsion to get over a history of racial trauma produces a crisis of time and objectivity; in order to get over anything, one must first objectify and then temporally demarcate injury. Building on this premise, Warren posits that such rhetoric "expresses a metaphysical 'will to power,' a desire to dominate time in the twenty-first century. Thus, it is not surprising that many proponents of getting over slavery use a restricted temporal grammar—slavery was 'back then,' 'this is now,' 'we're moving forward.'" According to him, this kind of language positions slavery as something to be conquered that we can fix and move past. He argues that the imperative to get over slavery is intertwined with "the constitutive violence of the metaphysical enterprise."

Concerned with the manifestation of the time of slavery in terms of psychic dynamics, Margo Natalie Crawford (chapter 4) examines the co-temporality of slavery and freedom through an examination of Toni Morrison's novel *A Mercy* and a set of texts that Crawford calls "post-neo-slave narratives." According to Sigmund Freud, melancholia is a state of being bound by a loss so significant that it cannot be overcome, leaving the individual unable to move forward. Mourning, conversely, consists of processes to work through past trauma. To explicate the simultaneity of slavery and freedom, Crawford argues that post-neo-slave narratives produce melancholy and mourning, which "[help] us learn to read a certain type of black resistance that is often illegible: the traumatized subjects' holding on to historical trauma in order to *repossess* the history that *possesses* them." The toggling back and forth between object (being possessed) and subject (repossessing) functions as a useful location for her because it affirms the unknowability of slavery and invites the reader to reclaim the liberatory properties of blackness.

Régine Michelle Jean-Charles (chapter 5) links the work of our book to the recuperative orientation of the black women writers' project of the late-twentieth century and draws attention to the relationship between memory and national building in France and Haiti. She explores the tropes of forgetting and remembering by analyzing works about the Haitian slave past: the film *Toussaint Louverture* (2012) and the novel *Rosalie l'infâme* (2003), translated as *The Infamous Rosalie* (2013). Her critique reveals how "memorial discourse is fraught with political anxieties about how best to represent group identity." She argues that collective memory reflects not only national desires about how to live in the present but also the way in which the public chooses to frame the past through acts of collective memory.

GerShun Avilez (chapter 6) explores contemporary meanings of *social death*, an influential theoretical concept that the sociologist Orlando Patterson coined to describe the status of the enslaved, which, arguably, situates them outside of western temporalities. In dialogue with prominent Afro-pessimist critics such as Jared Sexton and Frank Wilderson, Avilez rethinks the temporal boundaries that accompany Patterson's original theorization. Because social death, according to him, describes black lived experience, he turns specifically to drama, a genre "that is constitutively attuned to enactment and embodiment, as a means for exploring how social death anticipates the form and content of black expressive culture." The chapter analyzes Aishah Rahman's play *Unfinished Women Cry in No Man's Land While a Bird Dies in a Gilded Cage* (1977), "which presents the gendered dynamics that characterized U.S. enslavement as the dominant framework for articulating the possibilities of owning the self." Through its readings, the chapter shows how performance blurs the boundaries between times to demonstrate the psychic hold of slavery and undermine "the psychic and material spaces this institution has created."

In my analysis of Spike Lee's *Bamboozled* (chapter 7), I analyze how the history of commodity and cultural production in the United States circumscribes blackness in the twenty-first century and limits black people's ability to upset the governing norms of racial (mis)representation in film. I also show how filmic technologies upset perceptions of blackness's appearance as limited to the white gaze in order to call attention to twenty-first-century filmic techniques that demonstrate the possibility of black ontology within that frame.

Brandon J. Manning (chapter 8) examines a satirical piece of cultural production, "The Nigger Pixie" sketch from Dave Chappelle's *Chappelle's Show,* and argues that Chappelle's limited influence on the means of production interfered with the sketch's critique of racism. As *Bamboozled* did, *Chappelle's Show* sought to satirize U.S. race relations but instead became a satire of black cultural makers' attempts to critically intervene in racial hierarchies. Chappelle's attention to his inability to control the distribution and reception of his show ultimately led him to abandon the project. The unraveling of *Chappelle's Show* serves as the backdrop for chapter 8's questioning of the utility of satire as a form of racial critique in the post-soul era.

Exploring slavery's representation in a primarily visual form, Michael Chaney (chapter 9) examines the graphic novels *Nat Turner* and *Incognegro* and argues that "figuring the slave in cartoonal drawings permits artists a measure of distance from the prohibitions, interdictions, and martyrlogical sanctities of the slave." The chapter engages with our book's larger question of how to represent slavery, suggesting that the cartoonal offers a way to memorialize slavery without pinning it down to specific causal relationships, chronologies, or historical "facts." Similar to Morrison's claim in "The Site of Memory," the chapter asserts that the cartoonal reveals truths about contemporary culture but that those truths do not necessarily align with truths about slavery. Chaney suggests that the visual economy of the graphic novel avoids the limitation of language to express the loss associated with slavery, offering images instead. The images do not attempt to fill the gaps in the archive but provide another way of knowing.

Aida Levy-Hussen (chapter 10) redirects much of the book's conversation, shifting from the feasibility of representing slavery to the affective dynamics that motivate the desire to represent it. She examines Morrison's *Beloved* and David Bradley's *The Chaneysville Incident* to demonstrate that the psychic form of trauma inhabits and drives "the rhetorical form of the contemporary narrative of slavery." Her chapter meditates on investments in remembering and forgetting, taking into consideration impulses to "regard the contemporary narrative of slavery as redemptive on the one hand or inhibitive on the other."

In the book's brief conclusion, Robert J. Patterson reasserts its central questions. Why can't black people get over slavery? And why might they not want to get over it? He demonstrates how the long shadow of slavery serves to diminish black life and offers substantive evidence of the devaluing of black life as a provocation for action

We stand at the precipice, the re-rebirth of a nation. Although the physical conditions of nineteenth-century slavery do not resemble our twenty-first-century instances of disenfranchisement, the violent conditions of being black in the United States remain self-evident in the persistent killing of unarmed black children, men, and women. If slavery inaugurated the ontological condition of black being, we would do well to consider how the indiscriminate killing of black people in the twenty-first century relates to a long history of black life matters. Put another way, our book suggests that the persistence of antiblack violence in the present necessitates attending to that violence as the recurrence of not the thing itself but a nation-shaping psychic dynamic.

NOTES

1. For further discussion of the opening line of Bambara's novel and the trope of wellness in her work, see Linda J. Holmes and Cheryl A. Wall, *Savoring the Salt: The Legacy of Toni Cade Bambara* (Philadelphia: Temple University Press, 2008), part 6; and Robert J. Patterson, "Do You Want to Be Well? The Gospel Play, Womanist Theology, and Tyler Perry's Artistic Project," *Journal of Feminist Studies in Religion* 30 (fall 2014): 41–56.

2. Cheryl Wall, *Worrying the Line: Black Women Writers, Lineage, and Literary Tradition* (Chapel Hill: University of North Carolina Press, 2005), 7. Wall is one of several critics, including Hortense Spillers, Mary Helen Washington, Angelyn Mitchell, and Hazel Carby, who consider how black women write themselves into history.

3. See Avery Gordon, *Ghostly Matters: Haunting and the Sociological Imagination* (Minneapolis: University of Minnesota Press, 1997).

4. On the relationship between blackness and national narratives, see Toni Morrison, *Playing in the Dark: Whiteness and the Literary Imagination* (New York: Vintage, 1993).

5. Stephen Best and Saidiya Hartman, "Fugitive Justice," *Representations* 92 (autumn 2005): 5.

6. For arguments about the field-defining impact of *Beloved,* see Stephen Best, "On Failing to Make the Past Present," *Modern Language Quarterly* 73 (September 2012): 453–474; Walter Benn Michaels, *The Shape of the Signifier: 1967 to the End of History* (Princeton, N.J.: Princeton University Press, 2004); and Henry Louis Gates Jr. and Kwame Anthony Appiah, *Toni Morrison: Critical Perspectives Past and Present* (Princeton, N.J.: Princeton University Press, 2004).

7. For a consideration of the periodization of the civil rights movement, see Jacquelyn Dowd Hall, "The Long Civil Rights Movement and the Political Uses of the Past," *Journal of American History* 91 (March 2005): 1233–1263.

8. Thelma Golden, "Post-Black," in *Freestyle,* ed. Christine Y. Kim and Franklin Sirmans (New York: Studio Museum of Harlem, 2001), 14.

9. Ibid., 3.

10. Mark Anthony Neal, *Soul Babies: Black Popular Culture and the Post-Soul Aesthetic* (New York: Routledge, 2002), 3.

11. For an examination of the repeated newness of the New Negro, see Henry Louis Gates, "The Trope of the New Negro and the Reconstruction of the Image of the Black," *Representations* 24 (fall 1988): 129–155.

12. Evie Shockley, *the new black* (Middletown, Conn.: Wesleyan University Press, 2011), 1.

13. For analysis of the relationship between civil rights aspirations and Obama's inauguration, see Erica Edwards, *Charisma and the Fictions of Black Leadership* (Minneapolis: University of Minnesota Press, 2012); Gene Andrew Jarrett, *Representing the Race: A New Political History of African American Literature* (New York: New York University Press, 2011); Robert J. Patterson, *Exodus Politics: Civil Rights and Leadership in African American Literature and Culture* (Charlottesville: University of Virginia Press, 2013); and David Remnick, "The Joshua Generation," *New Yorker,* November 17, 2008, http://www.newyorker.com/magazine/2008/11/17/the-joshua-generation, accessed December 16, 2015.

14. Shockley, *the new black,* 1.

15. Frantz Fanon, *Black Skin, White Masks,* trans. Charles Markmann (New York: Grove, 1967), 110.

16. In *The Souls of Black Folk,* W.E.B. Du Bois considers black subjects' relationship to property as he describes Reconstruction and his direct engagement with Booker T. Washington.

17. Shockley, *the new black,* 60.

18. Robin Kelley, "The US v. Trayvon Martin," *Counterpunch,* July 15, 2013, http://www.counterpunch.org/2013/07/15/the-us-v-trayvon-martin/, accessed March 15, 2014.

19. Zach Baron, "Pharrell Williams on Advanced Style Moves and That Oscar Snub: My Song 'Will Be Here for 10 Years,'" *GQ,* March 25, 2014, http://www.gq.com/story/pharrell-williams-oscar-snub, accessed April 20, 2014.

20. See Ta-Nehisi Coates, "The Case for Reparations," *Atlantic,* May 21, 2014, http://www.theatlantic.com/features/archive/2014/05/the-case-for-reparations/361631, accessed December 28, 2015.

21. I borrow from W.E.B. Du Bois's well-known line from *The Souls of Black Folk* (1903): "the problem of the Twentieth Century is the problem of the color-line" ([New York: Barnes and Noble Classics, 2003], 17).

22. Tavia Nyong'o, *The Amalgamation Waltz: Race Performance and the Ruses* (Minneapolis: University of Minnesota Press, 2009), 10.

23. See ibid., intro.

24. Fred Moten, *In the Break: The Aesthetics of the Black Radical Tradition* (Minneapolis: University of Minnesota Press, 2003).

25. See Soyica Diggs Colbert, *Black Movements*, manuscript; and Thomas F. DeFrantz, "Performing the Breaks: Notes on African American Aesthetic Structures," *Theater* 40 (November 2010): 31–37.

26. Given the revolutionary aims of the civil rights movement and its primarily juridical victories during its classical phase (1954–1965), theorists such as Robert J. Patterson have made the case for its ongoing work. In contrast, Shockley's poem calls attention to the gargantuan effort that enabled the change of law and the possibilities for political action that the changes engendered.

27. George Wolfe's *The Colored Museum* (New York: Broadway Play Publishers, 1987) likens the slave past and traumatic histories to baggage that will be trashed if unclaimed. Christina Sharpe makes a similar point about usable and unusable pasts in *Monstrous Intimacies: Making Post-Slavery Subjects* (Durham, N.C.: Duke University Press, 2010), as does M. Jacqui Alexander in *Pedagogies of Crossing* (Durham, N.C.: Duke University Press, 2006).

1

12 Years a What?

Slavery, Representation, and Black Cultural Politics in *12 Years a Slave*

ROBERT J. PATTERSON

We tend to privilege experience itself, as if black life is lived experience outside of representation. We have only, as it were, to express what we already know we are. Instead, it is only through the way in which we represent and imagine ourselves that we come to know how we are constituted and who we are. There is no escape from the politics of representation.[1]

–Stuart Hall

The concept of American chattel slavery primarily animates Steve McQueen's Oscar-winning film *12 Years a Slave* (2013). Or, does it? Adapted from Solomon Northup's emancipatory narrative *Twelve Years a Slave: Narrative of Solomon Northup, a Citizen of New-York, Kidnapped in Washington City in 1841, and Rescued in 1853, from a Cotton Plantation near the Red River in Louisiana* (1853), the film has been acclaimed as one of the best filmic representations of slavery. Admirers note that it depicts the peculiar institution unflinchingly, accentuating how black life existed in a matrix of violence, evil, and immorality.[2] But in the extant criticism and reviews, the term *best* neither offers an aesthetic judgment nor assesses the accuracy of the adaptation. Rather, it draws attention to how the film, as an adaptation, engenders expectations about truth and accuracy that are central to the film's reception and that fit within a range of critical discourses about black cultural products and production. While directors and producers have the prerogative to choose the degree to which their representations will converge with an original narrative (which is also only a representation), the meaning of those choices cohere within, and always are informed by, a broader discursive context.[3]

Critical examinations of the film thus must ask a variety of questions that engage the complexities of these convergences and diverges. What does it mean, for example, to represent the violence of slavery on the big screen? Is the purpose to shock, inspire, or incapacitate? How do representational strategies compel or foreclose a range of affective responses, such as shock, inspiration, guilt, or terror? How might racialized audiences identify with or against the history of slavery? And how do representations of slavery mediate messages about the nature of antiblack oppression and the modes of agency and resistance that African Americans exercised? In thinking through these questions, I propose two interrelated arguments. First, by demonstrating how behaviorist discourses also inform McQueen's representation of Northup's life and chattel slavery, I contend that the movie's representation of black inequality privileges behavioral explanations over structural ones. Whereas structural examinations of black inequality examine how institutions are set up in explicit and implicit ways that thwart black thriving, behaviorist explanations contrastingly consider black people's (in)action as the cause and effect of their unequal access to and outcomes within America's institutions. Second, I question the degree to which representation—which is an important cultural force for catalyzing political action and engagement and memorializing history—can achieve our cultural and political desires.

12 Years a Slave reveals the remarkable story of New York citizen Solomon Northup (played by Chiwetel Ejiofor), whose life becomes unimaginably altered when, capitalizing on his talent as a violinist, duplicitous white men sell him into slavery. Viewers see Northup move through and survive horrid, life-threatening conditions in which slavery and owners repeatedly test his resolve. After a short period on the plantation of Master Ford (Benedict Cumberbatch), Northup is sold into *harsher* conditions as punishment for defending himself against the harassment of an overseer. His price for living is that he must endure a *Christian* master; he ultimately ends up on a plantation in Louisiana, where he and other enslaved African Americans are subjected to the cruelty of their owners, Master Epps (Michael Fassbender) and Mistress Epps (Sarah Paulson). Northup's lot finally changes when he meets an abolitionist (Brad Pitt), who works to *authenticate* his identity as a free man, and Northup leaves the plantation to be reunited with his family.

Northup's narrative guides the tale yet makes space for other important narratives to emerge. Most significant are the stories of Patsey (Lupita Nyong'o), whose status as the master's prized sexual object makes her the primary target of the mistress's venom, and Mistress Shaw (Alfre Woodard), a black woman who has married her former master and with him co-owns enslaved African Americans. Through Mistress Shaw's character, the film, like Edward P. Jones's novel *The Known World* (2003), highlights the historical fact that black people also enslaved Africans. Yet the movie does not invoke this historical anomaly to absolve white guilt. Rather, its inclusion demonstrates how, to borrow Soyica Diggs Colbert's logic, the institution of slavery unhinges "certain *givens* about will, agency, individuality, and responsibility" (see chapter 7). That is, the governing laws of the peculiar institution constrain Mistress Shaw's decision to co-enslave Africans; the ethics of choice cannot be understood outside of slavery's more general perversions.

Further demonstrating this idea, Alexander Weheliye astutely explains:

> As modes of analyzing and imagining the practices of the oppressed in the face of extreme violence—although this is also applicable more broadly—resistance and agency assume full, self-present, and coherent subjects working against something or someone. Which is not to say that agency and resistance are completely irrelevant in this context, just that we might want to come to a more layered and improvisational understanding of extreme subjection if we do not decide in advance what forms its disfigurations should take on.[4]

By drawing attention to the "extreme subjection" that governs the quotidian aspects of enslaved African Americans' lives, *12 Years* invites viewers to see how ubiquitous slavery was—from individual states to the country, from the national to the international, from the private to the public sphere, from the physical to the spiritual, from the impersonal to the intimate. The major and minor subplots and characters are essential for establishing this context. Through them, we see the inner workings of the institution and the significance of the community that the enslaved forge and build. Indeed, without them, it would be impossible to understand the full import of Northup's tale.

By dramatizing the enslavement of a *free* black man from the North, *12 Years a Slave* demonstrates how the institution of slavery threatens the freedom of *all* black citizens. It shows how slavery destabilizes the black, heterosexual, middle-class familial unit by removing the black patriarchal figure from the household, thus revealing "the perviousness of the family to the incursions of capital and the state."[5] In addition, it shows how slavery foregrounds black bodies as repositories for white sexual pleasure and pain by diminishing the possibility that those black bodies will experience sexual pleasure outside of the parameters of objectification. It also reveals how slavery impedes the development of an interracial feminist ethic by demonstrating the collusive forces of racialized patriarchies and how slavery attempts to destroy black agency, dignity, and psychological wholeness by thing-ifying black subjects.[6]

Our knowledge that the film is based on the autobiographical narrative of a formerly enslaved African American reinforces the point that the horrors of slavery are real and unexaggerated and that the violence McQueen represents is accurate. Yet such immediate authentication may miss the point that Northup's narrative, like Frederick Douglass's *Narrative of the Life of Frederick Douglass, an American Slave, Written by Himself* (1845), Henry Box Brown's *Narrative of the Life of Henry Box Brown, Written by Himself* (1851), Harriet Jacobs's *Incidents in the Life of a Slave Girl: Written by Herself* (1861), and Elizabeth Keckley's *Behind the Scenes, or Thirty Years a Slave, and Four Years in the White House* (1868), was a consciously constructed tale that responded to its multiple reading publics. Dwight McBride thoughtfully analyzes these "discursive audiences":

> This discursive reader, which the slave implied in his or her testimony, is in fact a confluence of political, moral, and social discursive concerns that animate, necessitate, and indeed make possible slave testimony itself. . . . The discursive reader, for the slave witness, is the imagined horizon wherein the pro-slavery advocates (and their arguments for slavery), the abolitionists (from the sentimental moralists to the staunchly political Garrisonians), and the ongoing debates between these two over slavery (which are characterized by such discursive sites as black humanity, natural rights, the Christian morality of slavery, the treatment of slaves under slavery, etc.) come together as an entity that will be the recipient of the slave's testimony.[7]

Suspending, for a moment, the question of authenticity, I argue that McQueen's film, even in the twenty-first century, has to be thought about in the context of both its historical and contemporary discursive audiences. Will contemporary viewers, for example, interpret the film's representations as overly politicized sensational accounts that misconstrue the horrors of the benign system? Will contemporary audiences identify parallels between slavery and modern black dispossession and disenfranchisement—that is, be able to distinguish between behaviorist and structuralist barriers to black political and social advancement? Can the film engage issues of racism without the label *racist* foreclosing upon substantive discussion and action? While the institution is certainly peculiar, it unequivocally is not benign.

In her essay "Tuning into Precious," Erica R. Edwards explains that adaptations can allow narratives "to find wider and more diverse audiences" but often do so by collapsing "radical, collectivist politics [of black feminism]" with "rhetoric of self-help and individual success." She posits that post–civil rights cinematic adaptations of radical black women's literary texts feed into a black popular cultural feminism and, as a consequence, undermine the radical politics that are central to the original narrative's unfolding.[8] That is, by omitting aspects of the narrative that eschew "rhetoric of self-help and individual success," adaptations reinforce the dominant order. As evidenced by Stephen Spielberg's (1987) adaptation of Alice Walker's novel *The Color Purple* (1982), commercial cinematic adaptations often fail to adequately analyze the political and cultural institutions—such as family and patriarchy—within which the plot unfolds. Instead, they focus on individual behaviors to explain black disenfranchisement and difference. I extend Edwards's claim to post–civil rights era cinematic productions of slavery to show how her critique applies more generally to adaptations of African American texts. For despite the film's commitment to more deeply examining slavery's intricacies and legacies, it does not explicate how ideas about capitalism, the nuclear family, hetero-patriarchy, masculinity, and femininity intersect with racist, sexist, and heterosexist ideologies to further contextualize the wide reach of slavery's arm. By noting moments when this critique might have occurred, we see how behaviorist explanations may become privileged over structural ones.

My preliminary overview of the film may seem to buttress arguments that situate slavery as the movie's primary concern. Yet slavery is only a *manifestation* of the larger, more complicated problem that propels that plot—a globalized antiblack racism—that is embedded not simply in American institutions, ideologies, and public policies. Racism, much to the detriment of black people, is also embedded in the ideas and dreams that black people are encouraged to have—the nuclear family and capitalist middle-class identity. This contradiction produces what Lauren Berlant theorizes as "cruel optimism: a relation of attachment to compromised conditions of possibility whose realization is discovered either to be impossible, sheer fantasy, or too possible, and toxic. What's cruel about these attachments, and not merely inconvenient or tragic, is that the subjects who have x in their lives might not well endure the loss of their object/ scene of desire even though its presence threatens their well-being."[9] The idea here is that racism is so deeply embedded within and occluded by the fabric of American society that almost any desire African Americans may have will be circumscribed by racist ideologies.

Slavery and antiblack racism arguably are both institutions and structures; but as analytical rubrics, their discursive power differs in significant ways. On the one hand, our post–civil rights era, post–Jim and Jane Crow era, and post-racial age of Obama has complicated any examination of slavery and racism: the prefix *post-* tends to render each of the eras into a bygone time period that lacks long-lasting historical effects. On the other, while the Thirteenth Amendment abolished slavery and the modern civil rights movement removed *legalized* Jane and Jim Crow segregation, global black racism has not ended. Instead, it has been restructured and, indeed, become more entrenched, calcified, and insidious.

One might cite the color-blindness movement that emerged on the political right in the 1970s as an example of how the shift away from structural analyses continues to haunt public conversations about race. By ignoring racism's structural embeddedness, the logic of color-blindness perniciously worked to characterize black disenfranchisement as a product of black people's own shortcomings. Perverting the *antiracist* rhetoric of color-blindness, which anti–civil rights proponents originally forged in the civil rights movement, opponents of black civil rights argued for the removal of race as a factor for consideration when such consideration would work to redress historical exclusion and its ongoing legacies of bias. (See, for example, the anti–affirmative action debates of the 1990s.) A consequence has been the erosion of civil rights gains for African Americans. Our best examinations of *12 Years* must then think about how McQueen's representation of slavery uses the peculiar institution to foreground how antiblack racism has continued to threaten the democratic nation and to demonstrate a historical teleology that maps out black disenfranchisement as a longstanding, institutionalized, and structural problem in the United States.

Behaviors and Structures: *12 Years a Slave* in Context

Northup's loss of freedom and citizenship rights draws attention to how slavery threatens the freedom of the entire republic and is not a sectional issue confined to the South. McQueen emphasizes this point by juxtaposing Northup's jail cell with the White House, the ultimate expression of democracy and freedom, to elucidate how black subjects live without basic citizenship rights. Early in the film, Northup arrives in Washington, D.C., with his "business partners" Mr. Brown and Mr. Hamilton and, after a successful week of musical performances, has a generally convivial dinner with them. When Northup becomes ill, Hamilton and Brown escort him to his room, assuring him that he will awake feeling "refreshed." Though they suggest that inebriation causes his illness, the fact that he awakens shackled and is then effectually sold into slavery suggests that he may have been purposely inebriated or drugged.

Now he has a new responsibility to prove his status as a free black man. While the chains mark his status as a bondsman, he remains self-assured, only to learn his first lesson in slavery—that assertions of manhood are incompatible with the servility slavery demands. When the slave breaker enters, for example, Northup asserts, "My name is Solomon Northup. I'm a free man, a resident of Saratoga, New York, the residence of my wife and children, who are equally free, and you have no right whatsoever to detain me. And, I promise, I promise you upon my liberation I will have satisfaction for this wrong."[10] At this early point in the film, he still believes that his liberation is imminent and reminds the viewer that he has two important markers of freedom and citizenship: a state-recognized family and the *legal* right to protect himself as a free man ("satisfaction for this wrong"). But the unnamed white overseers dispel this notion when they ask him to produce his "freedom papers."

The tenuous nature of freedom and the precarious nature of black masculinity during slavery quickly become visible. Northup lacks both the documentation to prove he is not "a slave, a Georgia slave," who has "run away," as well as the spirit of deference that unchecked submission requires. One overseer attempts to break Northup by beating him into submission. He breaks a paddle on Northup's back before whipping him, compelling Northup to acknowledge he "ain't a free man" but a "Georgia runaway" and, more precisely, a "runaway nigger." As the overseer leaves Northup crying in pain, he remarks, "You're not any free man." As Northup begins to stand up to look through his barred window, the scene fades, and directly across from his cell the viewer sees the White House. Simultaneously, his cries of "help me" become less audible. McQueen's introduction of the White House at this moment further demonstrates how the government remained (and continues to remain) deaf and otherwise indifferent to millions of bondsmen, bondswomen, and otherwise disenfranchised African Americans. If symbols of democracy and freedom are important because they draw attention to a paradox "of an American civic myth whose promise of equality continually disputes the reality of African American life," the juxtaposition of the cell and house accentuates the degree to which African American life falls outside of American civic myths.[11]

The unfolding of this scene is crucial to understanding behaviorist and structuralist explanations of black dispossession and black inequality as well as how this film, perhaps unconsciously, privileges behaviorist explanations to make its claims against racism. Heretofore, the movie has focused on the mundane aspects of Northup's life, including his relationship with his wife, Ann, his status as father, his economic mobility (as demonstrated by his modest home and ability to earn money by playing the violin), and his respected status within his community. In other words, as Andrea Williams suggests in her analysis of the "single" trope in the film, marriage has given Northup a way to avoid "civic and social marginality" insofar as social death is about "threats, affects, and experiences that accompany the conditions of living single."[12] That is, the movie presents him as an upstanding, middle-class black man who, having capitalized on his access to society's institutions, including marriage and paid labor, has succeeded in *becoming* "a (black) man." If, as Maurice Wallace argues, "man-making . . . is scarcely a different enterprise than image-making in either the private lodges or public lives of black men," this image of Northup confirms that he is a law-abiding citizen who has reaped the benefits of citizenship.[13] In other words, Northup embodies the black Protestant work ethic; it is at least implied that his hard work has aided his success. Contrast his case with those who exist in contemporary society, in which the "waning of the Protestant work ethic—hard work, deferred gratification, frugality, and responsibility," putatively explains and justifies black disenfranchisement.[14]

Northup's kidnapping, however, not only demonstrates the tenuous nature of freedom and manhood for black men but also upends the notion that the Protestant work ethic insulates him from the effects of antiblack racism. Nonetheless, the ethic's debt to the self-made man mythology gives McQueen an entry point for tapping into the consciousness and psyches of the audiences, encouraging an identification with Northup. As Monica Ndounou reveals in her important examination of the economic considerations that surround film production, movies that prominently portray black people or black themes (inasmuch as slavery is thought of as a black problem and not an American one), "studios want movies with crossover appeal, which Jesse Rhines defines as 'the potential of a film addressing nonwhite American concerns to secure a significant financial return from white American viewers.'"[15] In other words, pecuniary interests also shape McQueen's representation of Northup. Thus, however graphic, brutal, violent, and critical of whiteness it may be, his movie still invokes American civic myths and social values to resonate with white moviegoers. To achieve this identification, McQueen stages Northup as an ordinary man, whose blackness and productivity arguably make him extraordinary or exceptional. As I said in my discussion of the complicated relationship among adaptation, truth, and accuracy, this staging of Northup may have much to do with Northup's own representation in his original narrative, where black exceptionality was a central discursive context for the emancipatory narrative's genre and political aims.

This desire for audience identification is problematic, for it causes a more consequential disidentification with a broadly construed, transhistorical system of antiblack racism. That is, the tragedy of Northup's enslavement, as experienced and represented, is not primarily attributed to capitalist greed that is mutually constituted by racism, sexism, and heterosexism and a broader antiblack sentiment of which the institution of slavery is a structural manifestation. Sixteen years before *Dred Scott v. Sandford* will clarify that a black man "ha[s] no rights which the white man [is] bound to respect" and thirteen years after David Walker had declared slavery was just one manifestation of a more ubiquitous racism, Northup's loss of freedom and subsequent enslavement still does not stir an acknowledgment of the presence of slavery anywhere within the democracy as an always already inimical threat to freedom.[16] In fact, the film stages his enslavement as an isolated outrage worthy of sympathy and political action because he is a "good" nigger, a free African American man who embodies several ideals of American (black) manhood.

As a gainfully employed, respectable family man, Northup does not embody the dehumanizing stereotypes of the coon, sambo, or zip coon. This distinction is key to marking him as a productive black man who deserves citizen rights. By framing Northup within the context of a Protestant work ethic success story gone awry, the film enlists sympathy or empathy from spectators but misses the opportunity to engage in structural analysis. It remains *explicitly* inattentive to "subtle historical and sociological [analyses] of slavery" and its institutional descendants, such as "Jim Crowism, job and residential discrimination, skewed unemployment rates, inadequate healthcare, and poor education." As a result, *12 Years* may not help its audiences to capture the historical, contemporary, and future significance of the peculiar institution.[17] By focusing on Northup's behavior as the cause for outrage, the film and viewers perpetuate a problematic narrative of black exceptionalism, thus treating his uniqueness (the movement from freedom to slavery) as isolatable from a larger pattern of black suffering in which the common black man was neither middle class nor married.

Valerie Smith's contention that "Northup's sudden descent from freedom into captivity recalls the numbers of African Americans wrongfully convicted and incarcerated due to the racialized policies and profit motives that sustain a criminal justice system fueled by sentencing requirements" demonstrates one dimension of the film's contemporary resonances as well as a larger structural critique in which the movie engages.[18] Her framing of behavior—that is, her choice of the descriptor "wrongfully convicted"—actually turns attention to how structures—in this case, the legal system—obscure their discriminatory power by casting a behavior (here, one that leads to a conviction) as the explanatory force for an unjust justice system.

This point is important, for it raises a useful question: if Northup had not been a productive member of society, would his kidnapping and subsequent enslavement have been deemed so egregious? The overarching problem here is that, while their white counterparts enjoy the privileges and responsibilities of citizenship, black people must continually prove their deservedness. The rub is that, regardless of what they do, they cannot prove it. My argument that the movie privileges behaviorist explanations demonstrates the challenge of representing black political and cultural advancement as a desired and necessary political goal rather than points to this approach as a shortcoming of the film. On the one hand, representations never depict the real, no matter how much they mirror actual events; at best, they are approximations of the object or subject being represented. On the other hand, the assumed realness of negative and stereotypical representations of black subjects and black life has had real (that is, meaningful, substantive, and material) consequences for black people and thus contextualizes why representation has been an important force for the making of black cultural politics.

Representation and Black Cultural Politics

Representation remains a hotly debated topic in black cultural production and has long been conceptualized as a catapult in the shaping of black politics. Even as cultural theorists disagree on the types of representations that will politically benefit African Americans, they acknowledge that representation, as a form of informal politics, can affect formal political activity. "Informal politics," following Gene Jarrett, refers to "the context of cultural media, representation, and subjectivity." Formal politics, in contrast, "refers to the context of governmental activity, public policy, law, and social formations."[19] While this distinction does not inherently elevate formal politics, the cultural tendency in the post–civil rights era has been to emphasize the work and value of formal politics. Given the history of black exclusion from formal politics, first under slavery and later under Jim and Jane Crow segregation, this prioritization is not surprising. Yet the conspicuous disjuncture between the theoretical promise of equality that the modern civil rights movement fought to secure and the fact that this promise has been realized only partially might force a reconsideration of this belief.

In *In Search of the Black Fantastic,* Richard Iton historicizes the tension between formal and informal politics and demonstrates how popular culture—and its attendant modes of representation—remain important yet underexamined areas of informal political activity:

> The inclination in formal politics toward the quantifiable and the bordered, the structured, ordered, policeable, and disciplined is in fundamental tension with popular culture's willingness to embrace disturbance, to engage the apparently mad and maddening, to sustain often slippery frameworks of intention that act subliminally, if not explicitly, on distinct and overlapping cognitive registers, and to acknowledge meaning in those spaces where speechlessness is the common currency.[20]

On the one hand, Iton acknowledges one perceived danger of overemphasizing informal political activity. As critics including Adolph Reed contend, such arguments reinforce the notion that black people cannot engage in state-sanctioned, rational, organized politics (such as the electoral process).[21] On the other hand, Iton insightfully points out that black people's continued exclusion from and marginalization within formal politics have caused them to maintain a network of informal political activity.

As concerned with correcting oversimplified accounts of slavery that ignore the intricacies of slavery as it is with recognizing slavery's continued significance, *12 Years* positions itself as an important force in shaping black cultural politics vis-à-vis its representational possibilities. McQueen gestures toward this goal when responding to questions about the movie's graphic violence:

> I'm not going to apologize for the torture, the brutality, the cruelty that was done to African Americans in this country. That doesn't mean people are guilty for it here, that's what happened in the past. We had the recent situations with Trayvon Martin's unfortunate killing, we have a black president, the 150th anniversary of the abolition of slavery, the Voting Rights Act being taken away, the 50th anniversary of the March on Washington. It's a perfect storm for the conversation.

The conversation cannot just be about the brutality. It should be about what happened and why it happened. So as far as balancing the situations of violence in the film, there has to be a situation where you're telling the story, and it's not just people being beaten, whipped, tortured both physically and psychologically. If you take the violence out of it, you don't have a movie. Part of it is about the suppression of people.[22]

McQueen's project reveals to a larger public the magnitude of violence that enslaved African Americans experienced and demonstrates how the legacies of slavery—its abiding racism—still affect the contemporary period. In other words, McQueen suggests that the expendability of black bodies in the twenty-first century parallels the expendability of black bodies during slavery. Thus, a deeper understanding of slavery might engender a more nuanced understanding of systemic structural racism.

John Ernest contends that slavery and its legacy warrant further popular and scholarly attention:

Missing from such knowledge about slavery is any understanding of the systemic operations of slavery that shaped fundamentally virtually every aspect of American life, including the institutional and theological operations of Christianity and the economic and legal practices fundamental to American notions of civilization. Perhaps what is most striking about the film under discussion here is that it is still tasked to do roughly the same work that Solomon Northup tried to accomplish in the book *Twelve Years a Slave*, first published in 1853—that is, to effect a kind of historical eruption, an account of history (individually authenticated but shared by many) inexplicable by the usual assumptions about the social order.[23]

Likewise, the film's temporality works toward a dual disruption, one that is both historical and presentist. If McQueen were to rupture the social order, he would have to upset a matrix of representation that developed under slavery, that continues to cast black people as subhuman, while offering behaviorists unfounded explanations to justify disenfranchisement. Yet, as I have argued, the film's reliance on the performance of bourgeois masculinity to justify its abolitionist logic reproduces the social order. As the documentary *Ethnic Notions* adeptly demonstrates, caricatures and stereotypes, which prominently figure in American visual culture, have not only legitimatized and justified violence against blacks but have also materialized in laws and public policies that delineate which black bodies will live and die.[24] Thus, representation both shares an intricate yet problematic relationship with formal politics and is enmeshed with what cultural theorist Achille Mbembe terms *necropolitics*, wherein the state determines which bodies live or die.[25]

For black people, representation has been deeply connected to the state's sovereignty, which still adjudicates the conditions and terms of African American life and death—both literally and metaphorically. Northup's kidnapping demonstrates black bodies' tenuous position in the context of necropolitics while revealing the conundrum of representation, which demands authentic political representations that counter caricatures and simultaneously acknowledges cultural politics as limited.

The ubiquity of the visual field as a form of informal politics places it in a unique but tenuous position for altering popular discourses about black subjectivity. In *Troubling Vision,* Nicole Fleetwood examines "the larger cultural significance of the cinematic for the production of racial difference and subjectivity" by uncovering and responding to the denigration of racial difference that figures prominently in the history of cinematic production. When working to engage and counteract this problematic history, black cultural producers and their products are in a bind. There is "a weight placed on black cultural production to produce results, to do something to alter a history and system of racial inequality that is in part constituted through visual culture. . . . That something is . . . the desire to have the cultural product solve the very problem that it represents: that seeing black is always a problem in the visual field that structures the troubling presence of blackness."[26] Fleetwood's compelling argument allows us to think through the degree to which, within the context of structural and behaviorist explanations of black inequality, the film moves outside of hegemonic tropes.

In *In Search of the Black Fantastic,* Iton argues that by oversaturating the visual field, films can paralyze viewers and thus eclipse their effectiveness as tools for radical and transformative political activity vis-à-vis informal politics:

> It is worth noting as well that the heightened predominance of the visual as the primary mediator of communication might enable potentially novel forms of political campaigning and impede attempts to transmit more nuanced and substantive sentiments, because the crowding out effect of the visual and the tendency of the camera to seek out spectacular and merely shocking, perhaps exciting rather than provocative and paradigm shifting ones. These new data can also, with time, as a consequence of their ubiquity and intensity, depress certain forms of citizen engagement. At the most mechanical level, the visual demands of the post-soul era—the requirement that one look had an incapacitating effect.[27]

Iton's admonition raises important questions for thinking through McQueen's staging of violent episodes and how the audience might respond to these scenes. What, for example, are viewers to do once they see Northup whip Patsey or see Mistress Epps throw a jar at Patsey's head, knocking her unconscious?

What effect does this violence have on the viewer? And given that the film already relies on behaviorist theories that dissociate individual acts from larger structures and institutions, can white viewers rid themselves of what George Lipsitz refers to as a "possessive investment in whiteness"?[28]

Movies such as *12 Years a Slave* reveal the tension between reflecting, refracting, refuting, and reconstituting the representational and material politics of slavery and its legacies, particularly as they use brutality to demonstrate slavery's evil. When McQueen juxtaposes the representation of Northup as a morally upstanding man against the violence of the white owners and overseers, he does so neither simply to elucidate the brutality of slavery and how its ideologies adversely affect the white psyche nor to show how all black subjectivities remain threatened in an antiblack system of oppression. While Patsey's beatings may invoke tears and sympathy, beyond these responses, does more substantive action become possible? Do viewers separate these behaviors from more egregious institutional manifestations of racialized-sexualized patriarchy? Or do they feel that the problem is *so grave* that they do not have the capacity to try to engage it and would rather leave the problem unsolved and unresolved?

Between Structures and Behaviors:
Representations of Life and Death

As Mbembe notes in "Necropolitics," "the ultimate expression of sovereignty resides, to a large degree, in the power and capacity to dictate who may live and who must die. Hence to kill or to allow to live constitutes the limits of sovereignty, its fundamental attributes. To exercise sovereignty is to exercise control over mortality and define life as the deployment and manifestation of power."[29] Power, as instrumentalized through state apparatuses, becomes a central force in war politics, which, when compounded with biopolitics, orchestrates racialized enactments of necropolitics. Mbembe's discussion begins by examining the politics of life and death as the guiding force of war politics. Extending Michel Foucault's notion of biopower, he argues that, "in the economy of biopower, the function of racism is to regulate the distribution of death and to make possible the murderous functions of the state." Racism is, in Foucault's words, "the condition for the acceptability of putting to death." If racism is, in fact, the "condition for the acceptability of putting to death," slavery is the structure through which the state administers those deaths. The temporal continuity, then, between the historical, presentist, and futurist implications of *12 Years a Slave* resonates in how the state has been and remains a threat to (and not a protection of) black subjects' citizenship rights. While the film may purport ultimately to protect Northup, arguing that it shows slavery as a wrong turn for a U.S. state that has since corrected its flaws, it ultimately affirms the power of the state—its sovereignty—to return him.

Both Mbembe and Foucault provide an important point of entry into this consideration of the film insofar as their notions of sovereignty and biopower might be extended to demonstrate the complexity of racism in general and how black people since slavery have had to live with the ever-present specter of death. That is, both racism and slavery are discursive and material sites wherein black bodies constantly straddle tenuous positions between life and death—between being represented as the rational subject (Northup), whose ability to think and live within social codes gives him access to life, or as the dehumanized object (the other black men who are killed), whose thingness moves him closer to death.[30] By turning attention to the moments in the film in which the representation of slavery confounds structural and behaviorist etiologies of black disenfranchisement, I am questioning the degree to which this representation can be an effective form of informal politics, engaging in both revisionist historiography and futurity. Like Colbert (in chapter 7), I concur with Joshua Chambers-Leston's assertion: "Reparation, then, is not about the sublimation of past injury or forgetting of guilt, so much as it is a coming to terms with the past as a means of putting oneself together, or at least enough to be able to move into the future of possibility of love."[31] Revisiting and making use of the past, however challenging, remains important as the nation continues to grapple with slavery's afterlife—in particular, how its long reach continues to circumscribe black subjectivity.

While necropolitics poses a threat to black life and thriving in general, gender and sexuality fundamentally alter how black men and black women experience these politics differently. McQueen's depiction of black women's lives underscores these important discontinuities within the patriarchal, sexist, and heterosexist institution. Because the filmmaker pays attention to the lives of members of the enslaved and black community with whom Northup shares his life as a bondsperson, the viewer becomes familiar with one black woman in particular, Patsey. While the film casts her as an inversion of the tragic mulatta, she experiences a life that is equally, if not more, devastating. Unlike the tragic mulatta, whose biracial identity, as a sign of her proximity to whiteness, makes her the subject of her master's licentiousness and mistress's venom, Patsey is a dark-skinned woman who, much to her chagrin, has also garnered the sexual attraction of her owner.

Although Mbembe's idea of necropolitics is a useful analytic rubric, Hortense Spillers's gendering (and perhaps, as Weheliye notes, her racializing) of necropolitics better explicates the significance of necropolitics and representational politics as they operate along gender lines. As Spillers observes, slavery across the diaspora demonstrates that the "captive female body locates precisely a moment of converging political and social vectors that mark the flesh as a prime commodity of exchange."[32] Within the slave economy, Patsey's humanity is already devalued, but her productivity unsettles the concept of value because she is one of the most prolific cotton pickers on the plantation. As a metonym for the frustrated illogics of slavery, she thus emblematizes Spillers's larger notion that the system of slavery reveals its cleavages by showing the instability of social signs and relationships.

Even if the commodity and its attendant value change throughout the diaspora, and the black female body accrues different meanings across time, antiblack racism remains the overarching sign that structures how black people are positioned on scales of social value. If, as some argue, the age of Obama has reconstituted the meaning of blackness by demonstrating how racism can be overcome, this age of "posts" becomes increasingly dangerous precisely because it provides logics to evade structural analyses of slavery and its legacies. The age of Obama paradoxically allows viewers to isolate racism and slavery from contemporary manifestations of racism and de facto and de jure segregation, to relegate slavery to a bygone era that the civil rights movement fixed, and to contain racism to the individual acts that are divorced from institutional systems that encourage and sustain it.

Inasmuch as *12 Years a Slave* introduces twenty-first-century viewers to the brutality of slavery by foregrounding how the enslaved owners and jealous mistresses conspired to mark black flesh as an expendable commodity located in the interstices of life and death, McQueen unflinchingly projects onto the screen the ubiquitous violence that permeated slavery. He plots these scenes of subjection to demonstrate the true horrors of slavery. Yet his artistic project faces a dilemma. On the one hand, he wants to show the degree to which slavery, both the system and its perpetuators, brutalized and devalued the black bodies that were economically valuable. On the other, he risks revealing a violence so shocking (to return to Iton) that it impedes viewers' ability to act politically.[33]

Toward a Resolution? Gender Politics, Gender Problems

Patsey's narrative serves several functions in *12 Years a Slave*, emblematizing how the constructs of gender and sexuality particularize the types of suffering black women experience in slavery as well as how patriarchy inhibits the development of interracial feminist (with Mistress Epps) and intraracial gender (with Northup) allegiances. Consider the scene at the end of the film, when Master Epps commands Northup to whip Patsey. The events leading up to this moment (Patsey visits Mistress Shaw to obtain soap, which Mistress Epps refuses to give to her) are important for they reveal the degree to which slavery attempted to circumscribe every prerogative that enslaved Africans possessed, including the ability to take care of their personal hygiene. They also show how the enslaved refused to be subjected by these attempts of subjection and the price they were willing to pay in order to be agents. This scene is difficult to watch, not only because of its brutality but also because Northup executes the violence. How, some might wonder, can he whip Patsey, his fellow bondsperson, with whom he presumably has a racial allegiance and friendship? Northup easily might have refused to beat Patsey, but recall my earlier argument that slavery confounds contemporary understandings of the concepts of agency and will. Does Northup whip Patsey out of compassion in order to spare her from Epps's venom? Or is his decision *also* a way to protect himself from the physical and psychic threat that Epps's whipping might inflict?

In *his written narrative,* Northup recalls that, after having whipped Patsey thirty times so that she might avoid Epps's cruelty, he refuses to continue. At the same time he acknowledges the threat to his own personhood, which he has incurred for her sake:

> Throwing down the whip, I declared I could punish her no more. He ordered me to go on, threatening me with a severer flogging than she had received, in case of refusal. My heart revolted at the inhuman scene, and risking the consequences, I absolutely refused to raise the whip. He then seized it himself, and applied it with ten-fold greater force than I had. The painful cries and shrieks of the tortured Patsey, mingling with the loud and angry curses of Epps, loaded the air. She was terribly lacerated—I may say, without exaggeration, literally flayed.[34]

In the film, Northup has a compassionate attitude toward Patsey's suffering, but the narrative paints her as a dreamy simpleton. Thus, the writer's testimony in the narrative and his investment in particular modes of black masculine identity and sexual politics make it difficult to read the moment as *only* an act of altruism. In an earlier scene in the film, for example, Patsey approaches Northup to "help [her] end [her] life," an act that she herself "does not have the strength to do." Because she gets "no comfort in this life," she asks him to be an agent of God. Viewers see them as they stand across from each another, Patsey's passionate smile contrasting with Northup's disdainful frown. After interrogating her—"How can you fall into such despair [and] . . . cosign me to damnation with such an ungodly request?"—he literally turns his back on her, thus ending their conversation. This scene instructively anticipates the moment when he faces her back as he sears her with the whip.[35] His response does not solely signal his insensitivity to Patsey's suffering; rather, it shows his own investment in American manhood discourses, which cherish rugged individualism as requisite for survival.

In her examination of black subjection and the threat of violence after Emancipation, Saidiya Hartman refuses to reprint one of the most famous scenes of violence in African American literary history—the beating of Aunt Hester in Frederick Douglass's *Narrative*—because she does not want to perpetuate the image of black suffering as expected, commonplace, and unremarkable:

> The "terrible spectacle" that introduced Frederick Douglass to slavery was the beating of his Aunt Hester. It is one of the most well-known scenes of torture in the literature of slavery, perhaps second only to Uncle Tom's murder at the hands of Simon Legree. . . . I have chosen not to reproduce Douglass' account of the beating of Aunt Hester in order to call attention to the ease with which scenes are usually reiterated, the casualness with which they are circulated, and the consequences of this routine display of the slave's ravaged body. Rather than inciting indignation, too often they immure us to pain by virtue of their familiarity . . . [and] they reinforce the spectacular character of black suffering.[36]

While Salamishah Tillet has noted that McQueen's scene may also be an excessive representation of violence, she captures how the staging of the scene itself shifts the audience from Northup's to Patsey's point of view in order to "enable Patsey to assert her authorial control within Solomon's tale."[37] This shift is important for it shows Patsey as a thinking, feeling subject whose subjectivity extends beyond slavery's objectification of black women. Yet like Hartman, Tillet does not replicate the details of the moment.

While my argument has focused on the sexualization of racism and the racialization of sexism in the beatings of Patsey and Aunt Hester, critics have rightfully argued that the black male body remains vulnerable to sexual threat in such scenes. Returning to the scene in Douglass's *Narrative,* when he witnesses Aunt Hester's beating, Maurice Wallace argues that "Douglass reveals his own sexual vulnerability by a scopophobic worry betraying the spectagraphic surrogacy of the black woman's body for [his] frightful fantasies of male rape." To talk about the dynamics of gender and sexuality during slavery thus means to talk about the multiple ways that sexuality becomes regulated and social norms enforced vis-à-vis the sexual policing of men and women. Wallace's conclusion that "the erotics of slavery which, forsaking gender difference, places the enslaved biological male and the enslaved biological female equally within the reach of the master's wanton hand," does not negate the fact that "black women suffered far more sexual abuses in slavery." Yet it acknowledges black men as actual and potential "victims of sexual violence, including sodomitic rape."[38] While the historical archive of autobiographical narratives engaging black men's sexual experiences under slavery is slim, the general perversions of slavery support Wallace's claim; and liberatory narratives such as Morrison's *Beloved* fill this gap by showing overseers requesting fellatio from enslaved black men.[39]

As *12 Years a Slave* closes, Northup is returned to freedom—and I purposely use *returned to* as opposed to *returns to* to reinforce the state's sovereignty in defining who lives and dies. Patsey remains enslaved and subjected to unimaginable cruelties. The juxtaposition of his impending freedom with her continued enslavement leaves viewers wondering what will be next for the characters and the audience. If the scenes enlist sympathy for the plight of the enslaved and the movie's temporality operates in both the past and present, is that sympathy meant to extend toward the plight of contemporary disenfranchised African Americans? Beyond sympathy, does the film enlist action? If it does, what types of action will it engender, and how effective will they be?

In her analyses of nineteenth-century women abolitionists, Gay Cima argues that "Garrisonian women converted this idea of sympathy as involuntary correspondence into a voluntary exercise that necessitated a particular kind of *critical and partisan* spectatorship, distance, and self-judgment, as well as an activated awareness of another's material circumstances."[40] While Cima historicizes the performance of sympathy, which she carefully distinguishes from the later emerging concept of empathy, her assertion that sympathy engendered particular types of action—spectatorship, distance, self-judgment, and awareness—proves useful in thinking through how contemporary spectators view McQueen's film. If a viewer feels sympathy, or even empathy, but fails to engage in structural analyses of slavery and capitalism and their afterlife in the post–Jim and Jane Crow eras, what does this experience mean? Perhaps, then, Iton's contention is correct: oversaturation in the visual field may incapacitate and thus undermine the film's potential as a mode of informal politics.

A Final Word

The overlaying of physical violence in general, Northup's whipping of Patsey in particular, and Northup's depiction as an upstanding black man call into question the degree to which positive image vis-à-vis representation shapes black politics in a transformative manner. That is, these examples demonstrate the seemingly impossible tasks of representing what cannot be represented and attempting to do so by way of positive image making. For example, the desire to represent Northup as an upstanding middle-class black man does not call into question how the category of upstanding middle-class man is situated in antiblack, racist, and heterosexist understandings of black subjectivity.

Nor does it challenge, as Isaac Julien suggests, how representations are necessarily exclusionary and otherwise incomplete. As he explains, "the project of producing positive images is an impossible one. Though it may have the best intentions of redressing imbalances in the field of representation, it will be bound to fail because it can never address questions of ambivalence and transgression."[41] We are left to ask how, if at all, representations that are predicated on discourses whose function is to exclude may allow the excluded to demand their entrance into the body politic. Notably, McQueen's representation of black female gender and sexuality presses us to think imaginatively about how black women, even within the context of slavery and under the ideals of the cult of domesticity, expressed their sexual desire. There is, for example, an early scene in which an unnamed woman requests Northup's hand to help her to masturbate. The significance of this scene is that it complicates the notion that black women's desire was *totally* controlled or obliterated by slavery and suggests that they possessed a range of human emotions and desires, including sexual needs.[42] But do these acts of transgression or ambivalence fundamentally alter the discursive field in which ideas about blackness, tethered to ideas about gender and sexuality, circulate?

12 Years a Slave provides us with a useful way to engage with slavery and its legacies, and McQueen helps us attend to difficult issues that we often evade. I hope that this chapter's conversation about his representation of slavery will lead us to engage in a larger discussion of the possibilities and limits of representation, black cultural politics, and behaviorist and structural explanations of black inequality. To the degree that representation is concerned with the politics of identity and identity politics, representation remains central to discussions about political and cultural enfranchisement. Yet the notion of positive image making can be dangerous and undermine radical collectivist politics; as Julien has admonished, "identity politics in its positive-images variant is always purchased in the field of representation at the price of the other."[43] At whose expense, we might ask, is the representation of Northup purchased? Is it at the expense of Patsey, who is beaten and lacerated in one of the final scenes? Is it at the expense of ordinary black men, whose attempts to secure their freedom make them seem recalcitrant and therefore undeserving of citizenship rights? Or is it at the collective expense of all black people because such a focus on black behavior continues to obfuscate the structural and institutional challenges that nurture black inequality and disenfranchisement? After all, when he is stolen, Northup is technically doing what he is supposed to be doing—according to the behaviorist Protestant work ethic. Perhaps, then, the psychic hold of slavery has much to do with engaging the anxiety produced by behaviorist explanations of slavery; the inability to connect past, present, and future; and the desire for representations to perform Herculean tasks. Whether the psychic hold of slavery will diminish remains to be seen. However, as long as its vestiges are denied, it will rightfully continue to be a significant conversation within American culture. If nothing else, the issues that *12 Years* raise provide a platform to engage in and perhaps shift this conversation.

The release of *12 Years a Slave* raised questions about whether Americans want to see another movie about slavery and why black people cannot get over slavery. Yet analyses continue to deny the historical continuities between different disenfranchisements then and now. They continue to situate black people's lack of housing, education, and employment opportunities as solely consequences of their own actions and inactions. They ignore the significance of nihilism as an inherited psychological barrier that impedes progress and refuse to acknowledge how shifts in global capitalism have disproportionately truncated black people's social and economic mobility. This is why these movies continue to be made, why black people cannot get over slavery, and why all Americans might benefit from seeing such films, even if they do not want to. The vestiges of the peculiar institution run deep. Furthermore, as Weheliye notes, we must continue to place race in "front and center in considerations of political violence," taking note of how it functions "as a set of sociopolitical processes of differentiation and hierarchization."[44] If we fail to acknowledge and deconstruct the material and ideological institutions that circumscribe black life, we ignore how the modern epoch is deeply invested in racial, gendered, sexualized, and economic hierarchies that re-entrench black inequality and impede racial advancement. By drawing attention to how and why these institutions are cruelly optimistic, we might also begin to interrogate how to imagine new structures outside of the violence under which our current epistemes operate.

NOTES

1. Stuart Hall, "What Is This 'Black' in Black Popular Culture?" in *Black Popular Culture*, ed. Gina Dent (New York: New Press, 1998), 30.

2. See Manohla Dargas, "The Blood and Tears, not the Magnolias," *New York Times*, October 17, 2013, http://www.nytimes.com/2013/10/18/movies/12-years-a-slave-holds -nothing-back-in-show-of-suffering.html?pagewanted=all&_r=0, accessed October 29, 2015; Oliver Gettell, "'12 Years a Slave': A Captivating Story of Survival," *Los Angeles Times*, October 18, 2013, http://articles.latimes.com/2013/oct/18/entertainment /la-et-mn-12-years-a-slave-movie-reviews-critics-20131018, accessed October 29, 2015; Ann Hornday, "'12 Years a Slave' Movie Review: A Masterpiece of Form, Content, Emotion, and Performance." *Washington Post*, October 17, 2013, https://www. washingtonpost.com/goingoutguide/movies/12-years-a-slave-movie-review -a-masterpiece-of-form-content-emotion-and-performance/2013/10/16/1b158e76-34e8 -11e3-8a0e-4e2cf80831fc_story.html, accessed December 28, 2015.

3. Stephanie Li argues that McQueen's adaptation not only maintains important details from the original narrative but also affords access to the psychology and emotions of the enslaved—black women, in particular—that is typically excluded from emancipatory narratives. See her "*12 Years a Slave* As a Neo-Slave Narrative," *American Literary History* 26, no. 2 (2013): 326–328.

4. Alexander Weheliye, *Habeas Viscus: Racializing Assemblages, Biopolitics, and Black Feminist Theories of the Human* (Durham, N.C.: Duke University Press, 2014), 2.

5. Saidiya Hartman, *Scenes of Subjection: Terror, Slavery, and Self-Making in Nineteenth-Century America* (Oxford: Oxford University Press, 1997), 157.

6. See Soyica Diggs Colbert, "'When I Die, I Won't Stay Dead': The Future of the Human in Suzan-Lori Parks's *The Death of the Last Black Man in the Whole Entire World*," *Boundary 2* 39, no. 3 (2012): 190–195; Bill Brown, "Thing Theory," in *Things*, ed. Bill Brown (Chicago: University of Chicago Press, 2004), 4; and Robin Bernstein, "Dances

with Things: Material Culture and the Performance of Race," *Social Text* 27 (winter 2009): 69–70.

7. Dwight McBride, *Impossible Witnesses: Truth, Abolitionism, and Slave Testimony* (New York: New York University Press, 2002), 151.

8. Erica Edwards, "Tuning into Precious: The Black Women's Empowerment Adaptation and the Interruption of the Absurd," *Black Camera* 4 (winter 2012): 75. Edwards identifies Zora Neale Hurston's *Their Eyes Were Watching God* (1937), Alice Walker's *The Color Purple* (1982), and Toni Morrison's *Beloved* (1987) as three paradigmatic examples of black feminist texts that critique notions of self-help and structures, including the institution of marriage, while their cinematic adaptations support those notions.

9. Lauren Berlant, *Cruel Optimism* (Durham, N.C.: Duke University Press, 2011), 24.

10. *12 Years a Slave,* dir. Steve McQueen (Los Angeles: Fox Searchlight Pictures, 2013). DVD.

11. Salamishah Tillet, *Sites of Slavery: Citizenship and Racial Democracy in the Post–Civil Rights Imagination* (Durham, N.C.: Duke University Press, 2012), 13.

12. Andrea Williams, "Sex, Marriage, and 12 Years," *American Literary History* 26, no. 2 (2013): 347.

13. Maurice Wallace, *Constructing the Black Masculine: Identity and Ideality in African American Men's Literature and Culture, 1775–1995* (Durham, N.C.: Duke University Press, 2002), 67.

14. Cornel West, "Nihilism in Black America," in *Black Popular Culture*, ed. Gina Dent (Seattle: Bay Press, 1992), 37.

15. Monica Ndounou, *Shaping the Future of American Film: Color-Coded Economics and the Story Behind the Numbers* (New Brunswick, N.J.: Rutgers University Press, 2014), 7.

16. David Walker, *David Walker's Appeal to the Coloured Citizens of the World, but in Particular, and Very Expressly to those of the United States* (Baltimore: Black Classic Press, 1997).

17. Cornel West, "Nihilism in Black America, *12 Years a Slave*," *American Literary History* 26, no. 2 (2013): 37.

18. Valerie Smith, "Black Life in Balance: 12 Years a Slave," *American Literary History* 26, no. 2 (2013): 365.

19. Gene Jarrett, *Representing the Race: A New Political History of African American Literature* (New York: New York University Press, 2011), 13–14.

20. Richard Iton, *In Search of the Black Fantastic: Politics and Popular Culture in the Post–Civil Rights Era* (New York: Oxford University Press, 2008), Kindle ed.

21. Adolph Reed, *The Jesse Jackson Phenomenon* (New Haven, Conn.: Yale University Press, 1986), 41, 56–57.

22. "*12 Years a Slave*—Q&A with Director Steve McQueen and Chiwetel Ejiofor," *National Board of Review,* http://www.nationalboardofreview.org/2013/09/qa-director-steve-mcqueen-chiwetel-ejiofor/, accessed August 10, 2015.

23. John Ernest, "(Re)mediated History: *12 Years a Slave*," *American Literary History* 26, no. 2 (2013): 367.

24. *Ethnic Notions*, dir. Marlon Riggs (San Francisco: California Newsreel, 1987), DVD.

25. Achille Mbembe, "Necropolitics," *Public Culture* 15, no. 1 (2003): 11–12.

26. Nicole Fleetwood, *Troubling Vision: Performance, Visuality, and Blackness* (Chicago: University of Chicago Press, 2014), 2, 3.

27. Iton, *In Search of the Black Fantastic.*

28. Here I refer to George Lipsitz's notion that whiteness, as an ideological construct, possesses power in which white people are invested. This makes renouncing racism (and the privilege it confers) difficult. See his *The Possessive Investment in Whiteness: How White People Profit from Identity Politics* (Philadelphia: Temple University Press, 2006).

29. Mbembe, "Necropolitics," 11–12.

30. For a thorough discussion of social death in both the film and the narrative as well as a thoughtful consideration of how the film visualizes those images, see John Stauffer, "12 Years between Life and Death," *American Literary History* 26, no. 2 (2013): 317–325.

31. Joshua Chambers-Leston, "Reparative Feminisms, Repairing Feminism—Reparation, Postcolonial Violence, and Feminism," *Women and Performance* 16 (July 2006): 173.

32. Hortense Spillers, "Mama's Baby, Papa's Maybe: An American Grammar Book," *Diacritics* 17 (summer 1987): 75.

33. Some film critics have questioned viewers' willingness to see the movie, reflect on it, and move toward social change. For example, Betsy Sharkey argues that the violence of the movie makes it difficult to watch because the typical filmgoer does not want to view such spectacles ("Oscars 2014: For Many, '12 Years a Slave' Is Too Hard to Watch." *Los Angeles Times*, February 27, 2014, http://articles.latimes.com/2014/feb/27/entertainment/la-et-mn-12-years-a-slave-notebook-20140227, accessed December 9, 2015); Kenneth Turan echoes this claim ("McQueen's '12 Years a Slave' Impressive, and Hard to Watch," *Los Angeles Times*, October 17, 2013, http://articles.latimes.com/2013/oct/17/entertainment/la-et-mn-12-years-a-slave-movie-review-20131018, accessed December 9, 2015).

34. Solomon Northup, *Twelve Years a Slave* (Vancouver, B.C.: Engage, 2013), Kindle ed.

35. *12 Years a Slave.*

36. Hartman, *Scenes of Subjection*, 3.

37. Tillet, "I Got No Comfort in This Life," *American Literary History* 26, no. 2 (2013): 358.

38. Wallace, *Constructing the Black Masculine*, 86, 87.

39. Of course, Morrison's *Beloved* is a liberatory (neo-slave) narrative, and the author is thinking through these issues as she portrays slave owners who are forcing enslaved African men to perform fellatio on them. As black women historically resisted acts of sexual violation, so, too, do Morrison's fictive men, who are shot in the head and thus take a bit of foreskin with them to death.

40. Gay Cima, *Performing Anti-Slavery: Activist Women on Antebellum Stages* (Cambridge: Cambridge University Press, 2014), 21–22.

41. Isaac Julien, "Black Is, Black Ain't: Notes toward De-essentializing Blackness," in *Black Popular Culture*, ed. Gina Dent (Seattle: Bay Press, 1992), 261.

42. For a more in-depth discussion of this scene and how it fits into a larger trajectory of McQueen's depiction of a complex black female sexuality, see Li, "*12 Years a Slave* As a Neo-Slave Narrative," 327.

43. Julien, "Black Is, Black Ain't," 261.

44. Weheliye, *Habeas Viscus*, 5.

2

The Fruit of Abolition

Discontinuity and Difference in Terrance Hayes's "The Avocado"

DOUGLAS A. JONES JR.

In an 1847 appearance before the Female Anti-Slavery Society of Salem, Massachusetts, fugitive slave William Wells Brown delivered one of the most stunning pronouncements regarding slavery's representational history and future. He declared, "Slavery has never been represented. Slavery can never be represented."[1] If this is not the most thoroughly ironic claim in African American arts and letters, I don't know what is: not only did Brown proclaim it in the midst of a lecture on "Slavery As It Is," but he also devoted his life as a free man to representing slavery in a vast array of cultural media and literary forms, including his immensely popular *Narrative of William W. Brown, a Fugitive Slave* (1847), published only a few months before his speech in Salem.[2] Redoubling that irony (or perhaps nullifying it altogether), Brown's prodigious corpus—which includes pioneering work in autobiography, biography, drama, lyric writing, military and political history, the novel, oratory, the panorama, solo performance, and the travelogue—intimates the impossibility of representing "the real condition of the slave," engendered by chattel slavery's institutional and interpersonal effects, in any total kind of way.[3] That is, his ceaseless striving to recapture, for emancipatory ends, the affective, physical, and psychological particulars of slavery does not so much evince a series of representational successes as it does one of perpetual failure. His assertion that "slavery can never be represented" thus functions as a critical prolepsis of sorts, an anticipatory rejoinder against the inevitable shortcomings of his and others' renderings of the institution.

To be sure, deficiencies (and excesses) vis-à-vis the real define the ontology of representation itself, regardless of its subject. Yet facticity and historicity were what endowed artists and writers such as Brown with narrative authority and consequently furnished their redressive claims on behalf of the slave and her descendants with standing, however limited. Hence, the burden to represent "slavery as it is" fell mightily on abolitionist cultural producers, and the most lasting archive of the force of that burden remains the corpus of antebellum slave narratives. Under the editorial stewardship of William Lloyd Garrison, slave narratives not only gave rise to the documentary impulse that Barbara Foley theorizes as central to African American literature but also "helped to crystallize a [broader] taste for the 'real,' and thus to influence the development of literary realism as a genre," as Augusta Rohrbach has compellingly argued.[4] This "real"—whether the real suffering of the slave or, later, the real sociological forces that combine to produce a character such as Bigger Thomas of Richard Wright's *Native Son* (1940)—serves as the legitimating currency of much black cultural production and the ethical and political appeals enacted therein. But Brown's admonition to his Salem audience looms: if "we shall all fail to represent the real condition of the slave," then are the appeals for her repair that emerge from those unavoidably deficient representations unavoidably deficient themselves?[5]

This question has an acute relevance to contemporary black cultural criticism and theory, which, in the main, regards slavery as still deeply functional and a "ready prism for apprehending the black political present."[6] Such an understanding of the present as affectively and ethically bound by the slave past began to obtain in the late 1980s, precisely when an influential host of creative writers and scholars began to cast their work as revelatory, and thus corrective, of the representational deficiencies of slave narratives and testimony.[7] No person was more instrumental in this regard than Toni Morrison, and in her 1987 essay, "The Site of Memory," she was forthright in her insistence that writers from marginalized groups should take up such an enterprise:

> In shaping [their] experience[s] to make it palatable to those who were in a position to alleviate it, [slaves and former slaves] were silent about many things, and they "forgot" many things. There was a careful selection of the instances that they would record and a careful rendering of those that they chose to describe. . . . For me—a writer in the last quarter of the twentieth century, not much more than a hundred years after Emancipation, a writer who is black and a woman—the exercise is very different. My job becomes how to rip that veil drawn "over proceedings too terrible to relate." The exercise is also critical for any person who is black, or who belongs to any marginalized category, for, historically, we were seldom invited to participate in the discourse even when we were its topic.[8]

In this call to "extend, fill in, and complement slave autobiographical narratives," a "wish" she calls the "matrix" of her fiction, Morrison argued that the biggest obstacles to slaves' ability to represent the fullness of their experiences, especially "the more sordid details" and their "interior life," were, above all, the compulsions, constraints, and proprieties of the era rather than the limits of representation.[9] For her own writing, Morrison built from what Zora Neale

Hurston described as "memories within that came out of the material that went to make [her]," including a slave past that Morrison suggested still obtained in American life.[10] These "memories within" served not only as the "subsoil" of her fiction but also what she recognized as the affective and ethical remains of slavery that both enjoin and allow the contemporary writer to fill in the silences and remove the veils that constitute the stories that slaves forged.[11] In other words, because the United States maintained this proximity with the history of chattel slavery at the same time as the nation enjoyed unprecedented forms of cultural and sociopolitical latitude, present-day writers of fiction and nonfiction might *not* be certain to "fail" in representing "the real condition of the slave," as Brown believed he and his contemporaries inevitably did.

Indeed, whereas Brown claimed that, above all, the enormity of the trauma intrinsic to chattel slavery impeded his and others' ability to render the whole of the institution in any real way, Morrison argued that the social mores and representational norms of antebellum cultural production were what most hindered former slaves from fully rendering their lives as chattel and thus revealing a historical truth. With the abatement of these mores and norms in the late twentieth century, she suggested, writers might repair the constitutive holes in slave testimony that resulted from mid-nineteenth-century strictures on representation. Of course, she took up this work in her own literary practice when she first presented "The Site of Memory" as part of a lecture series on autobiography and memoir. At the time, she was in the process of completing *Beloved* (1987), the novel that epitomized the sort of narrative reparation she was calling for. One might even call *Beloved* the *urtext* of late twentieth- and early twenty-first-century African American writing about slavery, creative or otherwise. As Stephen Best explains the novel's ascendancy,

> Morrison no doubt played a major hand in . . . directing attention in African American studies straight toward the slave past and diaspora. It would not be going too far to add that her Nobel Prize in Literature in 1993 positioned *Beloved* to shape the way a generation of scholars conceived of its ethical relationship to the past. For a distinctive if not singular moment in the history of the interpretive disciplines, a novel set the terms of the political and historiographical agenda.[12]

He goes on to describe how "Morrisonian poetics," with its underlying ethic of "melancholic historicism," has become the dominant frame for the study of the so-called black Atlantic, leading several major scholars to consider periodization itself as paradoxical; that is, an "accepted truth . . . that the past is simply our present."[13] In construing slavery as ongoing, this critical disposition understands itself as engaged in the same struggle of historiographical recovery and revelation as Morrison believed *Beloved* to be part of—a struggle that strives to redeem both the past and the present (since they are one) by returning us, affectively and imaginatively, to the "site of origin and the scene of the fall," to some sort of "prelapsarian wholeness."[14]

The prospects of such a return must be horrifyingly sublime, this body of critical and imaginative histories suggests, because travelers must make their way back through all the loss that slavery occasioned. In other words, this journey requires accountings of all the death, physical and social, that the institution produced as well as accountings of all the ways of being and doing with which the institution's victims withstood those forms of death. By themselves, conventional forms of historiography are inadequate to produce these accountings because they are too rationalistic in both their methods and ends.[15] Imaginative forms of representation, however, offer access to the "awe and reverence and mystery and magic" that was the "milieu" of the slaves, as Morrison described it.[16] To reconstruct that milieu in all of its mundane and extramundane complexities is to evince the deepest truth of black/slave life, which is the central aim of Morrisonian poetics. Hence, questions of accuracy continue to orient prevailing rubrics for evaluating the historiographical and thus ethical worth of even fictive representations of slavery.[17] Willful inaccuracy is the greatest possible transgression here because in purposefully misrepresenting the slave past, one also misrepresents the conditions that produced the present and thus becomes complicit in perpetuating racial inequities and social injustices.

Though still few in numbers, an emerging cadre of critics has levied powerful critiques of the conception of an ongoing slave past that underwrites these protocols of critical judgment, historiography, and the literary imaginary. "At the risk of courting the sinister," Kenneth Warren writes, "it is my contention here that to understand both past and present, we have to put the past behind us."[18] Best seeks to replace "holding with letting go, clutching with disavowal," and he encourages a new critical poetics that recognizes that "the past is here to be appreciated as a falling away—slavery to be appreciated in the failure to make its racial legacy present."[19] Warren and Best, among similar-minded writers such as Walter Benn Michaels, do not dismiss chattel slavery's world-shaping impact but argue that the notions and rationales that animated and sustained the institution cannot fully explain our current racial moment. In their view, an "assumed continuity between the [slave] past and our present" yields imprecise if not wooly historiographies. Moreover, this assumption engenders a "sense of racial belonging rooted in the historical dispossession of slavery" and makes for "unstable ground on which to base a politics."[20] Simply put, the world *has* changed; thus, the conditions for black political belonging and the attendant terms of critical inquiry and imaginative narration, if they are to be efficacious, must change along with it.

This position accords with what Aida Levy-Hussen calls "postracial criticism"—that is, a critical orientation positing that, "since the gains of the civil rights movement, the legacy of racial slavery has ceased to be singularly, or even primarily, constitutive of African American experience" (see chapter 10). She grants that it is "right to warn against the ethical and methodological pitfalls of trans-historical overidentification" but ultimately distances her "own decidedly secular approach to criticism" from that of "postracial" critics. She rejects their animating set of "desires" that "are made disingenuous by their claims to objectivity and by their exaggerated projections of pathology, self-indulgence, or false consciousness onto competing articulations of historical desire."[21] For me, however, so-called postracial criticism does not necessarily emerge from "claims to objectivity" or make the sorts of "projections" that Levy-Hussen identifies; nor does it always rest on a conceptualization of history as a "fully conquerable object of knowledge," as she argues. Rather, the critical impulse to make intellectual and perhaps political "gains" by "extending the queer acknowledgment of nonrelationality between the [slave] past and the present in the racial case," as Best puts it, often reflects an acknowledgment of the considerable *unknowability* and thus *unconquerability* of the history of slavery. This encounter with history is based in humility, not the "desire for intellectual mastery"; it recognizes that we cannot fulfill the political projects of the slave past because they arose from, and maintained cogency within, a historical conjuncture that is no longer our own.[22] Thus, if a historical desire animates what one might call my brand of postracial criticism, it is the desire to cultivate a reading practice that is as attuned to defeat as it is to triumph, to alterity as it is sameness.

Terrance Hayes's poem "The Avocado" (2010) seeks to position its readers to approach history in this way, for it exemplifies an understanding of the slave past as distant and distinct from the contemporary moment. Hayes's sly manipulation of the form of the historical poem and his subtle juxtaposition of several epochs of African American history produce an alienating effect that ultimately rejects narratives of historical continuity and temporal compression. Rather than attempting to flesh out slaves' experiences and interior lives as acts of recovery and thus redemption of the history of black captivity, he dramatizes our relation to slavery as one of opacity and uncertainty. His irreverent and ironic treatment of slave history reanimates the past in a way that does not seek affective or psychic redress of slavery's injuries, for such repair is impossible. Instead, the poem strives to encourage new conceptual horizons with which to reconceive and thus inhabit our postslavery present—and such openings, it seems, might be the best we can hope for.

While the first African American writers to garner national and international acclaim were slaves such as Jupiter Hammon and Phillis Wheatley, whose poetic meditations on their lives as chattel were grippingly innovative, the institution of slavery and its history have not been dominant topoi of black-authored poetry until recently.[23] However unwittingly, most of these contemporary poets follow Morrison's entreaty to "fill in, extend, and comple-ment slave autobiographical narratives," and the historical poem has been their preferred form for this enterprise. As poet Major Jackson explains, "there is a political dimension to the historical poem. Regretfully, our education does not invite critical reflection of 'authorized' history. Yet the historical poem is political to the extent it encourages more rumination and challenges the supreme fictions and omissions from the official record that supports our damaged, partially developed democracy."[24] In this vein, the historical poem functions as a "site of memory," to recall Morrison's essay, that aims to recover what was lost or proscribed during slavery. It expands the contours of American democratic life by elucidating strides that persons have made, and must con-tinue to make, to achieve a more perfect union. Concerns of representativeness inevitably determine the thrust of such historical poems: "African American poets have . . . sought tenaciously to correct American history textbooks by writing volume after volume of poems that pull out of the shadows political and cultural figures deemed representative in the plight of black people's struggle for respect, equality, and dignity."[25] In other words, even if the acts and attributes such poets imaginatively ascribe to the personage of the historical poem lack historicity, they are worthy of memorialization because they signify this broader, collective struggle that dominant historical narratives too often render trivial and obscure.

The historical poem reveals more about the currents of history than it does about the history it ostensibly represents. For example, Paul Laurence Dunbar's 1895 elegy "Frederick Douglass" erects Douglass as a selfless demigod, whereas Evie Shockley's 2011 "from *The Lost Letters of Frederick Douglass*" depicts the nineteenth-century social reformer as a supercilious Victorian blind to the ways in which the oppression of women is homologous with white supremacy.[26] Do these poems reveal details of the historical life of Douglass as a person? Perhaps. But they unmistakably signify the intellectual preoccupations and political concerns of their eras: the world-changing uses of "great men" and the attainment of gender equality that feminist inquiry pursues. That is, if histori-cal poems "will come to constitute one of the most important and exhilarating containers of American cultural memory," as Jackson argued in 2008, then the firmest memories they contain involve the present in which they appeared, not the history they retell.

Hayes's "The Avocado," which appears in his 2010 National Book Award–winning collection *Lighthead*, ironizes the historical poem to uphold the form's limitations as historiography of the slave past. The title commences that irony because it does not orient its readers toward historical periods and personages in the way that the titles of historical poems almost always do.[27] Indeed, there is no initiatory denotation or even intimation of an effort to reclaim, redeem, or repair pedagogical and historiographical gaps concerning slavery. Even the most satirical and prurient treatments of the slave past, such as Ishmael Reed's parodic novel *Flight to Canada* (1976) or Kara Walker's sweeping silhouettes *The End of Uncle Tom and the Grand Allegorical Tableau of Eva in Heaven* (1995), rely on their titles to direct their audiences' attention to a specific, fairly restricted set of historical and cultural signifiers. Hayes's title lacks this force, offering no indication that the ensuing poem will take up historiography, let alone the historiography of slavery, in any meaningful way.

What makes the title choice even more striking is that Hayes's poem immediately launches into a scene featuring a lecturer ("the black man") and his audience (including the poem's narrator) that recalls a sweep of nearly a century of African American history. The poem begins:

> "In 1971, drunk on the sweet, sweet juice of revolution,
> a crew of us marched into the president's office with a list
> of demands," the black man tells us at the February luncheon,
> and I'm pretending I haven't heard this one before as I eye
> black tortillas on a red plate beside a big green bowl
> of guacamole made from the whipped, battered remains
> of several harmless former avocados.[28]

In this single, seemingly ordinary sentence, Hayes fuses an array of signifiers to express three distinct epochs of the black past: the post–civil rights present, the Black Power era of the late 1960s and early 1970s, and the Pan-Africanist Garveyite movements of the interwar period. The lecturer's anecdote of his participation in protests such as those that led to the demographic and curricular expansions in American colleges and universities, and the weariness that reminiscence produces in the narrator, clearly express the first two epochs. The fact that the occasion of this speech is the yearly "February luncheon," which is to say Black History Month, only doubles the narrator's weariness.[29] Yet Hayes's decision to date the anecdote within the poem as 1971 is significant because that is the year of his own birth.[30] He thus pays tribute to the history of the student efforts that led to the birth of black studies, among other departments and institutions, and links them to the provenance of his own life as poet and critic, even as he suggests the tedium of retelling history.[31]

These two time periods emerge clearly in the narrative of the first sentence of the poem, but the representation of the Pan-Africanist Garveyite epoch is far more elaborate. It appears, so to speak, in "a red plate," "black tortillas," and "a big green bowl of guacamole." Lateral, equal-sized bands of red, black, and green made up the flag of Marcus Garvey's United Negro Improvement Association (UNIA), the hugely popular black nationalist-separatist organization he founded in 1914. The tricolor was ubiquitous among UNIA members and sympathizers, who appropriated it into their sartorial styling and celebrated the colors in song and a war banner.[32] The UNIA flag has since become the dominant symbol of Pan-African unity, and a number of postcolonial African and Caribbean nations have based the designs of their flags on its color and compositional scheme.

After evoking these three epochs, the poem extends its historical reach back to slavery: "If abolitionists had a flag / it would no doubt feature the avocado, also known as the alligator / pear, for obvious reasons."[33] Here the narrator intimates that the UNIA flag could be the flag of abolitionism because the green of the tricolor is "a big green bowl of guacamole," a dish that features the green flesh of the avocado. Hayes's description of guacamole—"made from the whipped, battered remains / of several harmless avocados"—evokes the "several harmless" persons whose flesh an institution often reduced to "whipped, battered remains." The avocado, in other words, emerges as a metaphor for the slave before she was a slave. This seemingly random, nonsensical link compels readers and listeners to regard "our orientation toward" the slave past as "forever perverse, queer, askew."[34] That is, Hayes's figuration of the slave-as-guacamole represents, in poetic form, the critical estimation of the impossibility of recovery and redemption from slavery's injuries: we can never make guacamole whole again; we can never restore it to its state as an avocado.

As the narrator's reverie establishes this historiographical and ethical relationship between the present and the past, the lecturer is telling his audience what he and his "crew" wanted above all else: "Number one: reparations!"[35] Yet juxtaposed with the figure and figural significance of guacamole, reparations seem incidental and do little to hold the narrator's attention.[36] If anything, the lecturer's recollected appeal for money—"'Enough gold to fill each of our women's wombs, gold / to nurse our warriors waiting to enter this world with bright fists, / that's what we told them'"—brings into focus the "money-colored flesh of the avocado," as the narrator sees it, which, in turn, vividly recalls the "chattel principle" that underwrote American slavery. As per the chattel principle, "any slave's identity might be disrupted as easily as a price could be set and a piece of paper passed from one hand to another," the historian Walter Johnson explains.[37] Reparations, the poem suggests, affirm the chattel principle because even in death the slave's body and her labor accrue monetary value that someone else will receive. The idea of receiving compensation for the wrongs of slavery does not seem to interest the narrator, who, after hearing the demand for reparations, ponders the avocado's fat and oil and then turns to admire Yoyo's comeliness and "caterpillar locks."[38] (We learn later in the poem that Yoyo is the narrator's lover.) As a result, the second demand is missing from the poem because the narrator fails to notice it.

The lecturer's next demand does rouse the narrator, but only for a moment: "Three: we wanted more boulevards named for the Reverend Dr. Martin Luther King, Jr. An airport named for Sojourner Truth."[39] This demand, along with a later one calling for a "Harriet Tubman statue on the mall," suggests that the "president" whose office the crew marched into was Richard Nixon's, not a college or university president's, because the latter probably did not have the power to name streets and airports.[40] That said, it is still difficult to imagine a scenario involving black men and women, "drunk on the sweet, sweet juice of revolution," marching into the office of the president of the United States.[41] With this brilliantly ambiguous presidential identity in the balance, the third demand thrusts the narrator back into a state of reverie for the span of the next seventeen demands. Ostensibly, this interval is the most extended temporal gap in the poem's narrative unfolding. By way of this move, Hayes insinuates a general apathy toward, if not vexation with, nominal commemorations of African Americans and their cultural, political, and social achievements. Such commemorations often take shape in name only, as individuals, communities, and the state eschew fulfilling the commemorated person's legacy. Hundreds of boulevards and streets bearing the name Martin Luther King Jr. run through some of America's most violent, poverty-stricken, and collectively neglected neighborhoods, exemplifying this reality in a conspicuous and painfully ironic way.[42]

This critique of the lecturer and his crew's demand that public landmarks be named after African Americans does not emerge explicitly from "The Avocado," but its inability to capture the narrator's attention signifies dissatisfaction with the critique as both redress and narrative reclamation of race-based crimes and injustices throughout American history. Similarly, demands 4 through 20 are missing; and if we follow the logic of the poem's narrative time, we find that their omission gives way to the narrator's far more imaginative and productive meditation on the agricultural symbology of abolitionism:

> The roots of the avocado tree
> can raise the pavement, so it's not too crazy to imagine the fruit
> as a symbol of revolt on the abolitionist flag. We are all one kind
> of abolitionist or another, no doubt. And we are like the avocado too
> with its indelible ruby-colored seed that can actually sprout from the inside
> when the fruit is overmature, causing internal molds and breakdowns.[43]

Now that Hayes has established the avocado as a metaphor for the slave before she was a slave, "roots" sets off a chain of meanings that implicates the intellectual and social resources arising from the slave's African heritage, resources that she relied on to withstand the violence and horrors of enslavement. Hayes refuses to detail those resources in any realist way, modeling a refusal to presume personal access, affective or psychological, to those resources. Rather, he offers the evocative though aptly elusive image of the resources as "roots" that can "raise the pavement." Moreover, this passage recalls the UNIA tricolor as a metonym of Pan-African struggle and solidarity.

Because African "roots" produce the avocado (flesh), they must also be the source of the guacamole that gave color to the green stripe of the UNIA flag that surfaces earlier in the poem. (In fact, the designers of the UNIA flag used green to symbolize the natural resources of Africa, which they argued all black persons in the diaspora were heir to.) With the Pan-African tricolor framing the narrator's claim that all persons are "one kind of abolitionist or another," Hayes implies that twentieth-century black freedom movements such as African decolonization efforts were also forms of abolitionism.

Yet the poet carefully avoids equating these movements with the eighteenth- and nineteenth-century campaigns to end slavery: "We are all one *kind of* abolitionist or another" (my emphasis). The word *kind* performs much significatory work in this sentence, just as the word *like* does in the next. To be sure, the assertion that each of us is "like the avocado" (that is, the slave before she was a slave) denotes considerable similarities between the two, the most fundamental of which is the "seed that can actually sprout from the inside when the fruit is overmature." (Is this seed that bursts the confines of its skin a metaphor for a person's inherent need to be free?) But *like* also implies meaningful difference, and in the context of this passage it signifies that the "time" and "event" of slavery have "end[ed]."[44] Such qualifiers disrupt narratives of historical and affective continuity between the slave past and the present and, as a consequence, eschew the "melancholic historicism" so essential to Morrisonian poetics. Melancholy, as Best explains, "marks a refusal of such detachment and a persistent identification with the lost object. The melancholic historicism that is currently resurgent celebrates the commitment to remain 'faithful to the lost object' and to 'refus[e] to renounce [the critic's] attachment to it.'"[45] The narrative, poetic diction, and symbolic metaphors of "The Avocado" combine to refuse melancholy as a structure of feeling upon which to cultivate our relation to slavery. It never claims that what was lost in slavery is our loss to grieve today. If the poem espouses any sort of historicism, it is one that recognizes the slave past as fundamentally oblique and mystifying.

"The Avocado" registers slavery's constitutive opacities with striking clarity. Hayes abstains from what Hortense Spillers describes as the "search for a point of absolute and indisputable origin, for a moment of plentitude that would restore us to the real, rich 'thing' [slavery] before discourse touched it."[46] This search is an ever more "vain" one, which is why Spillers argues that "every generation of systematic readers is compelled not only to reinvent 'slavery' in its elaborate and peculiar institutional ways and means but also, in such play of replication, its prominent discursive features as . . . [a] field of enunciative possibilities."[47] Following this line of reasoning, practitioners of Morrisonian poetics and its critical and literary offshoots expose far more about their own generation than they do about the generations of those who lived during slavery. "The Avocado" marks an attempt to come to grips with the ineluctable failures that attend these and other critical and imaginative efforts to recover, and therefore redeem, the losses that slavery brought about. In large part, this is the substance of the poem's historiographical and ethical interventions: it calls on critics, writers, and cultural producers to reckon with the notion that the slave past will always remain irrecoverable because we are not part of it.[48] While evidentiary limits and problematics constrain any historiographical project, African American literary studies' current investment in remembering slavery is so prodigious that it has almost become unthinkable to acquire any sort of "critical agency" in the field without "making the slaves' 'hidden history' a vital dimension of the effort to define black political goals in terms of a model of representation."[49] "The Avocado" urges us to recognize that much of the slaves' history will forever remain hidden. Hence, the present and future usability of that history for building forms of political solidarity as means to achieve full democratic inclusivity is tenuous, even chimerical.

As if to reinforce why we must abandon slavery as the source for current and future forms of black political belonging and social affiliation, Hayes introduces the figure of Harriet Tubman in the second half of "The Avocado" to insinuate that an overinvestment in recovering slavery's unrecoverable leaves one heedless of, and dangerously vulnerable to, the realities of his own present.[50] The final demand that appears in the poem prompts the scene: "Demand twenty-one: a Harriet Tubman statue on the mall!"[51] Through "weeping" and "walking wet tissue to the trash can," the lecturer says, "Harriet Tubman was a walking shadow," or, "Harriet Tubman / walked in shadows," or, "To many, Harriet Tubman was a shadow / to walk in," and the meaning is "pureed flesh with lime juice, / minced garlic, and chili powder; it is salt, and the pepper / Harriet Tubman tossed over her shoulder to trouble the bloodhounds."[52] Here, Hayes uses the narrator's distracted attention to suggest that, no matter which story one tells about Tubman, its most elemental meaning always returns to "pureed flesh"; we can never restore the avocado to its state of wholeness. This reference to Tubman is the first explicit association between a slave and guacamole (and the word *slave* only appears once, as the last word in the penultimate line of the forty-three-line poem). Her appearance bewilders the narrator, who moves from commenting on the conditions that avocado trees need to pollinate, to interacting with Yoyo, to criticizing how the lecturer positions himself in the history he is lecturing on.[53] All of this unfocused musing comes to a halt when Tubman orders, "Hush now," which leaves the entire poem suspended, lingering in a state of spatiotemporal indeterminacy.[54]

Tubman's command endows her with narrative authority and begins to confuse the poem's historical time:

"Hush now," Harriet Tubman probably said
near dawn, pointing a finger black enough to be her pistol barrel

toward the future or pointing a pistol barrel black enough
to be her finger at the mouth of some starved, stammering slave
and then lifting her head to listen for something no one but her could hear.[55]

In these lines, Hayes uses the rhetorical figure of the chiasmus to destabilize the poem's final setting. While the first half of the figure keeps the poem in the present, the second half transports the narrator backward in time, alongside Tubman herself. The narrator becomes "some starved, stammering slave" because the narrator stammers in this moment by means of performative alliteration and has starved throughout the poem.[56] The scene imagines the slave past and the present as contemporaneous but only in order to bring into relief their distance and differences. Tubman points her finger-pistol "toward the *future*," toward undefined ends that emerge from the world of one person's present. This means for us that the future the slave craved should not be the future we crave; indeed, it cannot be because our presents are not the same. Moreover, when Tubman "lift[s] her head to listen for something," only *she* can hear it. She thus seizes the narrative reins, and the poem ends in what feels like a perpetual caesura—for no one (the narrator, Hayes, us) can complete her story. We can't hear even it.

Because it refuses to assume that we are coeval with the slave past, "The Avocado" does not mine the history of slavery in order to find affective, ethical, or political resources for mending the racial ills of the present. That said, the poem is not about "getting over" or "getting through" slavery because it recognizes we are unequipped to carry out the work necessary to achieve such repair and closure. Rather, "The Avocado" esteems institutional and interpersonal abolitionist struggles of the past even as it clarifies that the conditions that made those struggles necessary are different than those we endure. The poem tells a history of discontinuity and difference: now is not then. It offers advice to those of us who turn too readily and assuredly to the history of slavery to describe and thus respond to the social and political realities of the present: "Hush, now."

NOTES

1. William Wells Brown, "A Lecture before the Female Anti-Slavery Society of Salem, Massachusetts" (1847), in *William Wells Brown: Clotel & Other Writings*, ed. William Wells Brown and Esra Greenspan (New York: Library of America, 2014), 856.

2. Brown's *Narrative* was the second-best-selling slave narrative of the 1840s, behind Frederick Douglass's *Narrative of the Life of Frederick Douglass, an American Slave, Written by Himself* (1845).

3. Brown, "A Lecture," 856.

4. Augusta Rohrbach, "'Truth Stronger and Stranger than Fiction': Reexamining William Lloyd Garrison's *Liberator*," *American Literature* 73, no. 4 (2001): 727.

5. By the late eighteenth century, "it was not too late to imagine an end to slavery, but it was too late to imagine the repair of its injury" (Stephen Best and Saidiya

Hartman, "Fugitive Justice," *Representations* 92 [fall 2005]: 1). In the authors' view, slavery exacted such injuries upon the slave that full restoration of the person of the slave and full reparation for her descendants are impossible. Particularly onerous for those seeking some form of redress are the "prevailing formulas of political rationality"—namely, capitalism and the law—because they render the "political aspirations" and "yearnings" of the slave and his descendants "inaudible and illegible." Best and Hartman call these aspirations and yearnings "black noise," whose inability to signify within dominant conceptions of the law and political economy reflects the fact that, as Brown would have it, slavery continues to defy representation (9).

6. Stephen Best, "On Failing to Make the Past Present," *Modern Language Quarterly* 73 (September 2012): 453.

7. Contemporary narratives of chattel slavery began to appear as early as the late 1960s, with Margaret Walker's *Jubilee* (1966) as an exemplar. But the representational and critical vogue I am tracing here began to take hold in the late 1980s.

8. Toni Morrison, "The Site of Memory," in *Inventing the Truth: The Art and Craft of Memoir*, ed. William Zinsser and Russell Baker, 2nd ed. (Boston: Houghton Mifflin, 1995), 91.

9. Ibid., 99; 89–91. Brown himself noted these restraints, arguing that the "fastidiousness" of his Salem audience "would not allow him to . . . represent to [them] the Slave in his lowest degradation" ("A Lecture," 856).

10. Morrison, "Site of Memory," 92.

11. Ibid.

12. Best, "On Failing to Make the Past Present," 459. Consider, for instance, Salamishah Tillet's recent essay on the slave character Patsey in Steve McQueen's film *12 Years a Slave*, which exemplifies this critical approach ("'I Got No Comfort in This Life': The Increasing Importance of Patsey in *12 Years a Slave*," *American Literary History* 26 [summer 2014]: 354–361). In sketching the ways in which the film "asks us to reconsider the implications of seeing *woman* and *slave* as mutually constitutive terms," Tillet writes, "And while McQueen does not offer us a full chorus [of women], like the 'singing women' who literally save Sethe from the haunt of slavery in both the novel and film versions of Toni Morrison's *Beloved* (1987), he gives us an ensemble of African-American women's experiences during both freedom and slavery that *start* to complicate this American story and fill in those silences and omissions of the old and new historiographies of slavery" (355, 360.)

13. Best, "On Failing to Make the Past Present," 463. Pursing a different but related critique, Kenneth W. Warren recognizes "the way that the recent recourse to history in discussions of African American life and culture has tended to make discrete periodizations beside the point, and to attach a taint of injustice to periodization itself, which by its very definition has to be concerned as much with discontinuity as continuity and has to insist on some distinction between past and present. Accordingly, to proclaim the 'was-ness' of something so recent as the last century of African American literary production [as Warren does] carries with it an almost sinister cast" (*What Was African American Literature?* [Cambridge, Mass.: Harvard University Press, 2011], 84). Notably, both Warren and Best identify Ian Baucom's *Specters of the Atlantic: Finance Capital, Slavery, and the Philosophy of History* (2005) as an example of this historiographical approach and ideological persuasion.

14. Saidiya Hartman, "The Time of Slavery," *South Atlantic Quarterly* 110, no. 4 (2002): 774, 775. Preslavery black life in Africa, idyllic and pristine, became a trope in African

American writing very early. For example, see Russell Parrott's 1814 "An Oration on the Abolition of the Slave Trade," in *Early Negro Writing, 1760–1837,* ed. Dorothy Porter (Baltimore: Black Classic Press, 1995), 383–390.

15. Walter Benn Michaels, *Shape of the Signifier: 1967 to the End of History* (Princeton, N.J.: Princeton University Press, 2004), 129–168.

16. Morrison, "Site of Memory," 92.

17. Jelani Cobb, "Tarantino Unchained," *New Yorker,* January 2, 2013, http://www.newyorker.com/culture/culture-desk/tarantino-unchained, accessed November 3, 2015; Jasmine Nichole Cobb, "Directed by Himself: Steve McQueen's *12 Years a Slave,*" *American Literary History* 26 (summer 2014): 339–346.

18. Warren, *What Was African American Literature?,* 84.

19. Best, "On Failing to Make the Past Present," 456, 474. Ironically, Best argues that "Morrison herself has the condition" for this "undoing" in her 2008 novel, *A Mercy* (465–466).

20. Ibid., 454.

21. These desires are "the desire for intellectual mastery over an affectively charged, often unpredictable or even incomprehensible social world; the desire for release from uncomfortable feelings of guilt or impotence; the desire for a present whose possibilities are radically unhinged from the constraints of the past" (ibid.).

22. Ibid., 455–456.

23. Evie Shockley, "Going Overboard: African American Poetic Innovation and the Middle Passage," *Contemporary Literature* 52 (winter 2011): 791–792.

24. Major Jackson, "The Historical Poem," *American Poet* 35 (fall 2008): 5.

25. Ibid.

26. Paul Laurence Dunbar, "Frederick Douglass" (1895), in *In Memoriam: Frederick Douglass,* ed. Helen Douglass (Philadelphia: Yorston, 1897), 168–169; Evie Shockley, "from *The Lost Letters of Frederick Douglass,*" in *the new black* (Middletown, Conn.: Wesleyan University Press, 2011), 6–8.

27. On how these naming conventions take shape, see the titles of the historical poems in Jackson, "Historical Poem."

28. Terrance Hayes, "The Avocado," in *Lighthead* (New York: Penguin, 2010), 27.

29. Critics and cultural producers who came of age after the civil rights movement, the generation to which the narrator of "The Avocado" most likely belongs, have offered powerful critiques of Black History Month and the perfunctory ways in which the nation frequently observes it. For a fine encapsulation of these arguments, see the documentary *More Than a Month,* dir. Shukree Hassan Tilghman (Arlington, Va.: Public Broadcasting Service, 2009), DVD.

30. Events from his own life most likely inspired Hayes to write "The Avocado." In fact, the Yoyo of the poem probably refers to his wife, the poet Yona Harvey. Even so, I've refrained from assigning a gender to the narrator because the poem never does.

31. Noliwe M. Rooks, *White Money/Black Power: The Surprising History of African American Studies and the Crisis of Race and Higher Education* (Boston: Beacon, 2006), 31–60.

32. For lyrics, see Mary G. Rolinson, *Grassroots Garveyism: The Universal Negro Improvement Association in the Rural South, 1920–1927* (Chapel Hill: University of North Carolina Press, 2007), 119.

33. Hayes, "Avocado," 27.

34. Best, "On Failing to Make the Past Present," 456.

35. Hayes, "Avocado," 27.

36. Given our current political climate, the more compelling case for reparations for African Americans involves the legal and extralegal injustices of Jim Crow segregation in the twentieth century, not those of chattel slavery. See Ta-Nehisi Coates, "The Case for Reparations," *Atlantic*, May 21, 2014, http://www.theatlantic.com/magazine/archive/2014/06/the-case-for-reparations/361631/, accessed December 17, 2015.

37. Walter Johnson, *Soul by Soul: Life inside the Antebellum Slave Market* (Cambridge, Mass.: Harvard University Press, 1999), 19.

38. Hayes, "Avocado," 27.

39. Ibid.

40. Ibid.

41. Ibid. Of course, the speaker could be exaggerating in the heat of his speech. The important point here is that the circumstances that condition the word *president* make it productively equivocal.

42. Comedian Chris Rock captured this irony with biting humor: "You know what's so sad, man, you know what's wild? Martin Luther King stood for nonviolence. Now what's Martin Luther King? A street. And I don't give a fuck where you are in America, if you on Martin Luther King Boulevard, there's some violence going down. It ain't the safest place to be" (*Chris Rock: Bring the Pain*, dir. Keith Truesdell [New York: Home Box Office, 1996]). See also Alan Scher Zagier, "Along MLK Boulevards in the USA, an Urban Struggle," *USA Today*, January 19, 2014, http://www.usatoday.com/story/news/nation/2014/01/19/mlk-boulevard-urban-struggle/4648519/, accessed November 3, 2015.

43. Hayes, "Avocado," 27.

44. Hartman, "The Time of Slavery," 759, 758. Best argues that this article "represents a mere moment in the genealogy of melancholy historicism, and one that Hartman herself appears to have superseded, as the fundaments to her thought shift significantly in *Lose Your Mother* [2007]. In the latter text, dispossession forms the condition of relation for blacks in the New World, and the irredeemable past the grounds of any historiography of slavery. The title alone signals the book's deep attachment to what I am calling the abandonment thesis" ("On Failing to Make the Past Present," 464).

45. Best, "On Failing to Make the Past Present," 460. Here he quotes Slavoj Žižek, "Melancholy and the Act," in *Did Somebody Say Totalitarianism? Five Interventions in the (Mis)use of a Notion* (London: Verso, 2001), 141.

46. Hortense Spillers, "Changing the Letter: The Yokes, the Jokes of Discourse, or Mrs. Stowe, Mr. Reed," in *Slavery and the Literary Imagination*, ed. Deborah E. McDowell and Arnold Rampersand (Baltimore: Johns Hopkins University Press, 1989), 29.

47. Ibid., 29, 28.

48. In her analysis of Douglas Kearney's "Swimchant for Nigger Mer-folk (An Aquaboogie Set in Lapis)" (2009), Evie Shockley argues that it "takes another approach to honoring what has been lost; it instead underscores the irrecoverability of those voices by giving us in their place, so to speak, a spirited series of utterances that remind us of what is absent via excessive strategies of postmodernist play" ("Going Overboard," 805). In my view, "The Avocado" works similarly but is more concerned with exploring those silences.

49. Best, "On Failing to Make the Past Present," 453.

50. In 1972, the sociologist Orlando Patterson argued that African Americans must get "beyond 'blackness'" because "to survive they must abandon their search for a past, must indeed recognize that they lack all claims to a distinctive cultural heritage, and that the path ahead lies not in myth making and in historical reconstruction, which are always doomed to failure, but in accepting the epic challenge of their reality. Black Americans can be the first group in the history of mankind who transcend the confines and grip of a cultural heritage, and in so doing, they can become the most truly modern of all peoples—a people who feel no need for a nation, a past, or a particularistic culture, but whose style of life will be a rational and continually changing adaptation to the exigencies of survival, at the highest possible level of existence" ("Toward a Future That Has No Past: Reflections on the Fate of Blacks in the Americas," *Public Interest* 27 [spring 1972]: 60–61). Nearly forty years later, this position remains on the margins of black critical thought and literary practice; "[Toni] Morrison no doubt played a major hand in smothering Patterson's vision" (Best, "On Failing to Make the Past Present," 459).

51. Hayes, "Avocado," 27.

52. Ibid.

53. After the lecturer says, "We weren't going / to be colored, we weren't going to be Negro," the narrator responds, "and I'm thinking every time I hear this story it's the one telling the story / that's the hero" (ibid., 28).

54. Ibid.

55. Ibid. This scene alludes explicitly to part 2 of Robert Hayden's stirring poem "Runagate Runagate" (1962), which features Tubman leading a band of fugitive slaves northward: "*Hush that now,* / and she's turned upon us, levelled pistol / glinting in the moonlight: / Dead folks can't jaybird-talk, she says; / you keep on going now or die, she says" (in *Collected Poems,* ed. Robert Hayden and Frederick Glaysher [New York: Norton, 2013], 60). In a 2004 interview, Hayes listed Hayden as a poet whose work "helped broaden the scope of my poems" (Charles H. Rowell, "'The Poet in the Enchanted Shoe Factory': An Interview with Terrance Hayes," *Callaloo* 27 [fall 2004]: 1073).

56. The narrator's earlier rumination on the culinary, agricultural, and nutritional aspects of the avocado and guacamole culminates in his whispering to Yoyo, "'Goddamn, ain't you hungry?'" (Hayes, "Avocado," 27–28).

3

Black Time

Slavery, Metaphysics, and the Logic of Wellness

CALVIN WARREN

Exhaustion is the contemporary crisis of black studies. Though affectively unified, it takes various forms: the obsession with everything "post" (such as postblackness and postracial), the fetishization of progress narratives (such as the resurgence of liberal humanism in the academy), and the stigmatization of those who argue that emancipation was a political ruse—that slavery remains with us. Our critical climate is one of impatience, as if we've somehow exceeded a statute of limitations for discussing slavery. This exhaustion produces a set of "disavowed desires," in Aida Levy-Hussen's words, that recodify *exhausted temporal imaginings* as scientific or objective (see chapter 10). In other words, the desire of the exhausted to enter a temporality beyond slavery—to inhabit the present—has structured our discourse about slavery. The phrase "getting over" is yet another index of this intensifying exhaustion— one that figuratively subordinates the subject of the slave past, holding out the dubious promise that if we can somehow get over this incorrigible subject, this conceptual-historical surplus, then we might achieve something like wellness, success, possessive individualism, power, agency, and so on. But what exactly are we getting over? What is the slavery that we are so eager to move beyond?

At the heart of this compulsion to get over is a crisis of time and objectivity: to get over anything, one must first objectify something and then place this object within a schema of time. In a sense, this compulsion expresses a metaphysical will to power, a desire to dominate time in the twenty-first century. Thus, it is not surprising that many proponents of getting over describe slavery using a restricted temporal grammar—slavery was "back then," "this is now," "we're moving forward." Within this rhetoric, slavery becomes a conquerable object that we can temporize and leave aside; in turn, the act of leaving aside becomes the sign of wellness.

In my view, the critical compulsion to get over slavery is inextricable from the constitutive violence of the metaphysical enterprise. The aim of metaphysics is domination. Its function is to capture an event-horizon—something that exceeds metaphysical time—and then transform it into a historical object and dominate it. In contrast, I argue that slavery is not reducible to an object-event of metaphysics; moreover, it comprises an event-horizon that structures western thought itself. Slavery, in my analysis, is an antiblack episteme that enables the distinctions between human and nonhuman, citizen and property, self-possession and dispossession to have meaning. Thus, slavery exceeds the frame of the historical event that we are so eager to get over and indeed provides the condition of possibility for the liberal grammar of humanism that undergirds the compulsion to get over in the first place.

In essence, there is no meaning or world without slavery, which is why it is a horizon and not an object. Yet because slavery has become the metaphysical object of historiography, subjected to narratives of linearity, movement, and change, the event-horizon is distorted as merely one tragic event among others that we can somehow move beyond. I propose an alternative temporality of slavery—one that I call *black time*. Black time is time without duration; it is a horizon of time that eludes objectification, foreclosing idioms such as "getting over," "getting through," or "getting beneath." I use the idea of black time to critique the metaphysical hegemony and the complicit logic of black wellness predicated on a relinquishment of historical complaint.

Object-Events, Event-Horizons, and Metaphysical Violence

I understand metaphysics as constituting a particularly violent episteme, one that reduces the grandeur of being into a scientific plaything—an *object* of rationality, calculation, instrumentalization, and schematization.[1] Metaphysics' insatiable will to power attempts to crush spontaneity and projectionality (that is, the ability to engage in a unique life project) and to turn the individual into a docile, mechanical instrument. Philosopher Gianni Vattimo asserts, "Pain is the very essence of metaphysics[;] . . . there is no metaphysics except the metaphysics of pain."[2] By this, he means that metaphysics produces the source of its own nourishment: it produces the pain that sustains it. Indeed, if we reflect on the destruction, trauma, and devastation that structure existence, we will find at its root metaphysical thinking and organization of life. This enterprise of pain depends on certain strategies of domination to exercise control, and the strategy of objectification is, perhaps, the most destructive and pernicious of them.

Metaphysics works through object-events to establish its episteme: its violent organization of knowledge and claims to truth. In fact, there can be no metaphysics without them. An object-event is a scientific invention—a metaphysical entity—that colonizes the world through its imposition of the laws of metaphysics. Converting time into event in the name of knowledge, object-events are ironically *fraudulent*, for they present an impossible and orderly world that is fully knowable, transparent, and calculable within metaphysical logic. (This is what we call an object.)

Metaphysics seeks to dominate and to transform the event-horizon into an object-event. The event-horizon is that which exceeds metaphysical epistemes and incorrigibly escapes the clutches of metaphysics, even as metaphysics attempts to capture it through objectification. Slavoj Žižek, in *Event: Philosophy in Transit,* explains that "an event is the effect that seems to exceed its cause—and the space of an event is that which opens up by the gap that separates an effect from its causes." It is the "emergence of something new that undermines every stable scheme."[3] In this sense, events cause problems for the ontic approach—that is, metaphysical reasoning—because they defy established laws used to explain and govern our existence. (We might think of miracles as such an event.) Thus, metaphysics seeks to confine an event-horizon into a scientific box and invade it thoroughly to extract as much information as possible. In a sense, it attempts a forced translation of the ineffable into apodictic law, the opaque into the lucid. But event-horizons also defy the laws of temporality, or the vulgarization of time, as Martin Heidegger might describe it.[4] In dominating an event-horizon, metaphysics attempts to dominate time itself, transforming time into a mere object of scientific inquiry and calculation. Because our temporal sensibilities determine the orientation of our object-knowledge systems, time is always an issue in the translation from an event-horizon into an object-event. If metaphysical time relies on the stability of cause (beginning), effect (end), teleology (the calculation of cause and effect), past, present, and future, then part of the enterprise of pain is to stuff an event-horizon into the temporal categories of metaphysical reason. Thus, something that exceeds and defies metaphysical time is subjected to its logic; without this violent subjection we cannot know the event. In fact, we might suggest that disciplinary formations of knowledge emerge from vicious metaphysical domination.

What we call slavery can be seen as the result of metaphysical domination, both epistemologically and ontologically. In fact, *slavery is the triumph of metaphysics.* Through slavery, being becomes thoroughly objectified and instrumentalized; the African is transformed into "a being for the other," as Hortense Spillers has written—an instrumental-object infused with use value and traded within a perverse economy of cupidity, accumulation, and terror.[5] The ontological aspects of metaphysical domination are understood as they concern slavery, but the epistemological dimensions are often overlooked. This neglect, however, is far from benign. Epistemology anchors our ontological investigation of slavery. In other words, we know about this vicious ontological violence because slavery is *first* subjected to epistemological violence. In essence, slavery as an event-horizon is reduced to an object-event for our epistemological desires and interests. Our knowledge about slavery is inextricable from the metaphysical violence that preconditions it.

Slavery has become an object of historiography, and we can understand historiography as the violent metaphysical enterprise that objectifies time and space and reduces event-horizons into object-events.[6] Historiography reproduces metaphysical notions of linearity, cause-effect, progress, and schematization; we often refer to it as a science. It is one of the premiere metaphysical enterprises with the sole purpose of colonizing and objectifying time itself. Because historiography, probably more than any other disciplinary formation, claims slavery as an object, slavery is subjected to metaphysical time. Thus, when we are talking about slavery, we are always talking about time, either directly or indirectly. The temporal grammar that we use to discuss it distorts the event so that we can calculate it (for example, "When did it begin?" "When was or is it over?"). Perhaps describing slavery as an event-horizon seems awkward because we are conditioned to thinking about it as an object of science that can be traced and understood. If we follow Heidegger—who more than any other philosopher understood the violence of metaphysics—we can describe an event-horizon as that which discloses being itself or as Alain Badiou's meditation of the event as that which structures truth.[7] Event-horizons disclose and structure the condition of thought and existence. When we think about slavery as more than that thing, that object, that happened back then and that we are studying in our present, it discloses itself as an event that defies reason, rationality, and calculability. Indeed, it structures western thought itself. Psychoanalytically, we can suggest that slavery is a master signifier of antiblackness; it is the *phallus* of western philosophy and metaphysical knowledge formations. It is impossible to trace the non-sense of this phallus, to locate precisely its origin, because it is situated outside space and time. Thus, it preconditions both space and time. Because the phallus operates through substitution (meaning that it reproduces itself through a series of replaceable signifiers), slavery expresses itself in "endless disguise," as Spillers explains.[8]

In an interview with Mark Sinker, Greg Tate adumbrates this logic when he suggests that "the bar between the signifier and the signified could be understood as standing for the Middle Passage that separated signification from sign."[9] The structure of meaning in the modern world—signifier, signified, signification, and sign—depends on antiblack violence (slavery as master signifier) for its constitution. Not only does the trauma of the Middle Passage rupture the signifying process, but it also instantiates a meaningless sign as the foundation of language, meaning, and social existence itself. Following the work of Nicolas Abraham and Mária Török we could suggest that the meaninglessness of antiblack violence is the crypt-signifier that organizes the modern world and its institutions.[10] Any meaning that is articulated possesses a kernel of absurdity that blacks embody as fleshy signs. What I am suggesting is that slavery structures western thought; it is a violent metaphysical enterprise that reduces the grandeur of black being to an object of exchange and provides the condition of possibility for western institutions—trade, economy, philosophy, medical science, theology, and so on. (Can we envision modern civil society *without* slavery?) Slavery exceeds ontological violence—the reduction of black being to object. It structures the world itself; in Frank Wilderson's words, "no slave, no world."[11] When we limit our scope of slavery to the physical and the legal, we neglect other forms of violence that constitute slavery, such as epistemological and metaphysical violence. These other aspects are not easily quantifiable using historiographical instruments and positivists methods. We are just beginning to mine the depths of slavery as an epistemological, metaphysical (and ontological), and spiritual force. To suggest that slavery is a thing of the past is to deny the unsettling lifespan of violence; for certain forms of violence never die but are continually regenerated, reborn, and reincarnated. Slavery is such a violence.

Our conceptions of American slavery have overwhelmingly been historiographical, and historiography traffics in the metaphysical violence of temporality that engenders it. The event-horizon that structures modern thought and meaning is reduced to a mere scientific object with a beginning (supposedly 1619) and an end (supposedly 1865). This violence determines the way in which we talk about slavery; it turns slavery into something we can get over, control, calculate, and dominate. Perhaps our imagined need for control is at the root of our anxieties about slavery. If we can no longer objectify and monitor it, what might happen to our episteme of progress, movement, and change? Can we indeed be agents without the metaphysical instruments that ensure the exercise of such agency? Slavery is precisely a surplus that resists scientific capture, despite the indefatigable effort of metaphysics to dominate it.

The time of slavery, then, is a temporality outside of metaphysical time; it is time that fractures into an infinite array of absurdities, paradoxes, and contradictions. It is a time, much like time in the unconscious, in which the horizon of violence fractures the vectors of temporality. Present, past, and future all lose concrete meaning, and we are left with an accretion of undecipherable flashes. In other words, we distort the force of slavery by attempting to temporize it. Such violence cannot be said to ever end, even if we can attempt to trace its birth. It is precisely this time outside of duration that we must confront when we discuss slavery.[12] The problem is that our metaphysical grammar for discussing the event-horizon of slavery limits our understanding of the devastation of slavery. How do you discuss an event-horizon that provides the condition of thought? How do you determine the beginning or end of such a seismic force? The temporal vectors of past, present, and future are inadequate to capture the event, and the event fractures these vectors as we attempt to squeeze the event into them. We lack an appropriate grammar for discussing the time of slavery, and we carry this problem of grammar into our analysis.

Black Time

Slavery is the *extremity* of antiblackness through time. Imposing metaphysical temporality on the African body to accomplish the work of objectification is part of the internecine enterprise of slavery. What type of temporality sustains the black body in the hold of the dungeon or slave ship? How do you orient yourself in time and space without any reference, especially when the journey could take months? Temporal domination is essential to slavery; its purpose is to disorient, objectify, and terrify. Not knowing where you are, how long you've been there, how long this torment will continue, or if there is an end in sight is part of the domination that separates the white ship captain from the black cargo in the dark hold. Put differently, slavery works through temporal domination. Blackness is the product of such temporal domination, and metaphysical time is recoded as a feature of racial privilege. The time of slavery is multidimensional and cyclical, and antiblackness is a particular colonization of time through black bodies.

In "Possible Pasts: Some Speculations on Time, Temporality, and the History of Atlantic Slavery," Walter Johnson describes certain aspects of temporal domination. According to him, time is a site of contestation, imagination, and terror for beings captured during war, confined to dungeons, boarded on ships, and suspended in the ocean. Time, in a sense, is incalculable for the captive under such conditions. The "metaphysical horror of a 'middle' passage that some must have thought would never end and others might only have recognized as a trip across the '*kalunga*,' a body of water which separated the world of the living from that of the dead—a flight from time measured in the gradual physical deterioration of the worldly body"—compounds the ontological dimensions of domination.[13] Time is instrumentalized to pulverize and dominate the captive on the plantation. Perhaps this is why Frederick Douglass's master admonished him not to think about a future, for his time belonged to his master. The captive lives outside of metaphysical time, without a future, without an accessible past (natal alienation), and in a present overwhelmed with the immediacy of bodily pain, psychic torment, and routine humiliation. *Time is terror.* As Johnson writes:

> One of the many things slaveholders thought they owned was their slaves' time. Indeed, to outline the temporal claims that slaveholders made upon their slaves is to draw a multi-dimensional portrait of slavery itself. Slaveholders, of course, defined the shape of the day. Whether it ran from sunup to sundown, whether it was defined by the tasks that had to be done by its close, or was measured out into job scaled clock time, slavery's daily time was delineated by the master and often enforced by violence. Those who turned up late, quit early, worked too slowly, came up short, or failed to wait deferentially while the master attended to

other things were cajoled, beaten, or starved into matching the daily rhythms through which their owners measured progress. As well as quotidian time, slaveholders claimed calendar time as their own. They decided which days would be workdays, and which days would be holidays (or holy days); they enforced a cycle of yearly hires and calendar-termed financial obligations. And slaveholders thought they owned the slaves' biographical time: they recorded their slaves' birthdays in account books that only they could see; they determined at what age their slaves would start into the fields or set to a trade; when their slaves would be cajoled into reproduction; how many years they would be allowed to nurse their children they had, and how old they would have to be before retiring. . . . They infused their slaves with their own time—through the daily process of slave discipline, the foreign, the young, and the resistant were forcibly inculcated with the nested temporal rhythms of their enslavement.[14]

Not only did slave masters seize the captive's body as property, but they also seized his or her time, reifying it into a commodity of exchange and an instrument of torment. The "peculiar institution" of slavery could not exist without the violent metaphysical process of objectifying time; this process situated the black being outside the horizon of time that defines the human and into the indistinct zone of temporality—time without duration. We can call this black time. If we think about the way in which time orients the human existentially—birthdays, astrological signs, age, maturation, and so on—we see that time provides *meaning* for the human. So to seize time is, in essence, to seize the existential condition itself—to control the production and semiotics of meaning. Black beings are disoriented within metaphysical time; *they are temporally homeless.* This disorientation provides the necessary existential ground to discipline, punish, and destroy black bodies. Temporal domination is a vicious metaphysical enterprise; its aim is to break down the active will diurnally. Thus, we must consider a fourth temporal dimension in Johnson's distinctions (quotidian time, calendar time, and biographical time): existential time. Existential time is "the Time of Man," as Homi Bhabha writes: the "temporality of modernity within which the figure of the 'human' comes to be authorized."[15] *Ipseity*—that is, making the human proper to itself, the suturing of the self—is only accomplished through the time of man because it provides the necessary conceptual material to orient the self and concretize the boundaries between this self and the external world. To make a slave requires the foreclosure of *ipseity*, requires leaving the self in fragments. (Perhaps this was the existential riddle that W.E.B. Du Bois attempted to solve with his notion of "double consciousness.")[16] Black time is this foreclosure of the self, and we refer to this foreclosure as dispossession. The slave is dispossessed from the self only to the extent that the slave master can seize his or her time and *epidermalize* temporality (that is, black time and the time of man). *Slavery is the vicious enterprise of situating a being outside the time of man and in the abyss of black time.*

The inability or unwillingness of critical scholars to contend with black time diminishes the ontological and existential violence of slavery. In a sense, thinking in black time forces a reconsideration of the critical categories of analysis—history, linearity, progress, movement, and ethics. For this reason, scholars tend to reduce the event-horizon of slavery into the metaphysical object to conquer it and get over it. Perhaps our incessant desire to gain distance from the object animates this refusal of black time. How do you theorize an event that throws the past, present, and future into virtual crisis? Can we analyze slavery without these metaphysical distinctions? What is our investment in metaphysical time? Will thinking and writing in metaphysical time finally transform blacks into humans? In other words, does the performance of metaphysics resolve the ontological violence of dispossession and objectification?

In his essay "On Failing to Make the Past Present," Stephen Best argues for the "nonrelationality between the past and the present" to imagine a black politics unmoored from collective condition and racial solidarity. In his view, scholars infuse the slave past with both an affective and an ethical dimension, which results in the compulsion to analyze the present through the prism of this past; affect becomes axiom. This compulsion translates into a "melancholic historicism" in which the critic remains "faithful to the lost object and [refuses] to renounce the [critic's] attachment to it."[17] Best seems to aspire toward a certain traversal narrative, in the psychoanalytic sense—to traverse the fundamental fantasy of slavery as repetitive structure and accept the real of historical disjuncture. This idea represents, perhaps, another fantasy—and contemporary theories such as postblackness share it—about living independently from history that hurts and to invest the now with an ethical-political potency capable of restoring ontological coherence. Best advances this thesis through the rhetorical device of *erotema.*[18]

> In fact, why has the slave past had such enormous weight for an entire generation of thinkers? Why must we predicate having an ethical relation to the past on an assumed continuity between that past and our present and on the implicit consequence that to study that past is somehow to intervene in it? Through what process has it become possible to claim the lives and efforts of history's defeated as ours either to redeem or to redress? And if we take slavery's dispossessions to live on into the twenty-first century, divesting history of movement and change, then what form can effective political agency take? Why must our relation to the past be ethical in the first place—and is it possible to have a relation to the past that is not predicated on ethics?[19]

What structures Best's critique is a strong metaphysics of time: the "slave past," "our present," "assumed continuity," "relation to the past," and so on. He reduces the event-horizon of slavery into an object-event that can be easily catalogued using past, present, and future. But this reduction rebounds upon itself in certain ways; the ontological dimensions of slavery, which escape this categorization, create aporias in the analysis.[20] In other words, his questions circumvent the aporia of time and ontology that would render the critique ineffective. When he asks, "And if we take slavery's dispossessions to live on into the twenty-first century, divesting history of movement and change, then what form can effective political agency take?" he assumes metaphysical linearity, that history does move and change, and that blacks are situated within this time as agents. But divesting history of movement and change can only be a problem for the political agent, who can exercise agency because temporal linearity exists for him or her. Why do we assume that blacks are agents if the ontological problem of blackness is not resolved? Does Best assume that emancipation resolved the existential and ontological violence of foreclosed *ipseity* and dispossession? If so, how did the law resolve an ontological crisis? His question presumes a humanism that does not quite apply to blacks. Thus, the danger of losing political agency becomes something of a false alarm or non sequitur. Because his question theorizes blackness in the wrong time, Best creates a crisis that undermines itself.

The answer to this question, then, would be that blackness doesn't assume any effective political agency within an antiblack context because the ontological crisis of blackness is not resolved. An immediate reaction to this answer is that the ontological crisis *is* resolved; blacks are free. Yet what instruments ensured the end of this crisis? What is the evidence of such freedom? Does the exception clause in the Thirteenth Amendment force a rethinking of legal optimism and the law's ability, or willingness, to resolve the ontological crisis of blackness? To my mind, one must at least prove the ontological discontinuity of slavery before we can talk about political agency. Historical movement and change do not translate into eradication and resolution. Change and movement are mere metaphysical fantasies, not synonyms for ontological coherence. Because "slavery unhinges certain givens about will, agency, individuality, and responsibility," as Soyica Diggs Colbert avers, applying the term *agency* under extreme conditions of antiblack violence distorts, or disavows, the problem of coherency that slavery foregrounds (see chapter 7). According to Alexander Weheliye, "resistance and agency assume full, self-present, and coherent subjects working against something or someone."[21] Applying the grammar of coherency (agency) to fractured beings reflects more slavery fatigue than it does any substantial ability to eradicate antiblackness. If we are to assume that political agency can restore ontological coherence, then proponents must present this evidence. Every attempt to diminish or eradicate antiblackness with agency, political or otherwise, reproduces the very antiblackness that one is trying to eradicate.

Best also asks, "Why must we predicate having an ethical relation to the past on an assumed continuity between that past and our present?" But what does "our present" entail? The critique is predicated upon a neat distinction between "slave past" and "our present" because presumably we are no longer slaves. According to philosopher Mladen Dolar, "the subject and the present it belongs to have no objective status, they have to be perpetually (re)constructed."[22] Best mobilizes the word *our* as a collective identity, even as he aims to "clear space for a black politics not animated by a sense of collective condition or solidarity."[23] What is the status of this "our" that he at once mobilizes and disavows? What conceptual work does this "our" accomplish in the present? It seems to force a homogenization of time and refuses the disjunctive reality of both this "our" and the present. Furthermore, what is the present? Jacques Derrida would describe it as a condition of non-adequation—that is, the present always carries the trace of another temporality, or trace structure. The present fractures into the past, future, future anterior, future perfect, and so on. The coherent present is a metaphysical fiction designed to facilitate what Dolar would call "reconstruction" and to conceal what Derrida would call "disjuncture." Homi Bhabha captures this fiction in "the enunciatory present."[24] The present is nothing more than a discursive maneuver, a perspective within modernity, a way of continually enunciating the self into existence. Best *must* enunciate this present throughout the text to conceal the ontological crisis that undergirds it: there can be no present without the disjuncture of black ontology and black time.

This brings us to the question of ethics. Best inquires, "Why must our relation to the past be ethical in the first place—and is it possible to have a relation to the past that is not predicated on ethics?" To this inquiry we must ask, is it possible to have an ethics at all within a context of antiblackness? In *Red, White, and Black: Cinema and the Structure of U.S. Antagonisms*, Frank B. Wilderson III limns the underside of ethics—what he calls "unspeakable Ethics." For him, "ontological incapacity is *the* constituent element of Ethics. Put another way, one cannot embody capacity and be, simultaneously, ethical."[25] Ethics is a relationality between coherent ontologies that is predicated on fractured blackness, or the nonrelational landscape between the human and blacks. In other words, ethics assumes a human subject at the heart of this relation, but the human subject can only remain human to the extent that it is able to demarcate the boundaries between the human self and the world of objects. Slavery became indispensable for the institution of ethics because it enabled the human to define its boundaries *against* a sentient object.

Furthermore, Emmanuel Levinas considers "time . . . [the] very relationship of the subject with the Other."[26] The ethical, then, is nothing other than the experience of time in which the subject and the other relate. This becomes somewhat problematic, however, if we read Frantz Fanon with Levinas. For Fanon, blacks lack symbolic placement as both subject and other because antiblackness colonizes the sphere of the other, leaving blacks without a position within the temporal relation we call ethics.[27] Thus, ethics is a field that excludes blacks as a necessity, given that the subject cannot relate to something that lacks a symbolic position. It is an antiblack formation because its coherent subject is sustained only through black misery and suffering. The subject of ethics is the master, not the slave. It is interesting to return to the question of ethics within this context. Best assumes a symbolic position within *history* that secures the ethical relation. How can blacks have an ethical past if the field of ethics excises the instance of black-human relation? Perhaps "our" relation to the past is not predicated on ethics at all, and it never can be. We need a new grammar to describe black experience with the event-horizon as it fractures ethics and metaphysics. Best wants to capture the compulsion to engage this event-horizon, the necessity of it. The grammar of ethics, however, does not yield answers, only paradoxes and impasses.

If the ethical relation is really an experience of time between subject and other, as Levinas adumbrates, then the question of time becomes the circumvented aporia at the heart of Best's critique. Best resists the idea of historical repetition and reproduction—that the present is an assemblage of past repetitive grievances—but does not question the logic of presentism upon which the critique is grounded. What is the present? And how is it distinguished from the slave past? These questions challenge the critique of repetition and continuity because the critique assumes an objective distinction between temporalities. But does this demarcation of time between the slave past and our present fit the event-horizon of slavery? In "The Time of Slavery," Saidiya Hartman avers that "the distinction between the past and the present founders on the interminable grief engendered by slavery and its aftermath . . . the 'time of slavery' negates the common-sense intuition of time as continuity or progression, then and now coexist; we are coeval with the dead."[28] She shatters the logic of metaphysics with its commonsense narrative of linearity, progression, and change. For her, "interminable grief" escapes the confines of metaphysical enclosure and becomes a time without duration, a time outside of temporality—black time. The blackness of this time is what we might call grief; it is the black hole of time that resists linear narrativity. Best asserts that Hartman "solicits empathy with history's defeated through assertions that time has shown no movement" and questions the affective dimension of this solicitation. He, however, sidesteps her critique of metaphysical reasoning by focusing on the way in which feeling becomes axiom, not on the question of time itself. Does grief have a temporality? What temporal schema fully captures grief? Can we locate its precise beginning and end? This seems to be part of the complexity of Hartman's thinking about the time of slavery. If time shows movement, as Best seems to imply, does grief move with it in linear fashion? What would grief movement entail? Metaphysical time fails to account for the grief of slavery. The point is not so much that we need or have an affective relation to the past so much as the notion that black grief itself is untemporizable. The event-horizon of slavery resides precisely within the no-time of black grief. To assume that black grief is over or in the past misunderstands grief itself because grief is not subject to the metaphysics of time that orients historical subjects. The violence of slavery constitutes an interminable grief that resists the vectors of present, past, and future. To argue that slavery is a falling away from our present rests on a limited understanding of slavery—one that reduces it to a certain legal, material, and historical incarnation and neglects the epistemological, spiritual, traumatic, and metaphysical dimensions of such violence.

In *Trauma and the Politics of Memory*, Jenny Edkins suggests that "trauma time is inherent in the destabilization and production of linearity. Trauma has to be excluded for linearity to be convincing . . . [and] similarly, trauma time cannot be described in the language we have without recourse to linearity."[29] Grief and trauma both express a temporality outside of and fracturing through metaphysics; we cannot express it within the grammar of metaphysics without creating catachresis. If, indeed, slavery is the horizon of unspeakable ontological and existential violations, then we cannot properly place slavery into the past, present, or future. Our desire to do so is an expression of a certain will to power, as Friedrich Nietzsche might describe it—to control, objectify, dominate, and get over the event-horizon of black grief.[30] Best's critique may represent a class of discourses with this metaphysical will to power. Charting slavery along a temporal scheme distorts the very thing we wish to understand. Epistemology destroys much more than it illuminates in this instance.

The Logic of Wellness

How do you get over an event-horizon? What cartography enables us to map the existential coordinates to get over it? Can you get over something that provides the condition of possibility for getting over itself, meaning the structure of thought? The compulsion to get over articulates a metaphysical impulse to objectify slavery, to turn it into a conquerable object. What is the status of this "over" that we are supposedly getting when we objectify slavery? "Over" becomes a synonym for wellness. When we think about wellness, we are always already spatializing, creating the boundaries between wellness and sickness, between presence and absence. But when we get over slavery, we are attempting to dominate black time through the metaphors of spatiality. *Wellness, then, is the compulsion to dominate time, to turn it into an object that can be thoroughly understood, analyzed, and eventually discarded when no longer needed. Sickness, by contrast, defines the inability to objectify black time—to live within it.*

Are we able to get over an event-horizon with the tools of metaphysics: psychology, psychiatry, and therapy? If getting over signals an impossible desire, a neurotic compulsion to control the uncontrollable, what does wellness really mean? Doesn't it announce a certain sickness at its core—an antiblack pathology of dominating time through black bodies? And doesn't sickness embody the only hope for wellness—acceptance of the ineradicable nature of the event-horizon of slavery? Wellness is an aspect of what Lewis Gordon might call "bad faith."[31] It is an impossibility encoded as mandatory capacity.

The domination of black time, however, is a particularly violent process, and those who are unable or unwilling to engage in the impossible are stigmatized in various ways that perpetuate the sickness that advocates of getting over wish to achieve in the first place. Thus, we cannot separate the enterprise of wellness from the various forms of violence that sustain it in an antiblack order. In *Protest Psychosis*, Jonathan Metzl documents the way in which wellness, sickness, and psychiatric disorders (particularly schizophrenia) were used to justify incarcerating black civil rights activists.[32] Those who could not get over slavery were easily diagnosed as insane, sick, and unfit for society; wellness became an instrument of state-sponsored discipline, control, and terror. What would it mean, however, to get over slavery in this instance? Are lack of protest, silencing of discourse, and acclimation to antiblack violence signs of wellness? If you get over slavery, where do you land? Wellness is an expression of metaphysical logic, the logic of pain; it produces its own pathology and recodifies it as salubriousness. Perhaps it is time to get over "getting over" and to contend with slavery as a master signifier of antiblackness. Slavery is an event-horizon that expresses itself in endless disguise, through a time outside of duration—black time.

NOTES

1. My conception of metaphysics has been greatly influenced by Martin Heidegger's *Introduction to Metaphysics*, 2nd ed., trans. Gregory Fried and Richard Polt (New Haven: Yale University Press, 2014).

2. Gianni Vattimo, *Nihilism and Emancipation*, trans. William McCuaig (New York: Columbia University Press, 2004), 70.

3. Slavoj Žižek, *Event: Philosophy in Transit* (New York: Penguin, 2014), 12.

4. Martin Heidegger, *Being and Time*, trans. Joan Stambaugh (Albany: State University of New York Press, 2010), 320–333.

5. Hortense Spillers, *Black, White, and in Color: Essays on American Literature and Culture* (Chicago: University of Chicago Press, 2003).

6. For a provocative discussion of historiography and metaphysics, see Hayden White, "The Metaphysics of Western Historiography," *Taiwan Journal of East Asian Studies* 1 (June 2004): 1–16.

7. Alain Badiou, *Being and Event*, trans. Oliver Feltham (New York: Continuum, 2007).

8. Spillers, *Black, White, and in Color*, 208.

9. Gregory Tate, interview with Mark Sinker, unpublished transcript, 1991.

10. Nicolas Abraham and Mária Török, *The Wolf Man's Magic Word: A Cryptonomy*, trans. Nicholas Rand (Minneapolis: University of Minnesota Press, 2005).

11. Frank B. Wilderson III, *Red, White, and Black: Cinema and the Structure of U.S. Antagonism* (Durham, N.C.: Duke University Press, 2010), 11.

12. I borrow the phrase "time outside of duration" from Louis Althusser's description of "despotic time" in his *Politics and History: Montesquieu, Rousseau, Marx* (London: Verso, 2007), 78.

13. Walter Johnson, "Possible Pasts: Some Speculations on Time, Temporality, and the History of Atlantic Slavery," *Amerikastudien/American Studies* 45, no. 4 (2000): 489.

14. Ibid., 492.

15. Homi Bhabha, *The Location of Culture* (New York: Routledge, 1994), 240.

16. W.E.B. Du Bois, *The Souls of Black Folk* (New York: Barnes and Noble Classics, 2003).

17. Stephen Best, "On Failing to Make the Past Present," *Modern Language Quarterly* 73 (September 2012): 453–474, 460.

18. Erotema is a literary device in which one asks rhetorical questions to make an implicit argument. Best uses this device to make an implicit argument about the relation between time and slavery.

19. Best, "On Failing to Make the Past Present," 454.

20. An aporia is an irresolvable contradiction, paradox, or philosophical impasse. I have Jacques Derrida's concept of aporia in mind, and this indicates the moment in which the text undermines itself, creating conceptual chaos and instability. For an early demonstration of aporia, see his *Of Grammatology*, trans. G. Chakravorty Spivak (Baltimore: Johns Hopkins University Press, 1997).

21. Alexander Weheliye, *Habeas Viscus: Racializing Assemblages, Biopolitics, and Black Feminist Theories of the Human* (Durham, N.C.: Duke University Press, 2014), 2.

22. Mladen Dolar, *The Legacy of the Enlightenment: Foucault and Lacan*, cited in Bhabha, *Location of Culture,* 240.

23. Best, "On Failing to Make the Past Present," 454.

24. In *The Location of Culture*, Bhabha discusses Dolar's conception of reconstruction and Derrida's idea of disjunction as they relate to his idea of the "enunciatory present" (238–241).

25. Wilderson, *Red, White, and Black,* 49.

26. Emmanuel Levinas, *Time and the Other and Other Essays*, trans. Richard A. Cohen. (Pittsburgh: Duquesne University Press, 1987), 39.

27. Frantz Fanon, *Black Skin, White Masks*, trans. Charles Markmann (New York: Grove, 1967). Also see Ronald Judy's brilliant analysis of symbolic placement and blackness in "Fanon's Body of Black Experience," in *Fanon: A Critical Reader*, ed. Lewis Gordon, T. Demean Sharpley-Whiting, and Renee T. White (Hoboken, N.J.: Wiley, 1996), 53–73.

28. Saidiya Hartman, "The Time of Slavery," *South Atlantic Quarterly* 110, no. 4 (2002): 758.

29. Jenny Edkins, *Trauma and the Politics of Memory* (Cambridge: Cambridge University Press, 2003), 16.

30. Friedrich Nietzsche, *The Will to Power*, trans. Walter Kaufman and R. J. Hollingdale (New York: Vintage, 1968).

31. Lewis R. Gordon, *Bad Faith and Antiblack Racism* (Atlantic Highlands, N.J.: Humanities Press International, 1995).

32. Jonathan Metzl, *Protest Psychosis: How Schizophrenia Became a Black Disease* (Boston: Beacon, 2010).

4

The Inside-Turned-Out Architecture of the Post-Neo-Slave Narrative

MARGO NATALIE CRAWFORD

Does your house have lions?[1]

–Sonia Sanchez

Toward the end of Toni Morrison's *A Mercy* (2008), we learn that our reading of the entire novel is a reading of writing that the character Florens has spread over the walls, ceiling, and floor of a house belonging to a slave owner. Florens's furious writing makes the interior of the house seem to explode. She writes, "These careful words, closed up and wide open, will talk to themselves. Round and round, side to side, bottom to top, top to bottom all across the room. Or. Or perhaps no. Perhaps these words need the air that is out in the world."[2] With this image, Morrison unveils the *inside-turned-out* architecture of the psychic hold of slavery—the fact that remembering the trauma of slavery is often inseparable from the need to twist and turn this lingering pain *inside out.* The notion first occurred to me when I read Octavia Butler's *Kindred* (1979), a novel whose contemporary meditation on the slave past is imagined through the narrative device of time travel. Toward the end of the novel, an unforgettable passage provides a new grammar for how we talk about the psychic hold of slavery. As Butler imagines a black subject "being still caught somehow" in the material, bodily effects of slavery, she writes, "something . . . paint, plaster, wood—a wall. The wall of my living room. I was back at home—in my own house, in my own time. But I was still caught somehow, joined to the wall as if my arm were growing out of it—or growing into it."[3] "Growing out of it" may initially sound more liberating than "growing into it," but the protagonist Dana's inability to differentiate between the two suggests that the psychic hold of slavery makes actual escape impossible. It has made her an assemblage, a mix of flesh and plaster "caught" between the past and the present.

In "On Failing to Make the Past Present," Stephen Best argues, "If *Beloved* incites melancholy, *A Mercy* incites mourning." He describes a linear progression in the turn from melancholy (the "persistent identification with the lost object") to mourning (the "more baffled, cut-off, foreclosed position with regard to the slave past").[4] In contrast, I lean on the idea, prominently theorized by Fred Moten and Dagmawi Woubshet, that black mourning troubles the temporal logic of Freud's framing of melancholia and mourning. Moten writes, "The way black mo'nin' improvises through the opposition of mourning and melancholia disrupt[s] the temporal framework that buttresses that opposition."[5] Building on his theory of black mourning, Woubshet, in *The Calendar of Loss*, argues that the binary of melancholia and mourning assumes that there is a fixed time line of loss.[6] I argue that the antibinary, liminal space of melancholy that cannot be untangled from mourning is the space of *A Mercy* and other texts that are *space clearing* and *opening up* to such an extent that they could be called post-neo-slave narratives.

Florens's writing on the walls—the act that circumscribes the entire novel—is an act of melancholy, a *Beloved*-style linking of past and present that constructs a continuity between the nascent antiblack racism of *A Mercy*'s colonial America and the antiblack racism that is still in the process of being denaturalized in the twenty-first century. But Florens's writing is also an act of mourning and release: it hails a future that does not have to be the past. This "black mo'nin'" refusal of an opposition between melancholia and mourning helps us learn to read a certain type of black resistance that is often illegible: the traumatized subjects' holding on to historical trauma in order to *repossess* the history that *possesses* them.

In chapter 10, Aida Levy-Hussen explains that *Beloved*'s protagonist, Sethe, "becomes obsessed with the task of satiating the ghost." Sethe and any black subject swallowed by melancholia are starved subjects engaged in such satiation, but the "black mo'nin'" *remix* of melancholia and mourning refuses this starvation. The satiated mo'nin' enables black subjects to always be in the process of repossessing history even as history, as Levy-Hussen reminds us, keeps possessing them. Levy-Hussen's lucid attention (as she thinks about Cathy Caruth's words "possessed by history") to traumatized people's inability to have control and authority over the telling of their own stories should remind us that people stuck on a word or a sentence are still in the process of writing. This is why melancholia and mourning are not oppositional forces in black radical imaginations. When you fail to see the inseparable mix of melancholia and mourning, you fail to see the *logic* of continuing to write yourself into existence, even if you know the idea of self-mastery is a sham.

Ashraf Rushdy argues that the "social logic" of the neo-slave narrative begins in the 1960s, when the psychic hold of slavery meets Black Power and the critique of William Styron's *Confessions of Nat Turner* collides with revelatory new slave historiographies.[7] It follows, then, that the *post*-neo-slave narrative appears, nonlinearly, before and during the twenty-first century, when the psychic hold of slavery comes into full contact with the unknown. Texts such as Morrison's *A Mercy*, Edward Jones's *The Known World* (2003), Monifa Love's *Freedom in the Dismal* (1998), and Amiri Baraka's play *The Slave* (1964) are post-neo-slave narratives because they pivot on what Calvin Warren sees as the "event-horizon" of slavery as opposed to slavery as an object of melancholic identification (see chapter 3). The *post* in post-neo-slave narrative is not a chronological distinction; it is a space-clearing gesture that shows a conceptual rather than a chronological difference.

If the neo-slave narrative is revisionist history, the *post-neo-slave* narrative is a move from the literary imagination that fills in the gaps (what historians cannot know) to the refusal to fill in the gaps but to linger in the unknown. If the neo-slave narrative builds on the form of nineteenth-century slave narratives, the post-neo-slave narrative may be the narratives that stop building *on* and begin to improvise more fully in what *A Mercy* refers to as "ad hoc territory."[8] In a 2008 interview, Morrison uses the word *pre-racist* as a way of describing this ad hoc territory: the liminal racial formation that had not yet (in the late seventeenth-century setting of *A Mercy*) consolidated into the "black equals slave" formation of later American slavery.[9]

The idea of literacy as freedom is a familiar frame in the foundational studies of slave narratives, but post-neo-slave narratives pressure readers to gain a counter-literacy, to learn to read slavery against received epistemologies.[10] Rushdy argues that neo-slave narratives are a move to the intersubjective; for unlike the nineteenth-century slave narratives, they "undermine the coherent subject of narration by developing a series of other voices which sometimes supplement and sometimes subvert the voice of the 'original' narrator" (231). Post-neo-slave narratives, such as *A Mercy*, hold onto intersubjectivity and also reclaim subjectivity in a manner that differs from the "I write, therefore I am" formulation of many nineteenth-century slave narratives. In *A Mercy*, after the blacksmith accuses Florens of losing her humanity, she responds in a manner that shows that she is indeed the subject who refuses to prove her humanity and only needs "Lina to say how to shelter in wilderness."[11] The characters' exchange reworks a well-known scene from *Beloved*, in which Paul D. tells Sethe, "you got two feet, Sethe, not four." The text then reads, "Right then a forest sprang up between them; tactless and quiet."[12] In *A Mercy*, this forest is not quiet when Florens seizes her right to see herself with her own eyes, not through the blacksmith's charge that she has become a state of wilderness. Her answer is riotous: "You say I am wilderness. I am."[13] The excessiveness of this claim to self is what we need to imagine when we try to take seriously the idea that the entire novel is what she writes on the walls of the house. Florens's embrace of black subjectivity as wilderness can be understood, like Hortense Spillers's theory of flesh, as the black feminist critique of any self-determination that makes it impossible to imagine the unimaginable.

The architecture of the unknown (my metaphor for the psychic hold of slavery) is more than a metaphor. As Jacques Derrida explains in his 1986 interview with Eva Meyer, when architecture is treated as a metaphor, a technique, and a representation, there is a separation between thinking and architecture that parallels the insidious separation of theory and practice. Derrida tries to rescue the "architectural event" as a "way of thinking," reveling in the fact that language is "enmeshed" in and also moving through architecture.[14] When he writes of a "constant 'being on the move,' the habitability of the way offering no way out entangles you in a labyrinth without any escape," his imagery strikingly recalls the black mantra "make a way out of no way," arguably the most familiar phrase in the everyday practice of African American survival and resistance.

The architecture of the post-neo-slave narrative is the unknowable and the uncontainable, what Baraka anticipates, in *The Slave*, when the character Walker performing as an "old field slave," declares, "We need . . . a meta-language."[15] But what kind of meta-language could allow us to hear "slave" and "free" in the same temporal and spatial order? At the end of *A Mercy*, Florens writes, "Hear me. Slave. Free. I last" (189). Morrison disrupts the naturalized "from slavery to freedom" flow of the nineteenth-century narrative by making us understand visually that the words can occupy the same temporal and spatial location. The push, in post-neo-slave narratives, against the time and space of "slavery to freedom" is a push *outside* of the discourse that makes slavery legible and a push to the *wilderness* that slavery created for enslaved subjects.

We read the words in *A Mercy* on the page, but Morrison wants us to imagine reading them on a surface that has a material presence. I think of the names of enslaved Africans written on the reconstruction of a wall of a slave cabin that is a part of the Oak Alley Plantation tour in Vacherie, Louisiana (fig. 4.1). When I saw this wall of names, I felt that the only way to begin to honor the enslaved was to slowly read every name of every enslaved African who was reduced to property on this plantation. When I reached the name Do, I paused. The name may sound like a call for action, a slave owner's command reborn as a call for reparations. Yet the window in the middle of the list of names makes these names seem like a move to the interiority of slavery and also a way of looking outward at what cannot be contained in any exhibit approach to understanding American slavery.

Although Florens's writing on the wall is not a list of names, do we read her writing as we would a memorial? Because the entire novel is her writing on the wall, are we reading a novel or writing on a wall? The key difference may be the public interiority that the writing on the wall signals, a call for a memorializing that does not reinforce the boundaries between the public and the private in a manner that caters to the private zone of the national amnesia about slavery. When, in *A Mercy*, young Florens decides that she needs "Lina to say how to shelter in wilderness," Morrison subtly proffers a distinction between monuments that are built to control the experience of historical memory and

FIGURE 4.1. Interior of a reconstructed slave cabin, "Slavery at Oak Alley" exhibit, Oak Alley Plantation, Vacherie, Louisiana, December 2014. Photograph by author.

monuments that allow people to let go of the control they think they have. *A Mercy* made me cry the first time I read it in a way that is not so different from the way I cried when I visited the Oak Alley Plantation. The post-neo-slave narrative may offer some readers (among them, descendants of enslaved Africans) a way to break down and let go of the control we might think we have when we think about slavery. If *A Mercy* is a memorial (taking us back to the dedication of *Beloved*—to "sixty million and more"), it is a memorial "in the wilderness," a "shelter in the wilderness" (49).

In "Making the Memorial" (2000), Maya Lin analyzes her 1982 Vietnam Veterans Memorial to unveil a close relationship between books and memorials. She writes,

> The memorial is analogous to a book in many ways. Note that on the right-hand panels the pages are set ragged right and on the left they are

set ragged left, creating a spine at the apex as in a book. Another issue was scale; the text type is the smallest that we had come across, less than half an inch, which is unheard of in monument type sizing. What it does is create a very intimate reading in a very public space, the difference in intimacy between reading a billboard and reading a book.[16]

The idea of "a very intimate reading in a very public space" captures something essential in the architecture of the post-neo-slave narratives that make public the depths of the unknowability of the psychic hold of slavery.

At the same time, I am interested in the fact that post-neo-slave narratives are not memorials; they are antimemorial experimental forms. Consider, for example, Love's epistolary novel, *Freedom in the Dismal.* Formally recalling Florens's love letters that become her "letter to the world," the novel unfolds through a series of letters, written in 1983, that tell the story of a frustrated love affair between David, a young African American man imprisoned for thirty years, and Camille, a young African American woman. Despite the contemporary setting, lists of the names of slaves and free people of color who could be witnesses in a "Truth Commission" that shows the horrors of slavery appear abruptly between the letters throughout the novel. The first list appears in a multipage play within the novel. In these opening pages, Love plays with different fonts so dramatically that the book assumes a multimedia texture. The fonts collide voices and points of views, suggesting that the production of a testimonial space demands a capacity for improvisation. Love's use of improvisation as a foundation for the post-neo-slave narrative approximates Morrison's notion of the "ad hoc territory."

Freedom in the Dismal begins with the following boldfaced poster-like statement, which establishes, in the phrase of Florens's mother, that "there is no protection."

Your own Truth Commission.
Lights. Cameras. Notoriety.
Days upon days of probing our
insides. We show our insides
gladly. All we ask is that you not
eat them.[17]

The "[showing of] our insides" and the awareness of the threat of being consumed by an external, commodifying force vivifies the post-neo-slave narrative's heightened awareness of the forces of commodification that can create a slavery cultural industry that reduces the present of black people to the past historical trauma of slavery. Like Morrison, who emphasizes the "open wound that cannot heal" and the fact that "there is no protection," Love emphasizes both intersubjectivity and the threat of consumption.

Those keeping order at the Truth Commission claim that "everyone will be heard," but Love abruptly inserts the list of names throughout the novel as if to remind us that it is both a list of those who are not speaking for themselves and a list of the layers of what cannot be known. By way of these lists, Love signals that there is no closure to the event-horizon of slavery, though there is a release in the mourning that can be experienced as each individual's name is heard.

Please. All witnesses will be heard. We know many of you have been waiting a very long time. Please hold on to your numbers. Everyone will be heard.

21. *Daniel, a slave*
22. *Moses, a slave*
23. *Tom, a slave*
24. *Jack, a slave*
25. *Venus, a slave*
26. *Wallace, a slave*
27. *Thomas Hatchcock, a free negro*
28. *Andrew, a slave*

. . . .

44. *Bing, a slave*
45. *Nat, a slave*
46. *Dred, a slave*
47. *Arnold Artes, a free man of color*
48. *Nathan, a slave*

. . . .

58. *Elizabeth Crathenton, a free woman*
59. *Christian, a slave*
60. *Exum Artist, a free man of color*
61. *Bird, a slave*

Interspersed throughout the text, these lists convey Love's search for an archive of traces that will not inform us but force us to accept an unknowing. "Bird, a slave," is a witness waiting to be heard. The name itself speaks, even though what is being said remains a mystery.

Mimicking these lists that seem to never end, Love shows that the open wound of slavery has never closed. In the novel, the prison industrial complex is not just what Michelle Alexander has aptly named the "New Jim Crow." Love exposes it as the reenslavement of those suffering most from the lack of any reparations. As she brings prison literature and slave narratives together, she foregrounds the issue of wilderness in a manner that adds new dimensions to Morrison's use of the concept as a way of theorizing what the afterlife of slavery really is. Love anchors the emotional weight of the novel in the swamp area called the Dismal, an unsafe haven for runaway slaves where Nat Turner once hid. Her character Camille's father has heard about this swamp in the oral history passed on to him. Yet even though the area is life-threatening, the title of the novel, *Freedom in the Dismal*, signals the freedom by any means necessary that the Dismal represents. This is also what Florens embraces when she writes, "You say I am wilderness. I am."

In Jones's *The Known World*, the move to the unknown wilderness of slavery takes the form of foregrounding black slave owners and slaves owned by black masters. This Pulitzer Prize–winning post-neo-slave narrative was published in the early twenty-first century, a time when, arguably, there is more space for African American writers to address the lesser-known and more sensitive issues of slavery that complicate the totalizing assumptions of black innocence and white complicity in its evil. The architecture of turning the inside out is depicted literally in a passage describing the black slave owner Fern's "parlor dominated by trees, a peach and a magnolia, she and her servants had managed to domesticate." Jones describes this inside-out parlor: "The trees in Fern's house disoriented most people, those used to the inside always being inside and the outside always being outside."[18] As he imagines the life of white and *black* slave owners, he places his post-neo-slave narrative fully in the architecture of the unknown. His inscription of the psychological dimensions of being a black slave master and being a black person owned and reduced to property by a black person turns slavery inside out, making readers pause and think about the horror of a character such as Henry, who moves from slavery to slave master. It is hard to read this novel and not think about today's widening gap between the descendants of enslaved Africans who are poor and intensely disempowered and the descendants of enslaved Africans whose wealth protects them from the worst forms of antiblack racism.

The novel depicts the psychic hold of slavery most powerfully when Jones describes the pain felt by Henry's parents when he first tells them that he has bought a slave. His father, in utter bewilderment, beats his grown son with a stick and tells him, "Thas how a slave feel." His son then breaks the stick and says, "Thas how a master feels."[19] Henry's parents feel connected to the enslaved even though they are no longer slaves. In contrast, Henry enjoys being the mentee of Master Robbins, who owned him when he was a child. He lacks the inner urge to lift other black people from oppression. Some readers may connect this generational shift with the shift that separates civil rights and post–civil rights notions of racial solidarity. Jones shows that the psychic hold of slavery is sometimes black people's commitment (or lack thereof) to other oppressed black people.

The Known World's architecture of the unknown heightens when the novel creates new space for imagining how the psychic hold of slavery can also produce black suspicion of other black people. As Jones draws upon the limited historical records that prove the existence of black slave owners, he inserts these characters into the twenty-first-century literary tradition and adds new dimensions to the common focus in black studies on the divide and conquer techniques of white supremacy. Leaning into the unknowable, he imagines scars from these techniques that are much more than the familiar focus on the divisions between the field slaves and the house slaves. Malcolm X famously said, in his most cited speech, "And today you still have house Negroes and field Negroes. I'm a field Negro."[20] Imagine him delivering a speech about the difference between black slave owners and "field Negroes." *The Known World* takes us to a deeper sense of the antiblackness that black people participate in when they become part of the white supremacist power structure.

Yet Jones's move to foreground black slave owners also has the potential to liberate black people from the psychic hold of slavery; for if black slave owners existed, then being black cannot, in the deeper psychological registers, equal being a slave. Black people's legacy does not have to be the status of slave. Jones uses the word *legacy* in a passage that pivots on the melancholy that cancels out a black futurity that could be black prosperity, not black pain. Maude, mother-in-law of the recently deceased Henry, tries to convince her grieving daughter, Caldonia, not to abandon the slave-owning business: "But like your father, you have too much melancholy in your blood for your own good." Later, when speaking of Caldonia's brother, Maude reiterates this notion: "His blood has even more melancholy than yours. Leave it to him and your legacy will be out the door before morning."[21] The homonym *mourning/morning* signals how deeply invested Jones is, consciously or unconsciously, in the tension between melancholia and mourning. The melancholy is figured as the weakness that makes Caldonia unable to see her bright future or the legacy she has inherited.

But as this kaleidoscopic novel progresses with its steady introduction of new minor characters, Jones problematizes Maude's logical rejection of slavery. In chapter II he diverges from the main plot to offer an illustrative account of Morris Calhenny, a white slave owner who "suffered from a crushing melancholy." Beau, an enslaved African whom Morris owns, somehow understands that this melancholy has no remedy. He and Morris, when boys, had been "almost as close as brothers," and "Morris would seek out Beau when the melancholy hit because Beau never asked why he suffered like that, why Morris couldn't just get up and walk away from whatever was bothering him. Beau just stayed by his side until things got a bit better."[22] Jones crystallizes the feeling of stasis that melancholy produces, and his imagined meeting between Morris and Beau in this space is another example of the architecture of the unknown. We cannot know Beau's own inexpressible melancholy as he lives his life as a person owned by this "almost brother" whose melancholy he witnesses as he remains "by his side." Jones rechannels language that encapsulates the ethos of the post-race critique of the psychic hold of slavery—"just get up and walk away from whatever"—as he "cross-racializes the wound" (Jahan Ramazani's way of thinking about the cultural hybridity that trauma can create).[23]

The story of Morris ends with the intertwined story of Henry's father, Augustus Townsend, who is shot as he "gets up and walks away" from the man who believes he owns him. Augustus is a free man whose free papers are chewed up and swallowed by a slave patroller. He is sold back into slavery but refuses to live any longer as a slave. He decides that he would rather die. Morris's story begins with "crushing melancholy" and ends with crushing mourning incited by the image of Augustus being shot as he walks away from his "master." Jones shows what happens when someone "just get[s] up and walk[s] away from whatever."[24] Being stuck in the past is debilitating, but pathologizing the melancholy of the grieving leads to a misunderstanding of the psychic hold of slavery; that is, we often fail to recognize the resistance and power that have been created in the space of what appears to only be melancholy.

In *In the Break*, Moten asks, "Have you ever suffered from political despair, from despair about the organization of things? . . . What's the relation between political despair and mourning?" Here, we hear the power of a melancholy, a *stuckness*, that is more than stasis.[25] Moten uncovers this despair in Baraka's liminal pre–Black Arts/post-Beat work. The inside-turned-out architecture of Baraka's post-neo-slave narrative, *The Slave*, uses slavery as the frame (the beginning and the end) that encloses the 1960s setting of the play. The character Walker Vessels is a field slave who morphs into a radical black nationalist as the prologue ends and the play shifts in time. The same actor plays the role of the old field slave and the radical black nationalist. The temporal shift (between the prologue and the play proper) is also a tonal shift from the prologue's melancholy and mourning to the rage and exhaustion dominating the rest of the play, before we return at the end to the melancholy and mourning of the slave. The melancholic blues of the "old field slave," in the prologue, is inseparable from the jazz of the character's future-oriented push past the melancholy to the baffled "what now" sound of mourning.

I read the prologue and the epilogue as a subtle commentary on slavery's creation of the violent conditions of the 1960s race wars depicted in the interior of the play. Baraka makes the voice of the old field slave matter; he becomes the calm before and after the storm, the voice of ambivalence that rejects the master narratives that trap Walker (the black nationalist) and Bradford (the white antagonist) into a brutal, exhausting cycle of verbal warfare. Baraka's use of slavery as a frame suggests the complexity of the psychic hold of slavery. How has slavery produced the violent struggle between Walker and Bradford? How does the *living* room where the two characters (and Walker's wife, Grace) feud relate to the outside space of the slave, who refers to the need to recognize "personal phenomenological fields"?[26] What architecture of the psychic hold of slavery is Baraka exploring? How does the work done in this liminal play become the writer's attempt to let melancholy coexist with rage (and to let the psychic hold of slavery coexist with the psychic hold of black rage)?

The Slave's architecture of the unknown pivots not only on the mystery of the relation between the outer frame of the slave's voice and the inner textual and performance space of the 1960s but also on the utter unknowability of what happens to the daughters of Walker and Grace. Has Walker murdered them? Is the "child heard crying and screaming as loud as it can" at the end of the play the sound of one of the daughters?[27] The play closes with the trauma of reproductive futurity, and Gil Scott-Heron's iconic Black Power chant matches its tone: "Who will survive in America? Who will survive in America?"[28] The mystery of *The Slave* is the mystery of mourning encased in rage. How do we recognize the sadness that refuses to be quiet? Rage and resistance are often misread as having no connection to mourning and melancholy. Walker, dressed as the old field slave, addresses the audience from the space of before and beyond as he prepares for his role, in the play proper, as an angry, militant black nationalist. The consummate statement of the Old Man in the prologue—"your brown is not my brown, et cetera, that is, we need, ahem, a meta-language"—has another dimension when we read it as the older man talking to the younger generations.[29] The statement becomes a call for solidarity created through what cannot be known. Baraka implies that the meta-language, whatever it is, will allow the old field slave and the younger generations to find a meeting place in spite of their different relations to the psychic hold of slavery.

Baraka's stage directions describe how the actor playing the old field slave must morph into the younger man through the bodily and sonic expressions of one exhausted discourse moving into another. The writer implies that both slave narratives and 1960s black nationalism have reached the limits of their ability to explain the real meaning of black freedom and radicalism. The slave transforming into the 1960s character reveals the need for what Walker calls the "meta-language," a motion that allows black subjects to inhabit the past, present, and future at the same time. This "time of entanglement" (as Achille Mbembe describes it) produces the slippery "shift in an instant" labor that Baraka calls for in the stage directions: "Running down, growing anxiously less articulate, more 'field hand' sounding, blankly lyrical, shuffles slowly around, across the stage, as the lights dim and he enters the set proper and assumes the position he will have when the play starts."[30] As Baraka imagines the 1960s black radical as more "field hand sounding" than the old man who is actually enslaved, he gestures toward the possibility that some aspects of the psychic hold of slavery are produced in the larger event-horizon of slavery, after slavery ends.

Baraka's poem "An Agony. As Now" (1964) sheds light on this event-horizon's literal possession of Walker's body: "I am inside someone / who hates me. I look / out from his eyes."[31] In the lens of the poem, turning inside out would be the only way for blackened subjects to resist the brainwashing of a white power structure rooted in slavery. As Baraka reminds us that melancholia is, by definition, rage turned inward, he reimagines the nation as a person who feels white on the outside and black inside. The double consciousness of this nation is profound. The speaker of the poem is the black consciousness emerging from the interior of the white exteriority. The final words—"It [white hot metal] burns the thing / inside it. And that thing / screams"—provide another way of understanding the offstage screaming heard at the end of *The Slave*. The screaming is a type of fugitivity. Moten counsels, "The object vibrates against its frame like a resonator, and troubled air gets out."[32] Whatever escapes reshapes the container. The psychic hold of slavery is, sometimes, the psychic hold of fugitivity. As Haki Madhubuti advises, "DON'T CRY, SCREAM."[33]

This fugitivity is what Morrison foregrounds in *A Mercy* as Florens defines herself as wilderness. The character achieves a post-crying sensibility that screams words:

> You say you see slaves freer than free men. One is a lion in the skin in an ass. The other is an ass in the skin of a lion. That it is the withering inside that enslaves and opens the door for what is wild. I know my withering is born in the Widow's closet. . . . Still, there is another thing. A lion who thinks his mane is all. A she-lion who does not. I learn this from Daughter Jane. Her bloody legs do not stop her. She risks. Risks all to save the slave you throw out.[34]

The words "her bloody legs do not stop her" beg to be compared to Jones's words in *The Known World*—"why Morris couldn't just get up and walk away from whatever was bothering him."[35] Legs in pain really can move; there is a mourning that moves and screams and does not, like the classic neo-slave narrative, reclaim the humanity of the enslaved and the descendants of the enslaved but the wilderness of the unknown. Joan Anim-Addo and Maria Helena Lima, the editors of *Callaloo*'s special issue on the neo-slave narrative, argue that the "main reasons for this seemingly widespread desire to rewrite a genre that officially lost its usefulness with the abolition of slavery are to re-affirm the historical value of the original slave narrative and/or to reclaim the humanity of the enslaved by (re)imagining their subjectivity."[36] If the post-neo-slave narrative is invested, to any extent, in "reclaiming the humanity of the enslaved," the emphasis is on what Sylvia Wynter embraces as the radical black studies shift from the project of man to a new understanding of the human.[37] In the post-neo-slave narrative's approach to black humanity, being stuck in melancholy is not pathologized, and mourning is not set apart from rage, action, and resistance.

In chapter 6, GerShun Avilez reminds us that use of the words *social death* in relation to being black in an antiblack world should emphasize the living that exceeds this social death. Morrison's notion, in *A Mercy*, that being human is being wild allows us to see that black ontology is not set apart from social death. Indeed, black resistance to slavery and its afterlife resituates the meaning of being human as being unbound. The post-neo-slave narrative's architecture of the unknown pushes us to an understanding of ontology as inseparable from "hauntology," as Derrida shows in *The Specters of Marx*.[38] Colin Davis, in "Hauntology, Spectres, and Phantoms," explains, "For Derrida, the ghost's secret is not a puzzle to be solved; it is the structural openness or address directed towards the living by the voices of the past or the not yet formulated possibilities of the future. The secret is not unspeakable because it is taboo, but because it cannot not (yet) be articulated in the languages available to us. The ghost pushes at the boundaries of language and thought."[39] The post-neo-slave narrative impulse in Morrison's *A Mercy* is a push away from the "articulated" ghost in *Beloved* to the wilderness of the "not yet formulated possibilities of the future" that Florens represents. As she carves her words on the wall, she is refusing to allow anyone else to be the ghostwriter of her life. As she emphasizes "I am" after "You say I am wilderness," she becomes a ghostly *ghostbuster*.

Do these ghostly ghostbusters desire an ontology that is not shaped by hauntology? I want to hold on to Soyica Diggs Colbert's use, in this book's introduction, of Toni Cade Bambara's question "Are you sure . . . that you want to be well?" as a way of thinking about what is at stake when "we people who are darker than blue" hold on to slavery as a way of trying to know who we are and where we are.[40] Amus Mor's repeated questions in "Poem to the Hip Generation" (1972)—"who are we / where are we going / what are we here for"—still resonate.[41] Bambara's question gains another shape when we bring together these post-neo-slave narratives. It becomes, Do we want to know the depth of the unknowable? Morrison's reason for not ending *A Mercy* with the voice of Florens may be tied to her awareness that readers will barely know how to read the character's ferocious seizure of wilderness as an alternative to the skin enclosure her mother describes. It may indeed be more comforting to hear the voice of Florens's mother explaining how her skin became the enclosure of the wound of race. As she explains, after the Middle Passage, she was taken to Barbados and "seasoned" for slavery (slaveholders' own word for pre-slavery conditioning). She describes what has now become the familiar process of epidermalization, which Frantz Fanon has made a huge part of our grammar for talking about race.[42] Dreaming that she can talk to Florens, her daughter whom she has not seen for so many years, the mother says, "I was negrita. Everything. Language, dress, gods, dance, habits, decoration, song—all of it cooked together in the color of my skin. So it was as a black that I was purchased by Senhor, taken out of the cane and shipped north to his tobacco plants." The mother explains the cooking *in* "the color of [her] skin" after she painfully passes onto her daughter the inability to heal ("an open wound that cannot heal").[43]

The melancholy that the mother is passing on makes Best's argument in "On Failing to Make the Past Present" even more compelling. *A Mercy* does indeed "incite" mourning, as he says, but this mourning is produced through many melancholic moments. (The question of passing on the melancholy keeps rechanneling Morrison's words in *Beloved*: "this is not a story to pass on.")[44] The mother's mourning sounds so different from Florens's indignant, loud, angry mourning—for instance, her response to the "withering" created when the Widow makes her feel subhuman.[45] Florens's mourning sounds like Fanon's description, in *Black Skin, White Masks*, of the indignant response to being fixed by the antiblack gaze: "I was indignant. I demanded an explanation. Nothing happened. I burst apart."[46] This bursting apart is, finally, the deeper register of Florens's proclamation "You say I am wilderness. I am."

Our thinking about the psychic hold of slavery expands when we zoom in on this mourning that is not always legible—that makes Florens ask the black-smith, "Can you read?"[47] Everyday black vernacular, for example, such as "what had happened *was* . . ." sounds like melancholic language stuck on the emphatic "was," which becomes the energy that pushes blackened subjects forward. The everyday black vernacular sonic architecture of "what had happened *was*" may be turning inside out Carolivia Herron's simple and lucid diagnosis of African American family trauma in *Thereafter Johnnie* (1991): "What happened? Slavery happened."[48] Joy DeGruy Leary's use of the term *post-traumatic slave syndrome* may seem too simple a diagnosis for the psychic hold of slavery that persists in the twenty-first century, but her subsequent explanation of this phrase, in a 2003 grassroots community lecture, allowed me to see "shock" as a way in which people hold on precariously to the horror of the present as if it feels, sometimes, like the slavery past. She asked her skeptics, "Was any therapy ever given to the newly freed slaves? Do you think the *shock* of being so mistreated was passed on?"[49] Trembling hands hold on when they want to let go, not due to a patho-logical inability to decide to be well but due to the life and culture created in the architecture of the unknown. As Ntozake Shange told an interviewer, "I used to have boundaries up all the time, which is limiting. . . . I never want to feel limited. If anything is life-changing, being the descendant of a slave is. I went into therapy ten years ago because I needed to work that out. I've gotten better. Everything about me is more fluid, much less rigid. I'm gonna do everything I can, feel everything I can, until it hurts."[50] Shange implies that the real problem is a state of numbness that makes us unable to mourn what we cannot know.

The call for collective mourning in the space of the unknown sets the post-neo-slave narrative apart from the neo-slave narrative. Its mood is the impulse to privilege collective unknowing as collective mourning. This mood cannot be periodized; it appears in Baraka's 1964 play as well as twenty-first-century texts such as Jones's *The Known World* and Morrison's *A Mercy*. The psychic hold of slavery creates the external, collective work of culture; the inner, psychic hold is turned inside out as the unknown becomes the strange *structure* of feeling that made Gwendolyn Brooks write, "In the wild weed / she is a citizen."[51]

NOTES

1. Sonia Sanchez, *Does Your House Have Lions?* (Boston: Beacon, 1997).

2. Toni Morrison, *A Mercy* (New York: Vintage, 2008), 179, 188. According to the character Scully, "the instant he saw [Florens] marching down the road—whether ghost or soldier—he knew she had become untouchable" (179).

3. Octavia Butler, *Kindred* (Boston: Beacon, 1979), 261.

4. Stephen Best, "On Failing to Make the Past Present," *Modern Language Quarterly* 73 (September 2012): 472.

5. Fred Moten, *In the Break: The Aesthetics of the Black Radical Tradition* (Minneapolis: University of Minnesota Press, 2003), 210.

6. Dagmawi Woubshet, *The Calendar of Loss* (Baltimore: Johns Hopkins University Press, 2015), 18.

7. Ashraf H. A. Rushdy, *Neo-Slave Narratives: Studies in the Social Logic of a Literary Form* (New York: Oxford University Press, 1999), chap. 3.

8. Morrison, *A Mercy,* 15.

9. Michel Martin, "Toni Morrison on Bondage and a Post-Racial Age," *National Public Radio,* December 10, 2008, http://www.npr.org/templates/story/story.php?storyId=9807249I, accessed September 6, 2015.

10. Robert Stepto's *From Behind the Veil: A Study of Afro-American Narrative* (Urbana: University of Illinois Press, 1979) is one of the first foundational texts that links writing and freedom as a prime way of understanding the work of slave narratives.

11. Morrison, *A Mercy,* 49.

12. Toni Morrison, *Beloved* (New York: Vintage, 2004), 164.

13. Morrison, *A Mercy,* 184.

14. Eva Meyer, "Architecture Where the Desire May Live," interview with Jacques Derrida, in *Rethinking Architecture: A Reader in Cultural Theory,* ed. Neil Leach (London: Routledge, 1997), 319, 320.

15. Amiri Baraka (LeRoi Jones), *The Slave,* in *Dutchman and the Slave* (New York: HarperCollins, 1964), 45.

16. Maya Lin, "Making the Memorial," *New York Review of Books,* November 2, 2000, http://www.nybooks.com/articles/archives/2000/nov/02/making-the-memorial/, accessed September 6, 2015.

17. Monifa Love, *Freedom in the Dismal* (Kaneohe, Hawaii: Plover, 1998), 13.

18. Edward P. Jones, *The Known World* (New York: Amistad, 2003), 84.

19. Ibid., 138.

20. Malcolm X, "The Race Problem," speech to the African Students Association and the NAACP campus chapter. Michigan State University, East Lansing, January 23, 1963, http://ccnmtl.columbia.edu/projects/mmt/mxp/speeches/mxt14.html, accessed December 28, 2015.

21. Jones, *Known World,* 181, 182–183.

22. Ibid., 341.

23. Jahan Ramazani, *The Hybrid Muse: Postcolonial Poetry in English* (Chicago: University of Chicago Press, 2001), 70.

24. Jones, *Known World,* 345, 341.

25. Moten, *In the Break*, 93.

26. Baraka, *The Slave*, 45.

27. Ibid., 88.

28. Gil Scott-Heron, "Comment No. 1," in *Small Talk at 125th and Lenox* (New York: Flying Dutchman/RCA, 1970), LP; on the idea of reproductive futurity, see Lee Edelman, *No Future: Queer Theory and the Death Drive* (Durham, N.C.: Duke University Press, 2004).

29. Baraka, *The Slave*, 45.

30. Ibid. In *On the Postcolony*, Achille Mbembe describes the "time of entanglement" as "an interlocking of presents, pasts, and futures, each age bearing, altering, and maintaining the previous ones" (*On the Postcolony* [Berkeley: University of California Press, 2001], 16).

31. Amiri Baraka (LeRoi Jones), "An Agony. As Now," in *The Dead Lecturer* (New York: Grove, 1964), 15.

32. Fred Moten, "The Case of Blackness," *Criticism* 50 (spring 2008), 182.

33. Haki Madhubuti (Don L. Lee), "DON'T CRY, SCREAM," in *Don't Cry, Scream* (Detroit: Broadside, 1969), 27.

34. Morrison, *A Mercy*, 188.

35. Jones, *Known World*, 341.

36. This language was included in *Callaloo*'s 2015 call for papers for a special issue on Neo-Slave Narratives, ed. Joan Anim-Addo and Maria Helena Lima, https://call-for-papers.sas.upenn.edu/node/61602, accessed December 28, 2015.

37. Sylvia Wynter, "Making of the New Person" in *Black Metamorphosis: New Natives in a New World*, 246, an unpublished manuscript in the archives of the Schomburg Center for Research in Black Culture, New York City.

38. Jacques Derrida, *Specters of Marx*, trans. Peggy Kamuf (New York: Routledge, 1994).

39. Colin Davis, "Hauntology, Spectres, and Phantoms," *French Studies* 59 (July 2005), 378–379.

40. Curtis Mayfield, "We People Who Are Darker Than Blue," in *Curtis* (Chicago: Curtom, 1970), LP.

41. Amus Mor, "Poem to the Hip Generation" in *Black Spirits: A Festival of New Black Poets in America*, ed. Woodie King (New York: Vintage, 1972), 135.

42. Frantz Fanon uses "epidermalization" to describe what happens when the inferiority of the blackened subject is written on the body. See his *Black Skin, White Masks*, trans. Charles Markmann (New York: Grove, 1967), 11.

43. Morrison, *A Mercy*, 163, 194.

44. Morrison, *Beloved*, 324.

45. "They point to a door that opens onto a stoneroom and there, standing among carriage boxes and a spinning wheel, they tell me to take off my clothes. Without touching they tell me what to do. To show them my teeth, my tongue. They frown at the candle burn on my palm, the one you kissed to cool. They look under my arms, between my legs. They circle me, lean down to inspect my feet. Naked under their examination I watch for what is in their eyes. No hate is there or scare or disgust but they are looking at me my body across distances without recognition. Swine look at me with more connection when they raise their heads from the trough" (ibid., 133).

46. Fanon, *Black Skin, White Masks*, 109.

47. Morrison, *A Mercy*, 3.

48. Carolivia Herron, *Thereafter Johnnie* (New York: Vintage, 1991), 174.

49. Joy DeGruy Leary, *Post Traumatic Slave Syndrome: America's Legacy of Enduring Injury and Healing* (Portland, Ore.: Uptone, 2005), 28. The lecture I heard was delivered in 2003 at the Albany Branch of the Hartford Public Library, Hartford, Connecticut.

50. Ntozake Shange, "On 'What Is It We Really Harvestin' Here?'" in *In Fact: The Best of Creative Nonfiction*, ed. Lee Gutkind (New York: Norton, 2005), 118.

51. Gwendolyn Brooks, "The Second Sermon on the Warpland," in *In the Mecca* (New York: Harper and Row, 1968), 54. My words "structure of feeling" are used in the spirit of Raymond Williams's theory of the pre-formation, which compares to Morrison's use of "pre-racial" to describe the ethos of *A Mercy*. Williams writes, "It is a structured formation which, because it is at the very edge of semantic availability, has many characteristics of a pre-formation, until specific articulations—new semantic figures—are discovered in material practice: often, as it happens, in relatively isolated ways, which are only later seen to compose a significant (often in fact minority) generation: this often, in turn, the generation that substantially connects to its successor" (*Marxism and Literature* [Oxford: Oxford University Press, 1977], 134).

5

Memwa se paswa

Sifting the Slave Past in Haiti

RÉGINE MICHELLE JEAN-CHARLES

> History is often written by victors. Perhaps this is why, when discussing
> Haitian history, we tend to linger more on the battles we've won, rather
> than the ones we lost, the ones where we lost our people, our humanity,
> ourselves. . . . few people know what it meant for these eventual victors,
> or their parents and grandparents, to have survived the specific route of
> the Middle Passage.[1]
>
> –Edwidge Danticat

According to the Haitian proverb *memwa se paswa*, memory is a strainer,
always separating and dividing. Certain events vanish into the forgotten past,
while others stubbornly and prominently remain. A strainer sifts deliberately,
allowing the smaller matter to go through and leaving only the larger material
behind. It separates what passes through easily from what is more weighty or
substantial. The smaller the openings, the more refined the sifting will be. As a
metaphor for memory, the strainer proverb reminds us of our incomplete view
of the past. While revealing the past's inherent unknowability, it also reduces
memory to concrete, material terms. It is preoccupied with the deliberate act of
sifting. In this conception, memory is not simply about the organic processes
of the mind but about the creation of narrative for specific purposes.[2]

Memwa se paswa. This proverb can be aptly applied to intentional reanimations of the slave past in Haiti and, more specifically, to how slavery is treated
in academic and artistic memorial discourse. How does memorial discourse
serve as a sieve that can filter facts to the point of altering truth?[3] The distinction between memory and history is important here: I am interested in collective memory in terms of how institutions remember events and represent
the slave past through cultural production.[4] Although the proverb explicitly
refers to memory, I want to extend its reach to the politics of memory in fictive

imaginings of the past, which is why I invoke the relationship between fact and truth.

While writers, historians, artists, and scholars have enthusiastically turned to the Haitian Revolution as a generative source of analysis and inspiration, they usually examine what preceded it—the system of slavery regulated by Louis XIV's *Code noir* of 1685—in direct association with the revolutionary period.[5] That is to say, slavery is mostly important for what it can illustrate about revolution and freedom.[6] This is in part the problem of the archive. In contrast to other parts of the Caribbean, French-speaking countries in the region have had far fewer slave and ex-slave narratives, an absence redressed by Christopher Miller's *The French Atlantic Triangle* and challenged by Deborah Jenson's *Beyond the Slave Narrative*.[7] These two studies attempt to explain the void of slave voices by considering other ways in which to construct the history of French colonial slavery from the perspective of enslaved people. Historian Alyssa Goldstein Sepinwall offers another reason for the marked focus on the revolution, explaining that, "because of the difficulty of finding colonial-era sources from slave perspectives, scholarship on slaves has often worked backwards from the Haitian Revolution, reconstructing colonial life from revolutionary-era documents."[8] At the same time, according to Jenson, singular focus on the slave narrative genre has eclipsed the existence of other genres of slave writing, to the detriment of literary analyses on colonial Saint-Domingue.[9] Even with regard to the revolution itself, history has focused on those who led it because of the documents left behind, thus creating a scenario in which "we know much about its leaders, who left plentiful records of their actions and perspectives; we know far less about the experiences and views of the masses of slaves who so dramatically changed the world in which they lived."[10] Jenson's point reminds us that there is still a need for different perspectives on slavery in Haiti—histories "from below" are largely absent from the archive. This absence is also present in imaginative texts; as Brinda Mehta puts it, "the relative silence surrounding Haiti's former history of slavery also reverberates in contemporary Haitian literature."[11]

In my view, the marked preoccupation with the Haitian Revolution is a strainer that sifts the slave past, leaving behind the revolution while much else disappears. Disproportionate emphasis on the conflict obscures the significance of the nation's slave past, and there are costs to this forgetting. For instance, it hides the hypocrisy of France's universal-humanist ideals and flattens out the radical efforts of the enslaved that preceded and led up to the revolution. By turning to the representation of the slave past in Haiti, we can move outside of the context of U.S.-based slavery to consider what happens when the saturation of remembering slavery has not taken place.[12] In the absence of this flood of remembering the slave past, the imperative to forget becomes far less tenable.

My goal in this chapter is to explore ways of forgetting and remembering the Haitian slave past; and to do so, I consider a film and a novel that emblematize each approach: the film *Toussaint Louverture* (2012) and the novel *Rosalie l'infâme* (2003), released in English as *The Infamous Rosalie* (2013). As you will see, the process of sifting the slave past reveals that memorial discourse is fraught with political anxieties about how best to represent group identity. If collective memory concerns how the past of a group is lived again in the present, it also concerns what and how the public chooses to remember because of what it reveals about them in the present.[13]

This view differs drastically from the position of Douglas A. Jones Jr. in chapter 2. Unlike him, my interest is not in the failure of representation but in the need for attempts at representation, given the disparate histories that make up the Americas. Whereas Jones argues that Terrance Hayes's poem "The Avocado" "exemplifies an understanding of the slave past as distant and distinct from the contemporary moment," I want to express the need for representations that return to the slave past and their attendant ethical and political implications. This is especially the case for countries such as Haiti, where literary and cultural histories outside the canon of African American cultural production have been silenced and removed entirely from the present. My concern is that positions such as Jones's fail to account for the diversity of relationship to the slave past *within the Americas,* especially in Caribbean countries. The necessity for reanimations of the past that seek "affective and or psychic redress of slavery's injuries" is not only about a need to make the slave past present in the present. When anchored in the specificity of diverse locations, it can be about creating new narratives of slavery to move beyond the dominant representations. When we read what Jones calls for (and the Hayes poem allows for) as a need to enlarge our understanding of what reanimations of the slave past can and should do, we may see the central issue as not the impossibility or possibility of repair but the importance of cultural work that can create "new imaginative horizons." Jones's reading of "The Avocado" mines the ways in which the poem reinforces the unknowability and unconquerability of slavery's history. In contrast, my readings espouse the Morrisonian poetics that work through the "need to know" and "need to conquer," using the imagination as a space in which to do so. Despite the extant critiques of the realist models that are invested in repair, redemption, and recuperation, we cannot eschew the significance of the slave past in the current moment without exploring its different representations in the larger Americas.

While slavery is, in Salamishah Tillet's words, the "master trope for African American identity," revolution is the master trope in Haiti.[14] We could even say that the major contrast between Haitian and U.S. approaches to slavery's history is that the former focuses on what the latter represses: black agency and the glory of an enslaved population rising up to take its freedom. As Jenson has pointed out, "the literature of the Haitian Revolution and independence put the focus not on slavery per se, but on the means through which individuals and communities revolutionized the discursive sphere as well as the political sphere of Atlantic modernity."[15] The prodigious corpus of works on the revolution by both Haitians and non-Haitians speaks to its significance in the cultural imaginary.[16] Take, for example, the first Haitian novel, *Stella* (1859), by Émeric Bergeaud, an allegory that focuses on twin brothers and ends at the dawn of Haitian independence. As the author explains in the prefatory note, "La Révolution, . . . laborieux enfantement d'une société nouvelle, a donné naissance à quatre hommes qui personnifient l'excès et la gloire: Rigaud, Toussaint, Dessalines, Pétion. [The revolution, . . . laborious infancy of a new society, gave birth to four men who personify excess and glory: Rigaud, Toussaint, Dessalines, Pétion.]"[17] Bergeaud's consideration of the power dynamics among these prominent figures comments on the revolution and its immediate aftermath, and the novel was the first in an enduring literary tradition focusing on the ubiquitous heroes of the conflict.

Of course, it is no surprise that cultural workers turn to the Haitian Revolution as inspiration for their imaginative texts. My goal is not to question that impulse. Rather, what interests me here is the meaning this focus has for remembering slavery. If we frame the relationship between the slave past and the revolution in terms of the proverb that begins this chapter, we can understand the material remains as the presence of the latter in the archive and the imagination while the former is sifted away. As Edwidge Danticat writes in her foreword to *The Infamous Rosalie*, "when discussing Haitian history, we tend to linger more on the battles we've won, rather than the ones we lost, the ones where we lost our people, our humanity, ourselves."[18]

What if we shift the prism of the revolution to consider what it refracts about slavery? How do centuries of violence disappear into the memory of a thirteen-year war for independence? Rather than focusing on the glory of the revolution, what if we concentrate on the violence against bodies marked by race and sex on the slave plantation? What role do particular literary genres play in representing the slave past? What are the stakes of reanimating the slave past, and how are representational choices influenced by the past, the present, and projections of the future?

As Robert J. Patterson points out in chapter 1, representation is not reality, and a film or a novel will never be able to fully capture the indignities of slavery. Yet like him, I follow Stuart Hall in the belief that representation cannot be fully divorced from the real. Rather, social reality and representation are mutually constitutive.[19] According to this view, representation, while irreducible to the real, nevertheless has a material impact. Thus, reanimations of the slave past in Haiti will tell us something about how and why slavery is made to matter in the present.

Toussaint Louverture: Forgetting Revolution, Sifting Violence

The film *Toussaint Louverture* originally aired as a two-part miniseries in 2012 on the channel France 2, one of the country's most-watched channels.[20] It was also available throughout the French-speaking world, including in Haiti.[21] The film helps to illuminate how the violence of slavery can be easily elided in representation, even when the goal appears to be to expose silenced elements of the past. The film moves back and forth between Toussaint's memories of Haiti and his imprisonment in Fort du Joux in France, where he eventually dies. The scenes in Haiti display his childhood, his learning to read, his falling in love, and the increased politicization that leads to his involvement in the revolution. The lead role is played by Haitian actor Jimmy Jean-Louis, and the scenes in France unfold in the form of a conversation between Louverture and Pasquier, a man assigned by Napoleon to interrogate him. The narrative structure of the film lends itself to the framework of *memwa se paswa* because Pasquier's interview provokes (or sifts) Louverture's memories of Haiti, which the film presents as flashbacks. In other words, although Louverture tells the story, Pasquier sifts the narrative through his line of questioning.

The revolution's most prominent figure and its most popular subject of cultural production, Toussaint Louverture occupies a central, even singular, role in the history and representation of Haiti. The film follows the tradition of a large body of creative and scholarly texts, primarily written by non-Haitians, that exclusively focus on the male heroes of the revolution. C.L.R. James's *The Black Jacobins* (1938) is the best-known example of this tendency as well as the earliest. Almost twenty years later the Cuban novelist Alejo Carpentier published *The Kingdom of This World* (1957). Martinican Edouard Glissant published a lesser-known play, *Monsieur Toussaint* (1961), and Aimé Césaire later published another, *La Tragédie du roi Christophe* (1970). In the twenty-first century, Anglophone fiction has added to the corpus—among them, Derek Walcott's trilogy of plays (2002) and Madison Smartt Bell's trilogy of popular novels (1995, 2000, 2004).[22] More recently, Isabel Allende's novel *Island beneath the Sea* (2009) features a protagonist born in nineteenth-century Saint Domingue.

The film participates in this long tradition of mythification. Yet somewhat surprisingly, it begins with a fallen, imprisoned Louverture on the brink of death. This setting might be a way to wrest the figure of Toussaint from the shadow of omnipotence that he often casts, especially because "it is . . . probably impossible to separate reality from legend in the story of Toussaint," as Laurent DuBois observes in *Avengers of the New World*.[23] The film's opening departure from the cult of heroism could be interpreted as a way to complicate the towering figure. However, this reading ignores the context in which the film was created and for whom. *Toussaint Louverture* originated in France, is partially set in France, and is overall very *French*.²⁴ The French are central to the story and essentially move it forward. The opening sequence makes this point clear when it offers the viewer a contextual note: "Cette oeuvre de fiction s'inspire d'événements historiques ayant eu lieu à la fin du XVIIIème siècle dans la partie française de l'île de Saint-Domingue, connue aujourd'hui sous le nom d'Haïti. [This work of fiction is inspired by historic events that took place at the end of the eighteenth century in the French part of the island of Hispaniola known today by the name of Haiti.]"²⁵ The choice of words is telling. It is a work of fiction based on historic events in the French part of the island. The island's colonial heritage comes to emphasize the ownership status during the time period, as does the use of the colonial name, Saint-Domingue. The opening historical note mentions neither slavery nor the revolution. Its inclusion can be read as a conscious decision to foreground Haiti's colonial relationship to France. That this relationship can be highlighted without mention of slavery or revolution is the first sign of a deliberate sifting.

Following the note, the first scene of the film tells the story of captivity. Before seeing Toussaint for the first time, we hear the chains that restrain him and see French soldiers on horseback opening the cell. Looking far from heroic, he then stumbles through the snowy French countryside. The winter landscape is another index of distance from the tropical setting of the revolution. Although the scene also provides details of Toussaint's life, showing his forced separation from his wife, Suzanne, as well as his son and his nephew, few lines are exchanged during this interaction. Toussaint shouts in a combination of Kreyòl and French, "Pa pitit mwenyo, pa ma femme! [Not my children, not my wife!]" The use of language is telling here. While the Kreyòl precedes the French, the latter is clearly added for the benefit of the audience. As he approaches the cell into which Suzanne and the boys are being forced, the French soldiers strike him to the ground. Thus, the film's first act of violence is meted out to Louverture, forcing him into submission.

There is no real dialogue in the film until the French officers begin strategizing about how to get Toussaint to speak, which he has been refusing to do for a month. They decide to bring in a young officer, Pasquier, who will be responsible for getting to know the fallen general and writing his story. As Pasquier learns about Toussaint's life, viewers see the film primarily through his eyes. He is the mediator who presents the historical narrative of the revolution to a contemporary French audience.

When Pasquier arrives, he addresses the imprisoned general as "François Dominique Toussaint." Louverture corrects him: "General Toussaint Louverture." The young Pasquier tells the prisoner that he is no longer a general; the French have stripped his title. In response, Louverture says that he will speak only to Napoleon himself, not to a representative. Again, Pasquier makes him aware of Napoleon's orders. This exchange is no doubt a reflection of Louverture's habit of addressing his letters to Napoleon as "du premier des noirs au premier des blancs [from the first of the blacks to the first of the whites]."[26]

The scene is structured to dissolve the shroud of myth and heroism that surrounds Toussaint, and its attention to the French characters helps to achieve this goal. The men's interaction is one of the film's main focal points, and eventually Pasquier seems to become sympathetic to Louverture's vision. As the central French-Haitian interaction on screen, their relationship is presented as softened and amicable as the officer becomes enlightened by and empathetic toward the imprisoned general. But Pasquier is not a historical character. He is the fantasy of contemporary French filmmakers, a demonstration of their need to mute a contentious, historical relationship via an imagined mediator. Throughout the film, Toussaint's reliance on French benevolence for survival supports an idealized and unrealistic narrative about France, slavery, and the history of colonial rule. Pasquier's inclusion enables the French pretense of commitment to democratic universal values, which is often invoked to describe the nation's relationship to slavery in the past.[27]

Indeed, the entire film advances an uncomplicated and inaccurate view of slavery, which is especially evident in its effacement of the institution's violence. Whereas more recent films such as *12 Years a Slave* (2013) depict that violence in unflinching and unremitting detail, it is practically absent from *Toussaint Louverture*. One exception is the film's first scene, which takes place in Haiti. Here, a young Toussaint is on the auction block with a group of other slaves, including his father and his sister. The enslaved characters are displayed fully clothed and in chains. Toussaint's elderly father strokes the boy as a potential owner inspects them and then exchanges money for the son. Toussaint and his father are separated. Deemed too old for slavery, the father is pushed into the sea to drown; but when the boy runs after him, he is slapped. This display of physical and psychic brutality is immediately interrupted when another potential owner, Bayon, observes what happens, takes pity on Toussaint, and purchases him along with his sister. The sequence of events culminates with a French character who is moved to act sympathetically, and it is the first example of how the film is careful not to portray white slaveholders too negatively.

Other scenes of slavery show the enslaved working on the plantation or making exchanges in the marketplace, but there is almost no portrayal of violence in plantation life. This absence is not what Saidiya Hartman theorizes as "the terror of the mundane and the quotidian."[28] While the indispensability of the enslaved to the function of the society does come through in the film, it does not include the daily indignities that were an integral part of the institution. Perhaps its nonexistence can be attributed to the medium: because film is a visual mode, graphic scenes of violence can afflict viewers and risk causing them to turn away.

The violence that is present throughout the film involves not the slave owners but the uprising Haitian army. This reinforces the view that the revolution was more about barbarism than about freedom and is consistent with eighteenth-century French documents about the event.[29] Those accounts and subsequent histories focus on spectacular scenes of violence—for instance, describing slave rituals that demonize the freedom fighters who were furthering the spirit of the French Revolution. One scene in the film shows a white woman hanging from a tree after a series of massacres. The fact that this is the only lynching scene in a film about slavery exacts another kind of racial forgetting, one that ignores the scourge of violence that regulated the slave past. It is a glaring example of the costs of not reanimating the slave past, and it is especially insidious because it serves the French project of non-remembrance— what the historian Alyssa Sepinwall, among others, calls "French amnesia about the Haitian Revolution and ambivalence about slavery and colonialism in general."[30] By taking this approach to violence, the film actually inverts the social order of colonial Saint-Domingue. Moreover, its presence clarifies that the filmmakers did not avoid detailing the violence meted out to slaves because they were concerned about the visual impact of such scenes. By barely representing slavery and its violence, *Toussaint Louverture* removes the revolution from the context of a long tradition of black subjugation and atrocities perpetrated against slaves. This failure dangerously fortifies France's tendency toward silence, amnesia, and reckless forgetting when it comes to memorial discourse about slavery. The film serves as yet another reminder of the "layer of silence [that] has obstructed the memory of slavery [in France] throughout the centuries."[31]

I read the Frenchness of the film in terms of this long and disturbing legacy, which has gained traction in the past two decades. In 1998, when France publicly commemorated the 150th anniversary of the abolition of slavery in Guadeloupe and Martinique, the occasion highlighted the discrepancy between the official French memory of slavery and the collective memory of slavery in the French-speaking Caribbean. France cast abolition unequivocally in terms of the nation's universal and democratic values of freedom, equality, and brotherhood. The government focused exclusively on active and passionate French involvement in abolition without recalling what had preceded it.[32] The 2001 Taubira law, which admitted French culpability in the slave trade and acknowledged slavery as a crime against humanity, was one of the first steps toward redressing the nation's propensity for willful forgetting and steadfast denial.[33] This policy came into being thanks to the work of a number of activists, artists, and politicians, led by minister Christiane Taubira, after whom the law was named. The law simply states that the French Republic recognizes that the slave trade and slavery is a human rights violation.[34] According to the first article, "La République française reconnaît que la traite négrière transatlantique ainsi que la traite dans l'océan Indien d'une part, et l'esclavage d'autre part, perpétrés à partir du xve siècle, aux Amériques et aux Caraïbes, dans l'océan Indien et en Europe contre les populations africaines, amérindiennes, malgaches et indiennes constituent un crime contre l'humanité. [The French Republic recognizes that the transatlantic slave trade as well as the trade in the Indian Ocean, on the one hand, and slavery, on the other hand, perpetrated since the fifteenth century in the Americas and in the Caribbean, in the Indian Ocean and in Europe against African, Native American, Malgasy, and Indian people, constitute a crime against humanity]." Critics have rightfully noted that this trumpeted commitment to remembrance was preceded by decades of purposeful ignoring and outright denial of involvement in the slave trade.[35] These decades enabled an atmosphere of obsolescence that might have continued in France without intervention, activism, and policy changes.

The Infamous Rosalie: Slavery, Revolution, and Women

In contrast to the French-produced miniseries, Evelyne Trouillot's novel, recently translated as *The Infamous Rosalie*, concentrates on the period that preceded the Haitian Revolution. By foregrounding the quotidian brutalities and human atrocities of life on the slave plantation, the novel stands as an important example of the machinations of race, gender, sex, and power at work in 1750 Saint-Domingue. According to Renée Larrier, it belongs to a cadre of narratives by Francophone Caribbean women that "locate the normative femme as a black woman and narrate enslaved women's agency and subjectivity in a world of racial oppression and gender violence."[36] *The Infamous Rosalie* tells the story of Lisette, a young woman enslaved on the Fayot plantation during the mid-eighteenth century.

A Creole, Lisette was born in Saint-Domingue, unlike the female ancestors to whom she frequently refers in the novel—her mother, her great-aunt Brigitte, her grandmother Charlotte, and her godmother Ma Augustine—who survived the Middle Passage on the *Rosalie*, the ship for which the novel is named.[37] Lisette is a secondary survivor of this trauma, having lived through the stories handed down about the ship as well as the women's lives in the barracoons before they were enslaved. These inherited memories of the Middle Passage commingle with her lived experience on the plantation: "I fall asleep amid the beauty of this land that seems to bear the mark of our pain—Creoles, Aradas, Congos, Nagos, Ibos, newly arrived negroes, forever *bossales* confronting our chains. In my sleep I struggle against miasmas and stagnant waters, barracoons and the steerage of ships, the growl of dogs, bodies too hot and damp, the sound of bludgeons." At first she is eager to escape these inherited memories: "My youth wants to erase the stories of *The Infamous Rosalie* and the barracoons, to lift off this weight that clouds my vision whenever I try to dream." In her psychic space Lisette moves fluidly between the past and the present. While she dreams, she is unable to distinguish one temporal space from another.

Her relationship to the past is pregnant with fear and longing: "I feel the need to touch my talisman, to see these things that link me to Grandma Charlotte, to my mother, whom I didn't know, and to this great-aunt Brigitte they spoke so much about to me. I suffer from all the mysteries that surround me, from the stories that reveal themselves as pain comes and goes, from the days ahead that seem to extend immense tentacles of despair and anger."[38]

Lisette's thoughts reveal a relationship to time in which she is suspended between the past and the present, wanting to hope for the future but unable to imagine a future free from slavery. Her pain, in the words of Hartman, "might best be described as history that hurts—the still unfolding narrative of captivity, dispossession, and domination that engenders the black subject in the Americas."[39] This temporal understanding binds the past, present, and future, even if the past is made up of indirect experiences. The stories of the past operate as more than an invocation of the oral storytelling tradition; they are fodder for and eventually the catalyst of Lisette's future path as a maroon. Trouillot's use of the foremothers' stories also weaves Lisette's experience in the present into a continuous historical narrative.

Throughout *The Infamous Rosalie*, Trouillot explores different manifestations of women's agency on the plantation through the female characters that surround Lisette. One of the main characters, Brigitte, is based on an Arada midwife who, during her murder trial, reveals a rope necklace in which each knot represents one of the seventy babies she has killed at birth. In *The Infamous Rosalie*, the rope is passed on to Lisette, Brigitte's great-niece and the novel's protagonist, for whom it operates as a talisman throughout the story. Trouillot first encountered the story of the midwife in *La Révolution aux Caraïbes*, an archival history of slavery and resistance in the Caribbean; and in her novel's afterword, she quotes the woman's explanation: "To remove these young creatures from the shameful institution of slavery, I inserted a needle in their brain through the fontanel at the moment of their birth."[40] The Arada midwife exemplifies gendered resistance, embodied agency, and reproductive liberation. Her inclusion in the archive contrasts with the exclusion of women from official histories of the Haitian Revolution. As Mimi Sheller explains in *Citizenship from Below*,

> building black masculinity [was] a central task in the construction of Haitian national identity. In seizing the reins of power and constructing a militarized and masculine model of citizenship; the victors of this revolution created a paradox that still plagues Haiti: the egalitarian and democratic values of republicanism were constantly undercut by the hierarchical and elitist values of militarism. The paramount sign of this fundamental contradiction was the exclusion of women from the wholly masculine realms of state politics and citizenship.[41]

I suggest that another cost of not reanimating the slave past is losing sight of important ways in which women were also agents of resistance against the institution.

The case of the Arada midwife shows how enslaved women were involved in circuits of resistance ranging from poisoning their masters in the kitchen to killing their own and others' children at birth.[42] A gendered interpretation of this story has a triple significance: Trouillot's use of it functions as a form of historical recovery, one that salvages it from being sifted. The focus on reproduction and reproductive freedom as a site of resistance exists along the continuum of female-centered agency and heroism that Trouillot highlights in the novel. The characters in *The Infamous Rosalie* remember Brigitte's act of killing the newborn babies and, through the material object of the knotted rope necklace, a talisman that Lisette is determined to keep, also manage to memorialize her reproductive radicalism in the present. At the same time, reproductive freedom and female agency operate differently in Lisette's life by the end of the novel, when she, too, is pregnant. She chooses to become a marroon and to keep her child, to whom she whispers, "Creole child who lives in me, you will be born free and rebellious, or you will not be born at all."[43] Lisette accepts and revises the heritage of reproductive freedom into which the child will be born.

Enslaved women and their stories structure the plot of *The Infamous Rosalie* as their experiences with slavery are transmitted orally from one generation to the next. Lisette is constantly asking her grandmother to tell her the story about the slave ship. There are moments that Grandma Charlotte and Ma Augustine share, and others that they "have shrouded in mystery." Their sifting is deliberate, and Lisette notices. "What does their silence mean—this silence that intrigues and confounds me? I try to make up for it by gathering the small bits of information that I collect here and there from Grandma Charlotte and Ma Augustine over the years." When Grandma Charlotte does choose to share, the exchange follows the cadence of call-and-response storytelling: Lisette must ask for the story. The grandmother's decision to share is not simply based on tradition; she prefers not to repeat the stories and revisit the past. "After starting to tell the story, Grandma Charlotte always respected a moment of silence. I appreciated this pause, which brought us together and gave me permission to choose my story for that day. Grandmother would agree to my request except when I demanded she tell Brigitte's story or the one about the barracoons that she was keeping for a special day, a day still to come."[44] How the story moves from Grandma Charlotte to Lisette is determined by the older woman's perception of Lisette's state of mind. The exchange takes on a ritualistic air as Grandma Charlotte pauses, which Lisette understands as a signal for her to choose the story. But the pause can also be read as the older woman's reverence for what she is about to share. She pauses to honor the ancestors whose story she tells, to acknowledge the dignity of those who came before her. Trouillot's narrative strategies pull the reader into the question of how narrative is mediated by aesthetics and form.

In the following passage, Grandma Charlotte responds to Lisette's request for the story about *The Infamous Rosalie*:

> First there was this camp, which was like an enormous ditch surrounded by fencing. One day, I promise you, I'll tell you about the barracoons; one day, when you'll need wings to carry yourself beyond the present moment. One day, when your need will be greater than my fear of going back there in my memory. But not today. . . . On the ship I experienced a night I had never known, a night with no sky, no stars, no breeze; with bodies huddled against each other; without love or passion; with odors and movements stripped of their intimacy; with linked embraces and never-ending moans. . . . And no one hears your scream; it resonates only in your heart. . . . For there are hundreds of screams that mask your own.[45]

Trouillot connects Lisette's story to a generation of women that came before her to construct a female lineage that begins before the Middle Passage. For Lisette, memory is indeed a strainer because her godmother and grandmother pick and choose which stories to share with her. But the strainer works differently here: they intentionally sift what flows through more easily. Grandma Charlotte's promise to tell Lisette "one day, when your need will be greater than my fear of going back there in my memory" suggests that the material left in the strainer has greater weight because of the pain it causes the one who shares it. The more painful the memories of the past, the more fearful she is about revisiting it. At the same time her promise to tell Lisette "one day, when you'll need wings to carry yourself beyond the present moment," suggests that this pain ultimately will lead to her radicalization. According to this logic, the pain of the past can inspire the action of the future.

In the novel's afterword, Trouillot explains, "I wasn't intending to write a historical novel. May I be forgiven, then, for the few discrepancies and creative liberties I've taken. I only seek to acknowledge my characters' humanity. Yet I must refuse all responsibility for the torture and punishment described in the text. They are all unfortunately true, born of the cruel and perfidious imagination of those who proclaimed themselves to be civilized."[46] Trouillot's explanation of her method, which included significant archival research, recalls Toni Morrison's description of her approach to writing about slavery and the importance of the imagination: "Memories and recollections won't give me total access to the unwritten interior life of these people. Only the act of the imagination can help me."[47] For Morrison, as for Trouillot, the space of the imagination opens an additional space that is not accessible via history or memory.

Lisette experiences violence in different forms—as a firsthand victim, as a survivor of secondary trauma, and as a witness. Partway through the novel, the plantation owner's son rapes her. Not long afterward, she witnesses a slave being burnt at the stake, she runs through the woods and encounters a lynched body, and she has to nurse her lover back to life after his leg is severed. The scenes of torture are sometimes described in explicit detail, and they are constantly present in the protagonist's mind: "I don't dare think about what would happen to him if he were captured—or rather, I imagine all too well the atrocities to which he would be subjected. Marroons have severed legs, burned genitals, chained feet; they are cast aside to be sold with missing body parts maimed and half dead when they're not devoured by mastiffs."[48] This proliferation of violence does not compromise the centrality of resistance in Lisette's narrative; in fact, according to Grandma Charlotte, there is and should be a direct link between the two. The protagonist longs for a space of embodied freedom, recognizing that she is physically and psychically held captive. Lisette's longing, along with her godmother's stories about the past, allow her to imagine a different future for herself. Her resistance emerges again as a way to make sense of her condition as an enslaved woman.

One significant way in which *The Infamous Rosalie* moves beyond the dyad of Haitian exceptionalism is by highlighting the ordinary lives of ordinary characters. As the historian and anthropologist Michel-Rolph Trouillot has written, "the majority of Haitians live quite ordinary lives. They eat what is for them—and many others—quite ordinary food. They die quite ordinary deaths from quite ordinary accidents, quite ordinary tortures, quite ordinary diseases. Accidents so ordinary that they could be prevented. Tortures so ordinary that the international press does not even mention them. Diseases so ordinary that they are easily treated almost anywhere else. Exceptional, is it?"[49] Implicit in this paradoxical explanation is the notion that the extraordinary and the ordinary operate alongside one another. Such is the case for slavery when we consider that, within the confines of the extraordinary violence of the institution, slaves nonetheless lived life daily. It is this quotidian life, the desire to live and assert one's basic humanity despite the horror of the slave system, that Evelyne Trouillot describes in detail. The slaves in *The Infamous Rosalie* fall in love and make love. They argue, they question, and they plot. They dance, pray, play games, and flirt. They also witness many unforgettable scenes of violence. More than once Lisette is marked by the violence that unfolds around her each day: "I still can't shake the weight of those images of burned bodies swollen with water, floating on frothy waves."[50] The novel is set almost forty years before the beginning of the Haitian Revolution; and while reference to independence is not explicit, the theme of marronnage alludes to the freedom in Haiti's future. Yet despite the novel's marronnage trope, it is mainly concerned with the routine ignominy of life on the plantation.

The novel opens with Lisette running, a scene of violence stamped into her mind, for she has just witnessed a friend being burnt at the stake. Her focus as she is forced to watch this spectacle is on the two daughters whose father is being killed: "The screams of Paladin's children as their father is burnt at the stake on the Beauplan plantation still resound in my skin. . . . My tears began to flow, but I continued to watch the madness of the flames in spite of myself. The charred skin stuck to my pupils, darkening the depths of my soul. Before my eyes a human body turned to ashes."[51] Her understanding of this scene is essential information for the reader. First, we see that she is forced to be present as Paladin is made an example of for the other enslaved. Second, we understand that her immediate attention to the children processes the violence in terms of its effects on the plantation family system. Moreover, the opening scene underscores the juxtaposition of the ordinary and the extraordinary: Lisette must transition quickly from this scene of horror to her duties on the plantation.

The quotidian violence of life on the plantation is unremitting throughout *The Infamous Rosalie.* "Guilty or not, in the space of three weeks they've burned a coachman, two cooks, and a servant. Each week brings news of other poisonings from almost every part of the region."[52] Whether through her own direct experience, what she is forced to witness, or what the older women tell her, she is constantly aware of how violence defines life on the plantation. Likewise, the stories from the older women do not obscure the violence of what they experienced.

Yet the stories that she is told are also about freedom. As Grandma Charlotte recounts,

> Ayouba, your mother, had not yet understood the meaning of her destiny when the horror began. We were about twenty people, young men, beautiful and strong, young women, full of life, with high and beautiful chests, laughing eyes, and promising hands. Free. Brigitte could have told you how we were captured, how we resisted. Me, I only want to remember the simple joy that existed before, before the smell of those waves, those winds, and the sand moving beneath our feet. I don't just want to remember sand dunes and the bare shoulders of slaves. I want to think about the time before the kidnapping, before *The Infamous Rosalie.* Because afterward I'll have nothing warm to hold in my memory, except the weight of your hand against my cheek and the day of your birth.[53]

Here Grandma Charlotte develops her own theory of remembrance. She does not want to relive the passage and the barracoons because she wants to hold on to her memories of freedom. For an enslaved woman, there is a cost to recalling and reliving the violence of slavery. From this perspective, Lisette is in a position of privilege, which affords her the luxury of the listening to the story without being triggered. Grandma Charlotte engages the exact question that concerns many of the chapters in this book: what and whom does the remembrance or reanimation of the slave past serve.

When Grandma Charlotte does tell Lisette the story of the barracoons, her goal is to propel the younger woman toward resistance and a radical future. The anticipated exchange occurs in response to the young girl's acceptance of a gift from her mistress. Concerned that Lisette is taking pleasure in one aspect of her situation as a slave, the grandmother seeks to correct this egregious misstep. Lisette describes the moment: "My grandmother's voice sounded different; no doubt it was my fear of what was about to happen that made her voice sound like the tolling of a bell. Grandma Charlotte began slowly and spoke without pause, as if she had chosen her words a long time ago." By contrasting the story of the barracoons with the previous story about the slave ship, we, too, can observe that Grandma Charlotte perceives a difference. As Lisette notes, "Grandma spoke in a monotonous tone of voice, which was unusual, for she was always so incisive with her words and gestures."[54] In that ominous voice, the grandmother explains:

> This whole story is like a vast wound. Some parts of it bleed more than others. There are more recent marks, not as fatal. Then there are old wounds that have stopped bleeding but have filled the entire body with a smell of rotting flesh. From time to time this stench rises to the surface with a whiff of decaying bodies, masking makeshift lies, baskets woven with happiness bought on credit. The time of the barracoons is a festering wound deep in the bones, a humiliation for all to see. When one has experienced this kind of humiliation, defeat can call your name at any time and undo your memory. . . . Listen to the story of the barracoons! Perhaps one day we'll no longer be talking about any of this. Perhaps one day we'll no longer even remember this word; it will have perished with those of us who bored its mark—but the shame will remain until we root it out. . . . I've already told you about the slave ship, the ship's steerage, the ship's hold and the sea. There are some who found the days of the crossing to be the most horrible and painful. But for me the barracoons are the wound that will always bleed deep inside me. That was when I knew for sure that a large part of me had been buried.[55]

Grandma Charlotte's metaphor of the wound captures the searing pain of her experience. The moment of capture was a constitutive and transformative event in her life, one that would alter her identity and seal her fate.

As she continues, she expounds on the psychic, affective, and physical wounds of slavery that remain with her in the present; shame is chief among them. Yet she recognizes that the effects and costs of slavery are different for each of the individuals who experience it. Grandma Charlotte's insistence upon the singularity of her memory of humiliation makes an important point about the limitations of our ability to access the memories of others. Extending this lesson beyond the text, her statement that "perhaps one day we will no longer be talking about any of this. Perhaps one day we'll no longer even remember this word" seems to indict the way in which we, her readers, have forgotten the lives of slaves in the centuries before the Haitian Revolution. According to Grandma Charlotte, the shame will remain unless it can be rooted out. To have the luxury of forgetting, we must first share the memories of previous generations.

The different temporal layers at work in *The Infamous Rosalie* highlight the need for greater complexity in reanimating the past. In the novel we see the time of Grandma Charlotte and Tante Brigitte in the barracoons as well as before, the time of Lisette's life unfolding in the present, and the time of the reader. As she tells the story, Lisette refers to moments from her past, often without signaling to the reader that the temporal register has changed. As a result, her memories coalesce with her grandmother's and the stories of others to influence her present and help to determine her future as a marroon. These different temporalities assemble a layered view of the past that is multiple, dynamic, and collective. Taking into account the novel's paratext—the epigraph in which Trouillot dedicates the novel to historian Hénock Trouillot and the afterword in which she describes her discovery of the Arada midwife in the archive, the writer's focus on women-centered resistance occurs through the creation of a narrative that revolves around women rather than around male heroes.

Part of the power of *The Infamous Rosalie* is that, in Larrier's words, "Trouillot revises the dominant narrative; she restores subjectivity to enslaved people by specifying their ethnic origins, recalling their stable home communities in West Africa, validating their extreme sense of loss, honouring surrogate motherhood, and privileging the intergenerational transmission of culture."[56] Beyond this revision of the dominant narrative, the novel is a telling example of how representations of slavery can portray its violence without resorting to the dualistic logics of an exceptionalism in which slavery matters most because of its relationship to revolution. At the same time, resistance is not absent or even exceptional in the novel. By showing that resistance takes on many different forms and is engaged by different kinds of people on the plantation, Trouillot renders a representation of slavery that refuses to sift out the perspectives of enslaved women.

Shaping the Past through Sifting

Cultural production that focuses exclusively on the revolution foregrounds a post-slavery moment that allows the slave past to be too easily sifted and silenced. In view of the French amnesia about slavery—what Nelly Schmidt refers to as "the policy of forgetfulness of the past"—this sifting can enable us to assume that slavery was only about economic needs.[37] A film such as

Toussaint Louverture, in which the violence of slavery is practically erased, denies the human suffering of those who eventually successfully revolted. As Michel Trouillot reminds us, "any historical narrative is a particular bundle of silence . . . because power is constitutive of the story. . . . Silences are inherent in history because any single event enters history with some of its constituting parts missing. Something is always left out when something else is recorded. . . . Thus whatever becomes fact does so with its own inborn absences, specific to its production."[58] Cultural production uses the imagination to fill these absences. By imagining what may have existed in the space of silence surrounding slavery that emphasizing the Haitian Revolution creates, Evelyne Trouillot's novel begins with the archive of the slave past and works backward through the imagination.

Much scholarship and cultural production has been devoted to "assessing the significance and particularity of the Haitian Revolution as a cultural movement, an anticolonial struggle, an early assertion of black subjectivity, and an ambiguous claim on modernity."[59] The towering shadow cast by this historic event can often obscure the slave past. My aim here is not to deny the significance of the Haitian Revolution as a context for thinking about slavery but to show how it can become a potentially problematic site that sifts out parts of the slave past. In *Sites of Slavery*, Tillet argues that contemporary representations of slavery in African American literature, film, theater, and visual culture "reconcile what has been one of the fundamental paradoxes of post–civil rights American politics: African Americans' formal possession of full legal citizenship and their inherited burden of 'civic estrangement.'"[60] She believes that cultural workers grapple with this burden by foregrounding a "democratic aesthetic" that creates an imagined emancipatory space.

What kind of aesthetic would allow us to reimagine enslavement in the context of actual freedom achieved through revolution? Furthermore, why should we seek such representational forms? That is, when there is no paradoxical relationship to citizenship why depict realistic representations of slavery? My argument is that doing so allows us to conceptualize resistance in more nuanced and capacious ways, complicating and extending beyond the grand narrative of revolution. In contradistinction to the film *Toussaint Louverture*, Trouillot's novel demonstrates that foregrounding the slave past does not have to mean blotting out resistance. Central to the book is the relationship between the past, present, and the future imagined by a slave whose personal sense of agency develops in spite of her condition of enslavement. As Lisette remembers her grandmother's story about the barracoons, she holds onto the words that become her inspiration:

> [They] come back to remind me that I am a slave and it is in this truth
> that my strength lies. Whether a field slave or a house slave, man,

woman, or child, the slave is a creature who has lost his soul between the mill and the sugarcane, between the ship's hold and its steerage, between the crinoline and the slap in the face. Shame stains our every gesture. When we place our feet, undeserving of shoes, on the ground, we let our exhausted bodies fall on cornhusk mattresses, and when we swing the bamboo fans, we crush our souls under the weight of our shame. Only our gestures of revolt truly belong to us.[61]

While the novel is a portrait of colonial life from the perspective of the slaves who experience it, it is also a coming-of-age story about a young woman who moves from complacency to resistance within the confines of her existence as a slave. As Lisette becomes increasingly aware of her surroundings and reacts to them, her emotions lead her toward politicization, resistance, and radicalism. Ultimately, she decides to become a marroon herself and to let the child inside her live. Through this intimate portrait, Trouillot shows that it is possible to honor the Haitian Revolution without sifting out the memories of slavery.

NOTES

1. Edwidge Danticat, "Foreword," in Evelyne Trouillot, *The Infamous Rosalie*, trans. M. A. Salvodon (Lincoln: University of Nebraska Press, 2013), vii.

2. As Michel-Rolph Trouillot argues, history can be more accurately viewed as "the concrete production of specific narratives" (*Silencing the Past: Power and the Production of History* [Boston: Beacon, 1997], 22).

3. I borrow this language on the relationship between fact and truth from Toni Morrison, who points out that "the crucial distinction . . . is not the difference between fact and fiction, but the distinction between fact and truth. Because facts exist without human intelligence, but truth does not" ("The Site of Memory," in *Inventing the Truth: The Art and Craft of Memoir*, edited by William Zinsser and Russell Baker, 2nd ed. [Boston: Houghton Mifflin, 1995], 93).

4. Pierre Nora famously argues that memory is alive and carried out by living groups whereas history is an incomplete and complex representation of the past. Seeing memory as a strainer means that one also sees memory as incomplete, filtered, and complex. See his "Between Memory and History: Les Lieux de Mémoire," *Representations* 26 (spring 1989): 7–24.

5. Alyssa Goldstein Sepinwall explains: "The French colonial period is one of the most studied eras in Haitian historiography, its chroniclers include scholars trained in French history, Haitian historians interested in their country's origins and specialists in Caribbean and Atlantic history . . . [but] for much of the nineteenth and twentieth centuries, histories of Saint-Domingue focused on the colony's whites" (*Haitian History: New Perspectives* [New York: Routledge, 2013], 14).

6. For scholarship on the Haitian Revolution, see David Patrick Geggus, *The Impact of the Haitian Revolution in the Atlantic World* (Columbia: University of South Carolina Press, 2002); Carolyn E. Fick, *The Making of Haiti: The Saint Domingue Revolution from Below* (Knoxville: University of Tennessee Press, 1990); and Laurent Dubois, *Avengers of the New World: The Story of the Haitian Revolution* (Cambridge, Mass.: Harvard University Press, 2004).

7. "'We have at our disposal not a single written testimony on the reality of slavery coming from a slave' declared [Louis] Sala-Molins in 1987 concerning the literary legacies of the French slave-holding colonies" (Deborah Jenson, *Beyond the Slave Narrative: Politics, Sex, and Manuscripts in the Haitian Revolution* [Liverpool, England: Liverpool University Press, 2011], 2).

8. Sepinwall, *Haitian History*, 15.

9. Jenson, *Beyond the Slave Narrative*, 3.

10. Dubois, *Avengers of the New World*, 7.

11. Brinda Mehta, *Notions of Identity, Diaspora, and Gender in Caribbean Women's Writing* (New York: Palgrave Macmillan, 2009), 30.

12. As Aida Levy-Hussen points out in chapter 10, "African American memory scholars tell us that remembering history matters now more than ever." However, it is important to recall that considering the Americas at large gives us a more dynamic view of what is at stake in using representation to remember and forget slavery.

13. Ana Araujo, *Politics of Memory: Making Slavery Visible in the Public Space* (London: Routledge, 2012), 1.

14. Salamishah Tillet, *Sites of Slavery: Citizenship and Racial Democracy in the Post–Civil Rights Imagination* (Durham, N.C.: Duke University Press, 2012), 2.

15. Jenson, *Beyond the Slave Narrative*, 1.

16. This tendency in Haiti is also different from tendencies in other parts of the French-speaking Caribbean. For instance, as Bonnie Thomas notes, "Glissant's representations of the traumas of Caribbean slavery through a variety of media can be considered part of . . . a 'discourse of witness'" ("Edouard Glissant and the Art of Memory," *Small Axe* 30 [November 2009]: 27).

17. Émeric Bergeaud, *Stella* (Geneva: Éditions Zoé et Les Classiques du Monde, 2009), 19.

18. Danticat, "Foreword," vii.

19. Stuart Hall, "New Ethnicities," in *Critical Dialogues in Cultural Studies*, ed. David Morley and Kuan-Hsing Chen (New York: Routledge, 1996), 442–451.

20. *Toussaint Louverture*, dir. Philippe Niang (Paris: Eloa Prod, 2012), DVD.

21. In 2004, *Toussaint Louverture, Haïti et la France*, a documentary by Laurent Lutaud, appeared on France's TV5. It featured a number of Francophone Caribbean writers, including Aimé Césaire and Frankétienne.

22. For an analysis of non-Haitian literary works about the Haitian Revolution, see Philip Kaisary, *The Haitian Revolution in the Literary Imagination: Radical Horizons, Conservative Constraints* (Charlottesville: University of Virginia Press, 2014).

23. Dubois, *Avengers of the New World*, 172.

24. The miniseries was even filmed in Martinique, an overseas French department, rather than in Haiti.

25. All translations from the film are mine.

26. *Toussaint Louverture*, dir. Niang.

27. Examples of this apologist approach include the French focus on abolition of slavery in 1848 as well as the claim that there were no slaves in France.

28. Saidiya Hartman, *Scenes of Subjection: Terror, Slavery, and Self-Making in Nineteenth-Century America* (Oxford: Oxford University Press, 1997), 6.

29. For an extensive analysis of French responses to the Haitian Revolution, including the nation's depictions of slave barbarism, see David Patrick Geggus, *Haitian Revolutionary Studies* (Bloomington: Indiana University Press, 2002).

30. Alyssa Goldstein Sepinwall, "Happy As a Slave: Review of *Toussaint Louverture*," *Fiction and Film for French Historians*, http://h-france.net/fffh/maybe-missed/happy-as-a-slave-the-toussaint-louverture-miniseries/, accessed November 16, 2015.

31. Catherine Reinhardt, "Slavery and Commemoration: Remembering the French Abolitionary Decree 150 Years Later," in *Memory, Empire, and Postcolonialism: The Legacies of French Colonialism*, ed. Alec Hargreaves (Lanham, Md.: Lexington, 2005), 13. For more on this willful forgetting of slavery, especially in the context of its overseas departments, see Doris Garraway, "Memory As Reparation? The Politics of Remembering Slavery in France from Abolition to the Loi Taubira," *International Journal of Francophone Studies* 11, no. 3 (2008): 365–386.

32. Reinhardt explains that "the long historical period preceding 1848—three centuries of slavery—did not disrupt the unitary vision of the French government" ("Slavery and Commemoration," 12).

33. As Douglas A. Jones Jr. argues in chapter 2, "willful inaccuracy is the greatest possible transgression here because, in purposefully misrepresenting the slave past, one also misrepresents the conditions that produced the present and thus becomes complicit in perpetuating racial inequities and social injustices."

34. La loi tendant à la reconnaissance de la traite et de l'esclavage en tant que crime contre l'humanité, May 21, 2001, art. 1.

35. In 2006, then president Jacques Chirac "declared France's readiness to assume responsibility for an uncensored version of history by finally acknowledging its role in the slave trade" and announced the creation of a memorial center for the memory of slavery and its abolition (Thomas, "Edouard Glissant," 26).

36. Renée Larrier, "Inheritances: Legacies and Lifelines in Trouillot's *Rosalie l'infâme*," *Dalhousie French Studies* 28 (fall 2009): 137.

37. As Larrier points out, the ship is called "*Rosalie l'infâme* by the captives to reflect its perverted mission[;] this site of rupture, dispossession, and indignity has an oxymoronic nickname that juxtaposes rose—a beautiful flower, color, and the Christian name Lisette's mother Ayouba refuses—with *infâme*, an adjective used to describe a loathsome occupation, unspeakable act or disgusting odor, all of which are entirely appropriate in this context" (ibid., 140).

38. Trouillot, *The Infamous Rosalie*, 12, 64, 21.

39. Hartman, *Scenes of Subjection*, 51. Hartman's observation explicitly relates to "the Americas," a link I also make later in this chapter.

40. Trouillot, *The Infamous Rosalie*, 131.

41. Mimi Sheller, *Citizenship from Below: Erotic Agency and Caribbean Freedom* (Durham, N.C.: Duke University Press, 2012), 142.

42. Fick points out, "Slave women often resorted to abortion and even infanticide as a form of resistance rather than permit their children to grow up under the abomination of slavery" (*The Making of Haiti*, 48).

43. Trouillot, *The Infamous Rosalie*, 129.

44. Ibid., 30, 24.

45. Ibid., 25.

46. Ibid., 132.

47. Morrison, "The Site of Memory," 92.

48. Trouillot, *The Infamous Rosalie*, 13.

49. Michel-Rolph Trouillot, "The Odd and the Ordinary: Haiti, the Caribbean, and the World," *Cimarron* 2, no. 3 (1990): 12.

50. Trouillot, *The Infamous Rosalie*, 39.

51. Ibid., 2.

52. Ibid., 22.

53. Ibid., 24.

54. Ibid., 77, 78.

55. Ibid., 77–78.

56. Larrier, "Legacies and Lifelines," 142.

57. Nelly Schmidt, "Teaching and Commemorating Slavery and Abolition in France," in *Politics of Memory: Making Slavery Visible in the Public Space*, ed. Ana Lucia Araujo (New York: Routledge, 2013), 106. Also see Abdoulaye Gueye, "Memory at Issue: On Slavery and the Slave Trade among Black French," *Canadian Journal of African Studies* 45, no. 1 (2011): 77–107; and Garraway, "Memory As Reparation?" 365–386.

58. Trouillot, *Silencing the Past*, 26–28.

59. Doris Garraway, *Tree of Liberty: Cultural Legacies of the Haitian Revolution in the Atlantic World* (Charlottesville: University of Virginia Press, 2008), 6.

60. Tillet, *Sites of Slavery*, 3.

61. Trouillot, *The Infamous Rosalie*, 82.

6

Staging Social Death

Alienation and Embodiment in Aishah Rahman's *Unfinished Women*

GERSHUN AVILEZ

In recent critical discourse, the concept of social death has emerged as an important lens through which to describe and assess black lived reality. It has developed as a way to communicate how histories of racialized subjection inform the quotidian experience of African American existence. In his influential monograph, *Slavery and Social Death* (1982), Orlando Patterson uses the term to theorize slavery's institutional negation of the enslaved's capacity for self-determination.[1] More recently, Jared Sexton has refashioned the term as a tool for thinking through the phenomenon of *contemporary* communal and civic estrangement, particularly for racial minorities. "Black life," he insists, "is lived in social death."[2] His maxim consolidates the view of an emergent field of thought that has come to be known as Afro-pessimism in the context of U.S. critical theory.[3]

Afro-pessimism asks if the relationships between blacks and the state (and blacks and whites) are to some extent a series of irreconcilable encounters and considers how our understanding of the social world shifts if radical change or resolution is not imagined on the horizon.[4] More pejorative readings of this framework see it as mere hopelessness. Black citizens never seem to have agency and are unable to define themselves or have access to the social world—hence Afro-*pessimism*. Yet such assessments focus too heavily on the seeming incapacity (the death) of the black subject, missing the evaluation of the historically persistent restrictive nature of the civic realm (the social). In fact, a restricted yet existing black sociality has often been Afro-pessimism's chief concern. Sexton helps us to recognize that social death is more about recognizing seemingly unchanging social conditions and political structures and less about identifying a torpid black interiority that can appear will-less.

My approach to social death pivots on the idea that a distinct theorization of the body lies at the heart of this critical construct. In his comparative analysis of enslavement as a social system, Patterson explains that the slave was defined as a socially dead person. From the viewpoint of the majority of society, the enslaved person is deemed a "nonperson."[5] Patterson's larger point is that enslavement relies upon a particular institutionalized marginalization that deprives a specific group of rights and access to the body politic while still incorporating them into the social world precisely through that depriva- tion. That is, they become culturally legible through their abject status.[6] For the enslaved, there is no social existence outside the realm of the master. In effect, Patterson specifies a kind of civic death that results in a general social nonexistence or illegibility. The fact that there is no state of being beyond the affective circuit with the master figure means that social death has more to do with the *experience* of sociality than with subjectivity or the space of identity. In my reading, his point is not to evacuate the subject of interiority but to draw attention to how it is enmeshed in a set of networks that attempt to confine or obscure interiority. This constricting network creates the reality of social death.

Some readers conclude that social death *necessarily* implies an undesirable constricting of black interiority. However, the concept is also about the prohibi- tive boundaries of relationality. Social nonbeing becomes aligned closely with a specific racialization in the context of enslavement in the Americas. Racial embodiment becomes the basis and context for the marginalizing relation- ship. Accordingly, even after the official ending of enslavement, the circulating meanings already attached to blackness perpetuate the link between black corporeality and social death. The projection of negative values onto these sub- jects means that the experience of black embodiment can still be understood through this lens. In addition, the emphasis on experience clarifies that social death, from Patterson's work forward, constitutes a phenomenological assess- ment of black embodiment.

Social death is not only an important critical construct but also relevant to the world of artistic production; and drama, which is constitutively attuned to enactment and embodiment, is a particularly effective means for exploring how it anticipates the form and content of black expressive culture. In this chapter, I consider Aishah Rahman's play *Unfinished Women Cry in No Man's Land While a Bird Dies in a Gilded Cage* (1977), which uses the gendered dynamics that characterized U.S. enslavement as the dominant framework for articulating the possibilities of owning the self.[7] Rahman uses reproductive imagery and jazz musical references as figures for exploring her characters' limited social agency. The play features five fictional pregnant women and a fictionalized Charlie Parker Jr. (based on the well-known jazz musician), all of whom struggle to gain self-control and agency while being held captive by the state (the women) and by a rich patron (the musician).

The conceptual tension between individual freedom and imprisonment becomes the basis for Rahman's formal practices. She creates a dramatic form that exhibits structural collapse—specifically, the disintegration of the boundaries between scenes and different points in time—in order to enact her characters' striving attempts to challenge boundaries or limits. This performed collapsing becomes a means for recognizing the historical impress of enslavement and for refuting enslavement's totalizing influence through undermining the psychic and material spaces this institution has created. More importantly, the play represents a creative response to the conditions that underpin the notion of social death, and it stands as an unparalleled feminist intervention in Afro-pessimism.

Rahman presents what she calls a polydrama by having two sets with separate storylines on stage at once: the "Hide-a-Wee Home for Unwed Mothers" and the secluded boudoir of a French woman named Pasha. Wilma, Paulette, Consuelo, Mattie, and Midge—a group of young, pregnant women of different ethnic and class backgrounds—occupy the Hide-a-Wee Home. By the end of the day, all must decide if they are going to give their children up for adoption. The action depicted on the other set focuses on the saxophone player Charlie Parker Jr. and his white patron, Pasha.[8] Through these juxtaposed sets, Rahman uses the trope of reproduction to investigate how one's agency is delimited by social conceptions of her body. More importantly, the two sets together represent the paradox at the heart of social death. On each stage, reproductive imagery represents both gendered embodied agency *and* the mechanisms that link characters to limited social mobility. Juxtaposing freedom and restriction in her characters' gendered pursuits of self-determination, Rahman offers a performative exploration of the notion of social death.

A conflict between body and mind highlights the characters' collective vulnerability and informs the events in the play. The character Nurse Jacobs is central to the world of the Hide-a-Wee Home, and her presence helps to solidify the idea that the body makes one vulnerable to manipulation. Jacobs is in charge of the women's physical well-being during their stay at the home, but she also takes charge of their moral development. Her guidance develops from her belief that there is an internal competition going on within the women's bodies:

NURSE JACOBS: (*Examining Mattie*) Just what I expected! You're gaining too much weight. Too much salt. Lord, today . . . You're swollen and probably toxic.

PAULETTE: I told you not to eat that whole jar of pickles.

MATTIE: I like 'em. (*All of the girls laugh*)

NURSE JACOBS: You think it's funny, don't you. You think it's funny if she gorges herself with salt and swells up like a balloon. All right. Everybody off salt.

ALL THE GIRLS: What!

NURSE JACOBS: No more salt on the table. No salt in the crackers. No salt in
the ocean and no salt in your tears. No more salt, I say! Don't you know it's
a mortal sin to harm your babies. . . . I think you are purposefully trying
to cross God by harming your babies. . . . No salt for anyone I say. . . . Now!
You see the shame and burden loose ways bring upon a girl. . . . It don't
pay to be worthless![9]

Jacobs's insistence that these young women remove salt from their diets
leads her to a confusing yet suggestive hyperbole. In effect, to cry tears without
salt is not to cry at all. Her dietary request denies not only of food but also the
body itself. Her unfeasible demand (that they will no longer be allowed to have
salt in their tears or even in the ocean) also reflects her general tendency to ask
the impossible of these women: that they differentiate their desires from their
expectant bodies.[10] In arguing that physical pleasure is secondary to the health
of the fetus, Jacobs is asking the women to no longer fully inhabit and enjoy
their bodies for fear of fetal contamination. By having Jacobs place the needs
or rights of a fetus over those of the woman carrying it, Rahman consciously
invokes abortion discourses.[11] Moreover, pitting the body against the self adds
to the antiphonal effect of the polydrama.

Dorothy Roberts and Robert J. Patterson have both made the case that black
women in the United States have been historically manipulated and made vulnerable through reproduction, and the events of the play reflect a similar understanding.[12] The nurse insists that the women are only their bodies and places
herself in charge of them. Given that a place such as the Hide-a-Wee Home
would almost certainly be a state-run, publicly funded facility, she may be read as
an avatar of the state. The women's pregnancies have made them subject to state
influence. The thinking behind the nurse's directions also taps into commonly
held beliefs that working-class women and women of color in particular need
instruction on motherhood and require governmental intervention.[13] However,
rather than making Jacobs a simplistic, controlling apparatus of the state,
Rahman has created a heavy-hearted character who is herself alienated from her
corporeal existence. The nurse is asking the young women to do what she did
long ago: deny her body *and* her right to its issue. In a monologue in scene 4,
Jacobs explains that, when she was a young woman living in the Caribbean, she
fell in love with a Calypso singer. She got pregnant, but he left her, moving "from
island to island" to perform. After giving birth, she moved away, calling her
daughter a niece in an attempt to avoid dishonor and disgrace in her Caribbean
community. By claiming this tangential relationship, Nurse Jacobs demonstrates
that she feels she has no right to this child because of the circumstances of her
conception and birth. This feeling is linked to why she believes that the women
at the home have no choice but to sign their children over to heterosexual
couples with the wherewithal to raise them. From Jacobs's perspective, these

couples have more right to the issue of the women's bodies than do the women themselves. Accordingly, there are conditions on and limitations to the extent to which one can claim a right to her body. The nurse's shame about her own past has led her to become an agent of the state's circumscribing power.

This moralizing fracture of personhood and body leads the character Mattie to insist, "I don't know nothing except this baby is in my belly and gonna come out my pussy with blood and piss and shit. I'm scared."[14] Her assertion reveals self-concern and demonstrates that this home for unwed mothers does little to prepare the women for the actual act of giving birth. Yet it also locates her understanding of herself, the world around her, and the future in terms of her corporeal being. Another character, Midge, jokingly (and knowingly) responds to Mattie's statement: "We're just wonderful vessels of creation for the Lord!" Her sarcasm reveals the complexity of how the women are viewed and how they view themselves. If, as the nurse implies in her global moratorium on salt, they are simply vessels, pain should not and cannot be an issue. Nonetheless, the women and the audience know that this idea is false. Furthermore, the women are all aware that they are not deemed to be "*wonderful* vessels"; otherwise, they would likely not have to decide if they should hand their children over to strangers. The assertion, then, demonstrates the women's consciousness of the fact that they are seen not as people but as *unworthy* vessels. The statement acknowledges an understanding of their bodies that erases their sentience and value. It suggests that these characters occupy a space of nonbeing because of the public perceptions of their pregnant bodies; their access to both agency and self-definition has been co-opted. The body can make a person vulnerable because it situates her within the social gaze and exposes her to restrictive social meanings.

The disappearance of a woman's individuality beneath a pregnant body is a recognizable concept within feminist theoretical discourse. In "Stabat Mater," Julia Kristeva argues that no signifier is able to encompass the maternal body, which is overburdened with socially imposed values and ideas to the point of being hidden or obscured:

> The weight of the "non-said" (*non-dit*) no doubt affects the mother's body first of all: no signifier can cover [the maternal body] completely, for the signifier is always meaning (*sens*), communication or structure, whereas a mother-woman is rather a strange "fold" (*pli*) which turns nature into culture, and the speaking subject (*le parlent*) into biology. Although it affects each woman's body, this heterogeneity, which cannot be subsumed by the signifier, literally explodes with pregnancy. . . . These peculiarities of the maternal body make a woman a creature of folds.[15]

The theoretical model of the *non-dit*—the "non-said" or "not speakable"— does not indicate that the maternal body is beyond meaning or description.[16]

Instead, it intimates that this body has been drowned or submerged beneath layers of significations, which occasions a loss of personhood as the pregnant woman is transformed from a subject to a biological object: a belly. Hortense Spillers explicitly responds to and builds upon this understanding in her own thinking on black female identity, emphasizing the historical contexts that help constitute these ideas.[17] The "folds" describe the occluding layers of meaning that surround and ultimately stand in for the body in question. As Kristeva's work reveals, feminist theorizing is relevant to conceptions of black identity; the pregnant body functions as a productive site to connect feminism and black cultural theory.[18] Specifically, in considering the extent to which it is possible to gain control of or have agency over a body that is overdetermined with projected meaning, Kristeva reveals how social readings of the body persistently threaten to overwhelm the self-determining potential of individual interiority.

Acknowledging the emphasis on public perceptions of the women's bodies allows Rahman's readers to recognize how even the spatial locations of the play comment on the erasure of individual identity. The tangible space that the "unfinished women" inhabit, the Hide-a-Wee Home, symbolizes the place they occupy in public opinion. As the name of the home indicates, these women must be hidden from public view. When the character Consuelo's family decides to put her in the home and then lie that she is in Puerto Rico visiting relatives, they offer double evidence of the refusal to submit her body to community perusal and judgment. They create a narrative of her life and impose it on her because the conditions that surround the pregnancy threaten to shame her and them. Pregnancy has the potential to do social damage and must be kept from public view.[19]

The coextensive space of the private boudoir enhances the seclusion fundamental to the Hide-a-Wee Home. Rahman has the two sets occupy the same space and time on stage. Their proximity has nothing to do with geographical closeness; instead, it reveals that they have similar metaphorical values: the hidden and the private (both symbolically feminine domains). Whether literal (the pregnant characters) or figurative (Pasha's control of Parker), conversations about procreation take place in private because the pregnant body (or even the procreative body) is always on the cusp of becoming an unethical and offending body. Rahman makes the moral and ethical state of the body dependent upon its spatial location.

Rahman's dramatic work recognizes a link between this specific way of thinking about the pregnant body that Kristeva describes and the racialization of the black body/minority bodies in the social imaginary. Her play effectively links the concepts of the *non-dit* and social death. The disappearance of the subject beneath folds of projected meaning identifies precisely the cultural work done by racial and gender stereotypes. The racialized minority body, like the pregnant body, oversignifies and obscures individual subjectivity. This point is the one that Spillers makes in opening "Mama's Baby, Papa's Maybe":

> I am a marked woman, but not everybody knows my name. "Peaches" and "Brown Sugar," "Sapphire" and "Earth Mother," "Aunty," "Granny," God's "Holy Fool," a "Miss Ebony First," or "Black Woman at the Podium": I describe a locus of confounded identities, a meeting ground of investment and privations in the national treasury of rhetorical wealth. . . . Embedded in bizarre axiological ground, they demonstrate a sort of telegraphic coding; they are markers so loaded with mythical prepossession that there is no easy way for the agents buried beneath them to come clean. In that regard, the names by which I am called in the public place render an example of signifying property *plus*.[20]

The multiplicity of signifiers—here limiting stereotypes about black female identity—signals that, like the Kristevan mother, no signifier can cover the body of Spillers's "marked woman." Black female subjectivity lies hidden under these denominative folds. The subject remains effectively unspoken or unexpressed through the controlling and violent acts of misnaming. There are important theoretical ties between Spillers's assessment of the black female subject and the social world and the evolving theorization of social death. In both, meanings are projected onto a subject in ways that attempt to interrupt or bury identity. Both appear to describe a veritable loss of identity but actually illuminate the mechanisms by which identity is manipulated socially. By taking up these ideas and using them to construct her female and male characters, Rahman points to these exact mechanisms that are rooted in structures of power.

Social death has to do with corporeal vulnerability, not simply of the physical body but of the vulnerability to social scripts that the body expresses. The possibility of a troubled relationship to one's body also undergirds the second component of the polydrama, Pasha's boudoir. It may seem strange to juxtapose a group of expecting women with a dying musician and his mistress; however, Pasha's desire to be with Parker is itself a desire to conceive and to control through conception. When Parker arrives at the boudoir, she is tatting lace. Rahman purposefully makes use of this craft imagery because the act of creation relies on locking the lace into place; hence, Pasha creates by fixing and tying down. After complaining about his absence and her inability to contact him, she tells Parker that she will "tat" them a child. Her language links reproduction to confinement, and her comments throughout the play exhibit how this desire to procreate expresses her general desire to control him. As Pasha asserts that he should impregnate her because her patronage obligates him to do so, she explains that he is not only in her debt but also dependent upon her for personal development: "I am the farmer. You are the seed. I am the farmer that nurtures the seed. You are the genius but I am the power."[21] Her money gives her complete access to and governance of his body and future. Extending procreative understandings to the male body, she makes his body the site of (re)production in making him the seed but limits his creative output by making him dependent upon her will. She imagines him as will-less though necessary for the act of creation.[22] The procreative imagery, then, manifests her designs of controlling Parker and expanding her possession of him. He is figured as a vessel of creation that is effectively unworthy and incapable without her. Parker depends on Pasha for meaning and has little sense of value outside of their exploitative relationship.

The importance of procreation is enhanced by Parker's request for a womb: "Tat me a womb, Pasha . . . not attached to anybody . . . just some unattached place for me to lay my head. You can do it. You can do anything."[23] To make sense of this request, the reader must consider the "Playwright's Notes" that precede the text of the play. Here, Rahman emphasizes the importance of the "metaphor of birth and art" to the content and structure of her work.[24] If birth is connected to or equated with art throughout the play, then the womb that Parker requests represents artistic potentiality or a creative matrix. The character feels artistically stifled and at a standstill: "Music is my only motive. . . . My only alibi . . . for living. Clubs are named after me. Musicians make it . . . imitate me. And I can't even give it away. I stand around begging people to let me play. I . . . am . . . Charles . . . Parker, Jr. . . . and I beg people to let me play."[25] His frustration about not being able to create music is transmogrified into a request for a conduit for creation—a womb—for his horn, a phallic symbol, has failed him. More importantly, the desire for a womb that is "not attached to anybody" is a desire for its symbolic power minus the weaknesses connected to flesh. As his drug addiction confirms, Parker is a character who is especially vulnerable to such weaknesses: "Sometimes I wish I could be a thought, a sound / Anything, but flesh. . . . O! to be free. Not to a giant, not a god, not a man!"[26]

This rejection of flesh is a tacit acknowledgment of the vulnerability of the body, but it also points to a critical reading of racialized embodiment as fragmented. In "Mama's Baby," Spillers provides insight on the concept of flesh in the context of black cultural history. She makes a distinction between "body" and "flesh" in constructing captive and liberated subject positions:

Before the "body" there is the "flesh," that zero degree of social conceptualization that does not escape concealment under the brush of discourse or the reflexes of iconography. Even though the European hegemonies stole bodies—some of them female—out of West African communities in concert with the African "middleman," we regard this human and social irreparability as high crimes against the *flesh*, as the person of African females and males registered the wounding. If we think of the "flesh" as a primary narrative, then we mean its seared, divided, ripped-apartness, riveted to the ship's hole, fallen, or "escaped" overboard.[27]

In this view, the flesh precedes the body, which names one's placement within the discursive realm. The flesh thus represents the prediscursive realm, which exists before and outside of scripted meanings. The body has been mapped with designations and misrepresentations that can obscure histories as well as the scars of conflict. Spillers's goal is to illuminate the physical acts of destruction as well as to expose and remove the layers of pejorative meaning that are forcefully projected onto black corporeal being; these meanings give shape to the body as a social unit. She acknowledges the existence of the being who is outside of destructive designations. This understanding of the body lies at the root of and enables the conception of social death. The reference to flesh in the play therefore does not operate to signal a prediscursive positionality. Because flesh equals vulnerability, it is presented as a problem. More importantly, the desire to get away from the flesh can be read as an indication that there is no outside to the discursive realm. While Spillers's distinction clarifies that the body is a construct, my point is that Parker and the characters in *Unfinished Women* recognize how they are caught in a net of meanings because of their embodiment. The women know that their pregnancies have made them vulnerable, as Parker does with his addiction. Parker's desire to be a thought or a sound is a request for an escape from physical being and its social trappings. This yearning for escape gets coded or translated into a death drive.

It is important to recognize that Parker's desire to free himself from his flesh signals his impending death and the symbolic weight of death in the drama's general configuration. The space of the boudoir is itself a kind of burial plot: in it, Parker admits that his career is over, and he dies there under Pasha's watchful eye. His feelings of inadequacy and artistic impotence coupled with his approaching death suggest that his request for a womb reflects a longing for virility. In this way, Rahman alludes to recognizable formulations of masculinity that imagine reproduction as a tool primarily for manhood, as Robert Carr explains in the context of black nationalism.[28] Parker's necrotic presence in the drama also inserts death into the considerations of life that occur in the other space of the polydrama: the Hide-a-Wee Home. Ultimately, juxtaposing this dying figure with the fecund bodies of the young women shows how death provides the terms for depicting the contested nature of black and minority reproduction in Rahman's mind.

This representation of Parker's character also illustrates how he functions as a figuration of what Abdul JanMohammed calls "the death-bound subject." One might go so far as to say that the play as a whole offers a collection of death-bound subjects. For JanMohammed this subject "is formed, from infancy on, by the imminent and ubiquitous threat of death; he is one who inhabits a social environment in which the threat of death is constant yet unpredictable. As such, the death-bound subject occupies a deeply aporetic structure to the extent that he is 'bound,' and hence produced as a subject, by the process of 'unbinding.'"[29] JanMohammed develops the idea to describe the conditions of twentieth-century African American existence. In his view, the legal end to enslavement does not cease willful aggressions against black bodies, as lynchings and other acts of gratuitous violence throughout the twentieth century have shown. For him, such social realities mean that black subjectivity, as a social formation, continues to be defined in the context of the threat of death, which encloses and envelops the black subject and permeates the experience of the social realm. The emphasis on the threat means that the construction is not only about the cessation of the life function but also about undermining agency and willfulness.

JanMohammed's contention builds upon Patterson's earlier treatise, yet his work is also distinct from Patterson's and Sexton's. Patterson's construction of social death is rooted in ideas about civic death. Similarly, Sexton explores the terrain of compromised civic status in his thinking on social death. JanMohammed is more interested in shedding light on how the consistent and ongoing social *threat* of death—as opposed to civic marginalization and alienation—constitutes death-bound subjectivity. His discussion attempts to describe a position that this subject is forced to occupy because of historically ingrained conceptions about the social implications of black physical vulnerability caused by the ubiquitous threat of death. The constant context of death means that one is on the verge of losing personal identity and that agency is thwarted.

In chapter 1 of this book, Robert J. Patterson contends, "Both racism and slavery are discursive and material sites wherein black bodies constantly straddle the tenuous positions between life and death," and this understanding undergirds both the death-bound and social death concepts. This idea also describes succinctly the imagined world of *Unfinished Women*. Parker is actually dying and Pasha denies him any personal will outside of herself; he is figured as powerless outside of his relationship with this rich and influential white woman. The state's threatening denial of the young women's agency makes them appear similarly dependent, but it also attempts to present them as objects without autonomous subjectivity. In other words, Rahman's play depicts the cast of characters through the framework of being literally and figuratively death-bound to articulate the social restrictions that delimited certain racial and gendered agency well into the twentieth century. Part of the significance of the play is that it extends the death-bound subject formulation not only to the black female body but also to the female body in general by exploring the suffocating notions that are projected onto the pregnant body.

The curious figure of Charlie Chan enhances the contemplation of death that informs the presentation of the rest of the characters.[30] In the "Playwright's

Notes," Rahman describes Chan as "a black man in blackface, a minstrel who acts as master of ceremony, connecting between scenes, always remaining outside of the drama. He is a magic mimetic man."[31] In addition, he is dressed exactly like Parker—a conspicuous visual cue that he can be seen as Parker's double. On one hand, having the character in blackface allows Rahman to conjure up the idea of racial performance and embodiment as a historical phenomenon. Chan introduces the concept of minstrelsy, which, even with its problematic history, can function as an artistic tool for claiming ownership of historical means of representation and a gesture toward repair, as Soyica Diggs Colbert intimates in her discussion in chapter 7. Rahman's play seeks to highlight how certain recognizable notions about racial and gendered embodiment undergird the events on stage. It is Chan, as the figuration of these ideas, who links the disparate sets. On the other hand, the presence of a double for Parker in blackface that exists outside of the primary action also can be interpreted as a figure of death. It is not death in general but Parker's own death that threatens to emerge in the boudoir and that is announced and haunts the events at the Hide-a-Wee Home.

Besides his death-figure function, Chan's character also helps to illuminate how a different understanding of temporality emerges in *Unfinished Women*. One of the most important actions that this deathly doppelgänger performs is adjusting the hands of a broken clock on the stage, which he does at various moments throughout the play.[32] The clock keeps stopping, and Chan tries to make it show the right time. His actions, which only the audience notices, draw attention to the fact that time has stopped in the world of the play. The structural mechanisms of the drama gesture toward the possibility of halted time, suggesting the end of time, history, or life—arguably, the realm of death. The point is not simply that life is at a standstill but that the events of the play take place outside the normal circuit of the passage of time. For this reason the two sets of the polydrama can be juxtaposed. The events in the Hide-a-Wee Home happen on the day that Parker dies: March 12, 1955. The women hear about his death on the radio near the end of scene 1, yet Parker dies in the boudoir at the end of the play in the final moments of the last scene. The end of the drama beckons back to and is connected to the beginning. Although the audience experiences these events as a linear progression, the disruptive manipulation of time and temporal location is integral to the drama.

Chan offers the audience a lens for making sense of time in *Unfinished Women*. As the play opens, he explains, "Think of time as a circle going round and round, beginning at this place or any other place where we think we began. Where is the past? Up? Down?"[33] These comments enable a conception of time as cyclical and allow for an out-of-sync dramatization in which the temporal present of the Hide-a-Wee set is not the present of the boudoir set. Rahman's audience experiences a sensation of halted time; as Chan's comments indicate, this cyclical experience conflates and compresses different temporal moments.

(This idea is in line with Colbert's assertion that spatial logics can disrupt linear conceptions of time.) The notion that events have clear beginnings and endings and distinct boundaries is jettisoned in order to highlight how experiences can be constant or ostensibly unchanging regardless of the movement of time or space. This structure of the play, with its impossibly connected sets, reflects Rahman's theorization of death-derived time for her characters.

Whether reading or watching the play, the audience soon understands that Rahman is making extensive use of what critics have called a "jazz aesthetic."[34] It is formally apparent in the back-and-forth of the play's structure and content, the incorporation of music, and the suggestion of improvisation.[35] It is also discernible through Rahman's emphasis on the manipulation of formal structures within her work and the ultimate breakdown or degradation of formal boundaries and restraints. The drama tends to alternate between the two sets, with an occasional break in action during a monologue. There are also two scenes in which the boundary between the Hide-a-Wee Home and the boudoir falls away. In the last of these scenes, the dialogue and the syntax also break down so that words and songs run together. The idea of a polydrama gains its compound meaning from this enfolding and collapse, but the play's jazz aesthetic also has an important connection to Rahman's central concern with reproduction.

Parker's request for a womb signals a recurring cross-gender identification that is evident in the playwright's construction of a jazz aesthetic. The final death-bound depiction of Parker as feeling fatally trapped within his flesh contrasts with the young women's conception of him as free and liberated. The character Wilma explains in a monologue, "Secretly, I always wanted to be a man 'cause they can do things and go places. Bird [Charlie Parker] is the man I wanted to be."[36] She later sings, "I could be Charlie Parker / Oh the many selves of me / If I could be free, free / To be who I want to be."[37] Pasha may want to control him, but Wilma and the other girls want to be him. They imagine Parker as free because of his maleness and because of the improvisational form of his musical techniques, yet he feels constrained and limited. In other words, for the women, the idea of being this man, or cross-identifying in terms of gender, represents freedom. Conversely, Parker recognizes the symbolic potential in the women's ability to reproduce, but the young women feel subjugated by their bodies. Whereas he sees them as empowered because of their reproductive capacity, they feel that it pinions them. Rahman purposefully moves back and forth between these distinct, gendered perceptions.

Rahman gestures toward a collapsing of gender distinction in the play, which is represented in how the division between the two sets falls away as these statements are made. The two sets materialize the exact idea of a gender dichotomy: the Hide-a-Wee Home captures womanhood, the boudoir manhood. The polydrama, then, makes possible both the presentation and the undermining of the gender binary as well as the social ideas it sets into place.

In transgressing the boundary between the two sets of the polydrama, Rahman unweaves the dichotomy itself. She stages an enfolded gender collapse *conceptually* in the characters' requests and *performatively* by breaking the boundaries between the two sets of her polydrama. This technique helps to reveal the feminist strategies at work in the play. The primary goal is not to articulate womanhood but to reconsider the overall frameworks of gender expression; manipulating the structure of the play becomes a means by which Rahman can deconstruct the common understandings of black gender identity and express desires for their reformulation.

This notion of enfolded collapse also recalls Sexton's theorization of black life as social death: his insistence that "our grand involvement across the color line is structured like the figure of an envelope, folds folded within folds: a black letter law whose message is obscured, enveloped, turned about, reversed. Here a structure of violence is inscribed problematically in narrative, an inscription that can only struggle and fail to be something other than a writing-off, or a writing-over."[38] For Sexton, existence within the social world makes one aware of how power dynamics become imbricated with intimacy so that the experience of the social is only legible as a tortuous navigation through the conflicted layers of private and public meanings. He theorizes social life as a constant negotiation of imposed meanings, particularly those that pertain to racial and gender embodiment. Each fold of the metaphoric envelope that is social existence represents our entanglements in competing subjective significations. The idea that the "message is obscured" suggests that the blocked meaning must be unraveled and unbound to become legible or to be redefined. Sexton's discussion opens up space for strategies that seek to disentangle and unfasten the knotted significations that shape social life. Rahman's play takes up that challenge formally.

Laying bare the intrinsic connection between Rahman's jazz aesthetic and the drama's concerns with death, Wilma's monologue in the center of the play describes her first sexual experience. As she is lying beneath her boyfriend, she "crouches" inside of her self and listens to the "silence" of their activity. In the midst of this sexual silence, she feels, "very faint at first . . . the sound of Bird's horn . . . tugging at me, taking me back to a memory I was born with. Following the music's heartbeat I took a journey I could no longer avoid and along the way I helped a woman toss her newborn baby overboard a slaveship. I joined hands with my mother as she took her mother's hand and I took my place in the circle of black women singing old blues."[39] The sound of Parker's horn connects Wilma to a past of vexed reproduction and death. As a form shaped by the African American experience, jazz is arguably reflective of a complex history that entails manipulated, controlled, and forced reproduction. Accordingly, the first note Wilma imagines transports her to the Middle Passage and an African mother who would rather see her child drown than complete the journey.[40]

The monologue implies a continuum between Wilma and her forbears, between the living and the dead.

In *Raising the Dead*, Sharon Holland argues that references to the ancestors in African American texts function as strategic refusals of the clear distinction between life and death, the present and the past.[41] Amid such temporal and ontological confusions, black life occupies a liminal position. The blurring of the line between the living and the dead is like being caught in a net of conflicting significations. This liminality—being neither here nor there but both—defines the socially precarious state of black life, which functions as the foundation for constructions of social death, as Colbert reminds us in chapter 7. In Rahman's play, then, the sexual encounter evokes sacrifice and destructive histories. The character's vision does suggest unity and generative potential, but one routed through sorrowful songs from past violations.

The reference to the maternal chorus of ancestors sets the stage for the collective singing that constitutes scene 12, and this singing becomes an explicit and sustained strategic mechanism for crossing the boundaries between the two sets. In addition, it recalls and elaborates on Colbert's analysis of Manray's final performance in Spike Lee's film *Bamboozled* (see chapter 7). There, Manray's "dance of death" entails a performative negotiation of prescribed meaning: it "challenges the economies of legibility that render his movements commodifiable." Each step, skip, and slide embodies his precarious movement between his own claims of agency and the institutional forces that seek to deny that agency and claim him as their own. Likewise, in the boundary-breaking singing that closes *Unfinished Women*, the condition of compromised agency links the women to the musician. The collaborative vocalizing, singing, and chattering attempt to clarify this situation and repudiate the empowered individuals who seek to define and delimit the characters' sense of selfhood and their actions. According to Rahman, "the structure of this scene is nearest to a spontaneous jazz piece. Free-form saxophone music dominates and is played steadily throughout. . . . The entire drama bursts into music. The characters repeat the . . . dialogue over and over, weaving in and out of, on top and below, each other, accelerating in pace, volume and intensity."[42] The chaos of the scene and the fast-paced alternations among characters undermine each individual set's structural integrity and coherence. Having the drama "burst" into music infuses the jazz aesthetic into the fabric of the play but also destabilizes notions of structure, control, and order—the concepts associated with Nurse Jacobs's and Pasha's endeavors. The jazz-inflected structure offers the characters, both female and male, a momentary sense of agency in the context of manipulation. The fact that it is spontaneous and perhaps short-lived indicates the singing's and the characters' precariousness but does not erase the significance of the collective performance. The choral singing clarifies the characters' liminality, just as Manray's dancing does in Lee's film.

Thus, for every textual move that appears to lock the women into their bodies and into particular scripts, Rahman offers other artistic strategies that disturb such "tatting." The reader must always keep in mind that she characterizes Wilma, Paulette, Consuelo, Mattie, and Midge as "unfinished women"—a concept validated by the fact that all but Paulette have yet to give birth. At the same time, she aligns the women's embodiment with the seemingly unscripted or improvisational character of Parker's music. Unwilling to rest at any one level of meaning, Rahman pushes the reader to other understandings of "unfinished." The awkward expression functions as a response to the idea that these young women are "finished": no longer of value or written off by society. This state counters a description applied to the women before they ever appear on stage, and it operates in the text as a rejoinder to an interpellation.[43] The rights that the women characters claim to their bodies at the play's close are not sung in a vacuum. Rather, they engage with a social discourse that finds fault with them because of their choices and exposes public perceptions about each woman's body and character.

Wilma's perception of herself as connected to her ancestors extends Rahman's attempts to free her characters from understandings that confine or bind them. As Holland explains, "it is the dead, present as ancestors, who make the complete social death of the slave, and therefore the categories of freed and enslaved, unstable at best."[44] That the dead can be invoked and resurrected through embodied and imagined connection means that the condition of social death does not necessarily produce social isolates or characters without agency. Holland explains that such invocations function as devices that render social categories unstable and permeable, precisely because of the refusal of the division between past and present. Rahman chooses to have Wilma's sexual encounter become a meditation on her relationship to her ancestors. Conflating physical pleasure with historical pain, the dream vision confirms how death has saturated every encounter that Wilma has, but it also introduces the possibility of breaching boundaries that would stifle or limit her sense of self.

My exploration here of social death is not intended to assert the helplessness of the characters. Instead, it is a reckoning with how death informs minoritarian subjectivity. I follow Sexton, who argues that black social death as a critical concept does not concede defeat and acquiesce to the loss of agency: "A living death is as much a death as it is a living. Nothing in afro-pessimism suggests that there is no black (social life), only that black life is not social life in the universe formed by the codes of state and civil society. . . . Black life is not lived in the world that the world lives in, but it is lived underground, in outer space."[45] Black social death describes an environment in which a subject is expressly alienated from the rest of society—the metaphorical condition of being underground and or in outer space. In other words, it is more nuanced and nontransparent than its harshest critics have allowed.[46]

In *Unfinished Women,* Rahman may have set out to delineate the ubiquity of social death, but she does not then imagine characters without agency and the right to define themselves. Perhaps it is only by recognizing the penetrating yet non-annihilating character of social death that black life can be redefined.

Unfinished Women unveils a conceptual connection between black reproduction and death because of the social history that haunts black embodiment. This association grounds the drama and situates reproduction as a crucial conduit for the concept of social death. Rahman's emphasis on reproduction uniquely clarifies the contention that social death is about life, not about the act of dying or the absence of will or personal agency. The playwright works at the intersection of contemporary discourses on race and gender, and her play is a significant feminist appraisal of social death and an artistic contribution to critical discourse. In addition, her investment in feminist frameworks allows us to reimagine the coordinates of gender identity in the context of social death.

Rahman's play also uses the concept of social death to illuminate the boundaries of masculinity and femininity and the means for transgressing them. The fact that she chooses to explore death and black identity in these ways on stage or through embodied enactment illuminates the idea that social death concerns itself with lived experience and embodiment. The genre itself helps to root the concept within the realm of the performative, staging the body's experience of discursive confinement. Ultimately, *Unfinished Women* helps to explain the attraction of social death as a critical construct, one that elucidates the coordinates of the legacy of enslavement as an experiential reality. To speak of social death is to acknowledge how we must all continue to negotiate the past's presence in our expressions of self. The question of wellness that frames the chapters in this book can also be understood as a question about freedom. Cultural explorations of social death, like Rahman's play, propose that we turn our attention to the social conditions and structural forces that might impede the routes to desired freedom and wellness.

NOTES

1. Orlando Patterson, *Slavery and Social Death* (Cambridge, Mass.: Harvard University Press), 1982.

2. Jared Sexton, "The Social Life of Social Death: On Afro-Pessimism and Black Optimism," *InTensions* 5 (fall/winter 2011): 29.

3. The concept of Afro-pessimism, which gained traction in the 1980s and 1990s, initially was an attempt to describe how sub-Saharan African nations might be so plagued with social and political dilemmas that any effective change or progress would be difficult to realize. David Rieff argues for the value of the framework in "In Defense of Afro-Pessimism," *World Policy Journal* 15, no. 4 (1998–1999): 10–22. For work that details the historical and political contexts that fed this understanding, see George B. N. Ayittey, *Africa Betrayed* (New York: St. Martin's, 1992); and his *Africa in Chaos* (New York: St. Martin's, 1998). Also see Robert Jackson and Carl Rosberg, *Personal Rule in Black Africa* (Berkeley: University of California Press, 1982).

4. See Frank Wilderson, *Red, White, and Black: Cinema and the Structure of U.S. Antagonisms* (Durham, N.C.: Duke University Press, 2010), 58–59.

5. Orlando Patterson, *Slavery and Social Death* (Cambridge, Mass.: Harvard University Press, 1982), 5.

6. This relationship between abjection and cultural legibility resonates with Giorgio Agamben's argument that a subject can be included in the community through his or her exclusion. This included exclusion is crucial to the formation of communal or national identity. See *Homo Sacer: Sovereign Power and Bare Life*, trans. Daniel Heller-Roazen (Stanford, Calif.: Stanford University Press, 1998).

7. Rahman's title invokes Harold Pinter's play *No Man's Land* (1974) and Maya Angelou's autobiography *I Know Why the Caged Bird Sings* (1969). Her play thus revises both the canonical play and black feminist theorizing.

8. Charlie "Bird" Parker Jr. was one of the most influential jazz musicians of the twentieth century. He is known for his innovative musical style, his excessive sexual appetite, and his drug abuse. The character Pasha is modeled after Baroness Pannonica "Nica" de Koenigswarter, Parker's real-life friend and patron. He died in her suite at the Stanhope Hotel in 1955. See Ross Russell, *Bird Lives: The High Life and Hard Times of Charlie (Yardbird) Parker* (New York: Charterhouse, 1973); and Brian Priestley, *Chasin' the Bird: The Life and Legacy of Charlie Parker* (New York: Oxford University Press, 2006).

9. Aishah Rahman, *Unfinished Women Cry in No Man's Land While a Bird Dies in a Gilded Cage*, in *Plays by Aishah Rahman*, intro. Thadious M. Davis (New York: Broadway Play Publishing, 1997), 16.

10. By having Jacobs attempt to exert power over their development, Rahman is linking desire to agency and subject formation.

11. On ethical questions and politics linked to the relationship between the fetus and the female body, see Lynn Morgan and Meredith Wilson Michael, *Fetal Subjects, Female Positions* (Philadelphia: University of Pennsylvania Press, 1999); and Barbara Duden, *Disembodying Women: Perspectives on Pregnancy and the Unborn* (Cambridge, Mass.: Harvard University Press, 1993).

12. Dorothy Roberts, *Killing the Black Body* (New York: Vintage, 1998); Robert J. Patterson, *Exodus Politics: Civil Rights and Leadership in African American Literature and Culture* (Charlottesville: University of Virginia Press, 2013).

13. Patricia Hill Collins, *From Black Power to Hip Hop: Racism, Nationalism, and Feminism* (Philadelphia: Temple University Press, 2006); Roberts, *Killing the Black Body*.

14. Rahman, *Unfinished Women*, 17.

15. Julia Kristeva, "Stabat Mater," in *The Female Body in Western Culture: Contemporary Perspectives*, ed. Susan Rubin Suleiman, trans. Arthur Goldhammer (Cambridge, Mass.: Harvard University Press, 1985), 115.

16. The idea of the non-dit resonates with Toni Morrison's concept of the "unspeakable." See her *Beloved* (New York: Vintage, 2004); and Marc Connor, *The Aesthetics of Toni Morrison* (Jackson: University of Mississippi Press, 2000).

17. Hortense Spillers, "'An Order of Constancy': Notes on Brooks and the Feminine," and "Black, White, and in Color, or Learning How to Paint: Toward an Intramural Protocol of Reading," both in *Black, White, and in Color: Essays on American Literature and Culture* (Chicago: University of Chicago Press, 2003), 131–151, 277–300.

18. The idea that the pregnant body connects feminism and black cultural theory lies at the heart of Roberts's *Killing the Black Body*.

19. It is important to note that the women are "hidden" in a public institution and become publicly marked by that fact.

20. Hortense Spillers, "Mama's Baby, Papa's Maybe: An American Grammar Book," *Diacritics* 17 (summer 1987): 65.

21. Rahman, *Unfinished Women*, 20.

22. See Patterson, *Slavery and Social Death*. The will-lessness apparent here is a white-imposed conception; Pasha's construction of Parker results in an eviscerated agency.

23. Rahman, *Unfinished Women*, 19.

24. Rahman, *Unfinished Women*, "Playwright's Notes." The section is unpaginated.

25. Ibid., 28.

26. Ibid., 29.

27. Spillers, "Mama's Baby, Papa's Maybe," 67.

28. Robert Carr, *Black Nationalism and the New World* (Durham, N.C.: Duke University Press, 2002).

29. Abdul JanMohammed, *The Death-Bound Subject: Richard Wright's Archaeology of Death* (Durham, N.C.: Duke University Press, 2005), 2.

30. Chan's name also alludes to Chan Parker, Charlie Parker's common-law wife, and Charlie Chan, the fictional Asian American detective. These connections enhance the connotations of racial performance.

31. Rahman, *Unfinished Women*, 7.

32. Ibid., 8, 33, 34.

33. Ibid., 7.

34. Brandi Wilkins Catanese, "'We Must Keep on Writing': The Plays of Aishah Rahman," in *Contemporary African American Women Playwrights*, ed. Philip C. Kolin (New York: Routledge, 2007), 115–131.

35. On this understanding of the jazz aesthetic, see Alicia Kae Koger, "Jazz Form and Jazz Function: An Analysis of *Unfinished Women Cry in No Man's Land While a Bird Dies in a Gilded Cage*," *MELUS* 16, no. 3 (1989–1990): 99–111. The concept of improvisation is integral to the characterization of Parker's musical style.

36. Rahman, *Unfinished Women*, 21.

37. Ibid., 29.

38. Sexton, "The Social Life of Social Death," 30.

39. Rahman, *Unfinished Women*, 22.

40. The fact that Wilma is transported by means of Parker's phallic horn suggests that black hetero sex is immersed in a complex history of subordination but is also a tool for escaping from that history.

41. Sharon Holland, *Raising the Dead* (Durham, N.C.: Duke University Press, 2000), 43.

42. Rahman, *Unfinished Women*, 34.

43. On the idea of interpellation, see Louis Althusser, "Ideology and Ideological State Apparatuses," in *Critical Theory Since 1965* (Tallahassee: Florida State University Press, 1992), 244–246.

44. Holland, *Raising the Dead*, 14.

45. Sexton, "The Social Life of Social Death," 28–29.

46. See Howard Winant's critique of Patterson in *The New Politics of Race: Globalism, Difference, Justice* (Minneapolis: University of Minnesota Press, 2004), 84.

7

Dancing with Death

Spike Lee's *Bamboozled*

SOYICA DIGGS COLBERT

The texture of freedom is laden with the vestiges of slavery, and abstract
equality is utterly enmeshed in the narrative of black subjection.[1]

−Saidiya Hartman

As time goes on, the direct impact of slavery on American social life seems to
become less and less clear. As the new millennium opened, the United States
turned a page in race relations, with many deciding that we no longer need the
protections of key parts of the 1965 Voting Rights Act or the use of racial criteria
in college admissions decisions. As the saying goes, everything has a season,
and the short season of racial repair enacted through juridical means seems
to have run its course. The notion of the natural and progressive propulsion of
time underpins the logic that historical distance has diminished the affect of
slavery on the lives of twenty-first-century Americans.

Set at the critical juncture of the new millennium, Spike Lee's film
Bamboozled (2000) questions how far U.S. audiences have come, since the nineteenth century, in their perceptions of blackness as well as how far removed
we are from slavery's legacy. The film situates abject blackness as central to the
formation, maintenance, and proliferation of American society and culture,
presenting blackness in "a dialogical rather than a strictly oppositional way."[2]
The dialogic relationship between the constitution of blackness and nationalism also calls attention to time as a progressive and contrapuntal force with
the ability to mark the progress toward fulfilling the promise of the democratic
and the counterpoint of transatlantic slavery. Much like Hortense Spillers, who
famously claimed that "my country needs me and if I were not here I would
have to be invented," *Bamboozled* dramatizes the ongoing tension between the
national necessity of blackness and the particular ways in which twenty-first-
century culture makers remake it.[3]

The film depicts minstrelsy as a toothless nineteenth-century relic and uses it to question how blackness is reinvented in and for a twenty-first-century national imagination. Instead of emerging as the constitutive property of the progeny of the enslaved, blackness becomes coded as a synonym for *urban*, a mode of adornment, a style, or a social or political position. Nineteenth- and twentieth-century biological formulations of blackness that emerged in relationship to the transatlantic slave trade ascribed fixed and debasing character traits to an emergent class of African Americans. In contrast, twenty-first-century formulations of blackness more often depict race as an unfettered experience of individualization through self-willed agency that does not fully account for the ways in which identity appears as a function of the injurious past.

Wrestling with a key distinction between new millennial blackness and its instantiation in the nineteenth century—the difference between owning and being property—*Bamboozled* depicts the stratification of black people in New York City, from the most elite sectors of society to the homeless. Though it is often criticized for its multiple and meandering plotlines, the film critiques black hatred (self and otherwise) as it manifests in egalitarian and dehistoricized notions of commodity production. It does not condemn capitalism per se but calls into question the labor conditions that require the abjection of blackness as a prerequisite for American filmic representation.

In *Powers of Horror*, Julia Kristeva explains abjection as the casting off of objects that threaten the subject in order to demarcate between life and death: "The corpse, seen without God and outside of science, is the utmost of abjection."[4] In her view, the disentanglement of individual and mother produces the individual's first experience of abjection. The instantiating and commonplace loss defines abjection as the threat of deathly embodiment, which results from not heeding the necessity of individualization. According to Darieck Scott, "abjection is a way of describing an experience, an inherited (psychically introjected) historical legacy, and a social condition defined and underlined by a defeat."[5] Focusing on the interface of sexual violence and the social production of blackness, he theorizes ways of inhabiting an identity category that is preemptively constituted as abject: defiled, shameful, and repulsive positions. I am indebted to his original formulations of a specifically racialized abjection, yet my use of the term emphasizes different properties of abjection—namely, how it describes the bodily presence of death in the form of the corpse. Abjection, then, can account for the jettisoning of several forms of waste, but I contend that the installation of the national subject requires production of the black corpse.

In *Bamboozled*, the mundane and quotidian violence usually associated with minstrel shows transforms into the dramatic murder of the central minstrel. The major plotline depicts the development of Pierre "Peerless" Delacroix's (Damon Wayans) television show, *Mantan: A New Millennial Minstrel Show*, which features the tap-dancing virtuoso Manray as Mantan (Savion Glover), the comedian Womack as Sleep 'n Eat (Tommy Davidson), and the hip hop band the Roots as the Alabama Porch Monkeys (fig. 7.1). With his assistant, Sloan Hopkins (Jada Pinkett Smith), Delacroix has tried to create a show so offensive that it will force his boss, Thomas Dunwitty (Michael Rapaport), to fire him as a writer for the Continental Network System (CNS). Instead, the show is an accidental hit.

Bamboozled revises the plot of the 1976 film *Network*, which depicts a failing network that saves itself by transforming informational news programming into propagandistic editorializing. The shift in the direction of news programming coincides with a change in the management of the show from a male to a female producer. As with *Bamboozled*, the leadership of an individual from a historically marginalized group results in the deterioration of popular media. Although one could say that both films imply that the inclusion of minoritarian groups in executive positions enables the production of deleterious television programming, such an interpretation tells only half the story. Both films also emphasize how corporate structures facilitate certain modes of television production that garner the widest audiences and therefore reflect the viewing appetites of the consumer. They show how individuals from minoritarian groups are used to signal the progressive politics of the networks through the diversification of hiring and the loosening of strict racial hierarchies. Yet the regressive appetites of popular audiences undercut this ostensible gain.

FIGURE 7.1. Screenshot of Womack (Tommy Davidson, left) and Manray (Savion Glover, right) in blackface, from Spike Lee's *Bamboozled*, New Line Cinema/40 Acres and a Mule Filmworks, 2000.

Delacroix conceives of a television show that sutures the loss of racial legibility. On screen, it secures a fantasy of national desire for black degradation; off screen, it demonstrates individual black Americans' freedom to compete in the workforce. New millennial blackness thus frees black subjects to become the authors and finishers of their fates, abject and otherwise, with the putative assurance that they have chosen freely as individuals.

Unlike the news show depicted in *Network*, Delacroix's show is initially meant to be offensive. Instead, *Mantan* succeeds, illuminating how mainstream entertainment remains invested in black humiliation. Its success demonstrates how black suffering remains fundamental to the elaboration of liberal identity, which attempts to forget how an individual's choices function within historical contexts that precede the individual. For the idea of unyielding individual freedom to cohere, one must understand oneself as having unfettered opportunity. Yet historical contexts limit such notions of liberal identity.[6] In a new millennial context the operation of liberal identity depends on having the former owners of such histories authorize their appearance in the public sphere. The notion of individual ownership obfuscates the function of black abjection as fundamental to national and therefore collective belonging. Greg Tate charges, "What Lee eloquently reminds us of in *Bamboozled* is the degree to which the dehumanization and commodification of Africans that occurred during slavery lingers on as a fetish in American entertainment."[7] As he proposes an ongoing longing for the fulfillment of national natal desire, Tate points to the incompleteness of black people's commodification through the peculiar institution.

The film's central characters, Pierre, Sloan, Manray, and Womack, have access to capital and the privilege it provides. Nonetheless, they all struggle with caricatures of blackness that mediate their ability to act as culture makers. In their various roles, the characters contend with desire, in the Lacanian sense, as "the desire of the Other," the national necessity of black abjection as the means by which they may achieve recognition.[8] Yet the metrics of desire represented in the film prevent the characters from being, in Stevie Wonder's words, "a misrepresented people." An analysis of *Bamboozled* demonstrates how the history of commodity and cultural production in the United States circumscribes blackness in the twenty-first century and limits black people's ability to upset the governing norms of racial misrepresentation. At the same time, filmic techniques may upset the notion that the appearance of blackness is limited to the perception of white optics and instead show black subjects in a new light.

Adjusting the Frame

The opening scene of *Bamboozled* offers a spatial metaphor for how the vestiges of blackness as property compete with new millennial exceptional blackness, which is marked by owning property and producing cultural commodities. In this scene we see a rotating and descending shot of a transparent clock that comprises a wall in Delacroix's apartment. Moving from a high angle to an eye-level shot, the orientation of the clock transforms from a hovering image to the backdrop of the first scene (figs. 7.2 and 7.3). The rotating view offers different yet reinforcing perspectives of New York City, intertwining time and place. The first angle presents a picturesque scene of the city skyline and reveals, through the multi-million-dollar view, the privileges of access to capital. The second angle, a grandiose view of the inside of the apartment, further solidifies not only Delacroix's access to the privileges of capitalist consumption but also his place within the frame of the film.[9]

Dwarfed by the massive clock, itself a sign of the dawning of a new day, progress, and change, as well as by the sleek furnishings that include a massive wardrobe and large pendant lights, Delacroix becomes a minor detail within the visual order. The frame draws the eye to the graphic composition of the space filled with circles and lines rather than to the figure sitting on the bed in the shadows. Although Delacroix blends into the cool tones of the furnishings, the hand of the clock, which rotates backward from the viewer's perspective, points to him. The arrow-shaped minute hand (similar to the visual sign in the 2006 issue of Kyle Baker's *Nat Turner*, discussed in chapter 9), points to Delacroix's involvement in time's disjointedness. By being in both the background of the shot and the forefront of the film, he splinters the film's

FIGURE 7.2. Screenshot of a window in Delacroix's apartment, from Spike Lee's *Bamboozled*, New Line Cinema/40 Acres and a Mule Filmworks, 2000.

FIGURE 7.3. Screenshot of Delacroix (Damon Wayans) in his apartment, from Spike Lee's *Bamboozled*, New Line Cinema/40 Acres and a Mule Filmworks, 2000.

commentary on black ontology vis-à-vis the mise-en-scène and the use of digital technologies. His ability to be at the center and the periphery establishes the nature of black being as a relational. The opening frames introduce his extraordinary access, which he purchases by attenuating the hold of stereotypical blackness, and simultaneously his unimportance to the structuring of the room. The room establishes a predesignated order that privileges progress and profit, which he affirms. The two empty chairs positioned in the foreground of the frame anticipate the participatory structure of meaning making, inviting the viewer to enter the frame and foreshadowing later scenes that include a live television audience. Although Delacroix sometimes finds it difficult to deny his racial heritage and assimilate fully to the demands of commodity culture, all the structures around him—from the spatial logics of his apartment to the audience's responses to his new show—invite such cruel optimism. Cruel optimism, according to Lauren Berlant, describes a situation in which, "something you desire is actually an obstacle to your flourishing."[10]

The opening sequence suggests that place and time must be read concurrently in order to decipher how blackness operates in the twenty-first century. To borrow from Stuart Hall's definition, race is "not an essence but a *positioning*. Hence, there is always a politics of identity, a politics of position, which has no absolute guarantee in an unproblematic, transcendental 'law of origin.'"[11] The opening camera angles indicate that, if the viewer loses focus on how Delacroix

figures within a network of cultural production, she consents to being, to quote
Malcolm X, "Hoodwinked! Bamboozled! Led astray! Run amok!"[12]

Questions of consent and agency are at the heart of understanding how
black subjects appear within the frame of the film and inform that framing.
In *Bamboozled,* temporal and geographical locations circumscribe agency and
conscript African Americans' desire for recognition as a part of the national
body. Delacroix functions as the cautionary tale of the black bourgeois when
members' social gains are predicated on abject blackness. From his name, to
his address, to his associations, he exudes and privileges European culture.
As the narrative unfolds, the audience learns of the self-hatred at the heart of
Delacroix's drive toward racial amnesia; and by film's end, the main character
pays for his choices much as the ill-fated protagonist (Clay) of Amiri Baraka's
Dutchman does—with his life.

Conversely, to show how cultural production can be a liberatory practice,
the film presents Delacroix's father, Junebug, as an example of living well.
Junebug's choices mirror Lee's decisions to forgo financial support from the
film industry to maintain artistic control of his work. Paula J. Massood explains,
"Lee is the quintessential inside/outside man, often working with the industry,
but just as often looking elsewhere for financing." The politics around financing inform the crafting of his films. "[He] has experimented with cheaper
technologies as a means of cutting production costs. . . . Since [he] received no
studio interest in his film about the Million Man March, he and his producers solicited private investors, eventually raising $2.4 million from a variety
of African American celebrities." Using his ingenuity in fundraising and film
production, Lee "shot the film on Super-16 mm film stock, a cheaper and more
flexible format, thus enabling his exploration of African American masculini-
ties to make it on the screen. This technological experimentation continued
with *4 Little Girls* and *Bamboozled,* both of which were shot using digital video
technology."[13]

Junebug (Paul Mooney), a standup comedian who works the Chitlin'
Circuit, understands how aesthetic choices constrict an artist's market share.
His act exercises the power of critique while bearing the material consequences
of not playing to mainstream audiences. In an interview with Michael Sragow,
Lee discusses the link between the character and the actor who plays him:
"Well, to me, Paul Mooney is really playing himself. You know, he wrote a lot
of Richard Pryor's standup material. He's a great talent who could've maybe
had a much bigger career, but just wouldn't play along. He wouldn't play the
Hollywood game."[14] For both Delacroix and Junebug, positioning works as a
function of history by enabling each individual to act as an agent, an author.
In Junebug, *Bamboozled* presents self-authorship as a mode to redress antiblack
racism, yet the film makes it clear that there is a high price for speaking a true
word about oneself. Lee is not alone in suggesting that authorship functions

as a viable strategy of repair. In *Joe Turner's Come and Gone* (1988) and *King Hedley II* (1999), August Wilson also presents the transformative power, in Toni Morrison's words, of "claiming ownership of that freed self."[15]

Inventing New Millennial Blackness

Lee's notion of authorship situates the act of repair as the task of the injured, thus imparting some agency and urgency to the dismantling of racial hierarchies. At the same time, his remedy seems to excuse the wrongdoer from playing a role in enacting justice. Engaging with the work of another black filmmaker, Robert J. Patterson argues that director Steve McQueen's film *12 Years a Slave* "relies on behaviorist discourses to frame his representation of [Solomon] Northup's life and chattel slavery" (see chapter 1). Contending that "the movie reinforces discourses that ignore the continued significance that structural barriers present for black political and cultural advancement," he argues that the distinction between behaviorist and structural critique does not elide how an individual's actions reinforce oppressive structures. Instead, it emphasizes how structures draw from social contexts and conventions within which certain acts become not only possible but conceivable. "The transformation of social relations becomes a matter, then, of transforming hegemonic social conditions rather than the individual acts that are spawned by those conditions. Indeed, one runs the risk of addressing merely indirect, if not epiphenomenal, reflections of those conditions if one remains restricted to a politics of acts."[16] As Judith Butler argues, social relations precede and intercede into individual acts, prescribing the possible and conceivable. The black cultural tradition offers only one caveat to the compelling arguments of Butler and Patterson: its condition of being animates the impossible and inconceivable.

McQueen's and Lee's proactive strategies respond to the long history of American culture predicated on the denial of black suffering and subjection as a structural component of nation building. The imperative of their "why we can't wait" directorship parses the individual's desire for healing from a national desire to forget slavery in order to elide ongoing practices of black subjection. In "The Case for Reparations," Ta-Nehisi Coates makes a strong case for how racism structures social contracts from mortgages to zoning laws, which, he argues, contributes to the wealth gap between black and nonblack Americans. He contends that the nation-state owes a debt to black America that has little to do with individuals, living or dead, and much more to do with how communities are organized and governed.[17]

The thrust of Coates's argument follows the provocation of Stephen Best and Saidiya Hartman: that repair must be focused on structural and institutional changes and must be a future-oriented project. They make the case for a perpetual state of unfreedom that characterizes black life in the United States and therefore the afterlife of slavery. Asserting that "Fugitive Justice," a justice project "on behalf of the slave (the stateless, the socially dead, and the disposable)," takes place "in the political present," they explain that, "in posing the question of slavery in terms of the incomplete nature of abolition, we are concerned neither with 'what happened then' nor with 'what is owed because of what happened then,' but rather with the contemporary predicament of freedom, with the melancholy recognition of foreseeable futures still tethered to this past."[18] The retention of the past in the present that characterizes the melancholic state puts pressure on a future-oriented vision that wonders how to make use of the unfinished past of abolition, what has *yet* to be done.

In many ways the two seem at odds. Melancholy tethers the subject to the past, yet the innovation at the heart of Best and Hartman's assertion to tell the story "that we *ought* to tell out of the present" would seem to require some flexibility with the past, some mechanism to shape, attenuate, or bolster the status of the past in the present.[19] Nevertheless, given that notion of repair, Coates's provocation toward proactive social planning as a reparative act and Lee's notion of self-authorship appear less oppositional. In the words of Joshua Chambers-Letson, "reparation . . . is not about a sublimation of past injury or a forgetting of guilt, so much as it is a coming to terms with the past as a means of putting oneself together, at least enough to be able to move into the future and possibility of love."[20] Lee's filmmaking practice is reparative in that it invites the spectator to see the world through a lens that disrupts some of the fundamental assumptions of filmmaking as an index of what Lev Manovich calls "prefilmic reality." It also shows nation building through blackness "as the imaginative surface upon which the master and the nation came to understand themselves."[21] Within the context of the United States, if we are to understand nation building as a function of collective desire, how do the representational fields that we create shape the institutions that we inhabit?

While many of this book's contributors consider how representation informs the ongoing projection of abolition, *Bamboozled* does not presume to represent the past, given the impossibility of such knowing outside of the realm of the imagination (see chapters 1 and 2). Instead, the film considers how representational fields operate as dynamic social fictions that mediate and expose the threat of loss that produces, sustains, undercuts, and calls into question national identity and belonging. The film's indexical presumption invites such investigations of constitutive national fantasies and the specific ways in which they relate to bodily difference.

Bamboozled institutes its structural critique by manipulating the frame and exposing the history of film as a racialized technology, from *The Birth of a Nation* (1915) to *Django Unchained* (2012). Following the angles that position Delacroix within the frame of the opening scene, the camera zooms in on him as he recites a definition of satire. The tracking shot moves him from the margin to the center, almost belying his instrumentality. The close-up presents him in the midst of dawning—of a new day, a new era in race politics, a new opportunity for the realization of self-authorization. At the same time, the shot disrupts the film's sense of realism and troubles the idea of natural progression. "Pierre [Delacroix] moves along the circular path the shot traces, passing by the backwards clock that looms behind him with each revolution," once again calling attention to how spatial logics (in this case, circles) may disrupt linear conceptions of time.[22] The camera focuses on Delacroix as he defines "Satire. 1a. A literary work in which human vice or folly is ridiculed or attacked scornfully. b. The branch of literature that composes such work. 2. Irony, derision or caustic wit used to attack or expose folly, vice or stupidity."[23] Satire lobbies critique in order to produce shame, recognition, and reform of political, social, and cultural conditions. It seeks to reorient the gaze from looking at others to self-reflection. Like the opening shots of the film, it questions positioning—in this case, the audience's.

As the film unfolds, stereotypical depictions of blackness become the object of satirical critique. Yet instead of producing derisive laughter, the representations of black people as dimwitted, buffoonish, lazy, and greedy engender humorous moments of recognition, affirming the audience's deeply held beliefs and desires. In a turning point, during the live premiere of Delacroix's new millennial minstrel show, the audience shifts from looking at the show with shock, horror, and embarrassment to snickering, laughing, and guffawing at the display. Lee recalls that the screenplay did not script the audience's reaction to the premiere: "They weren't acting. Not everybody knew that Tommy [Davidson] and Savion [Glover] were gonna come out there in blackface. And we did that *live*. By live, I mean we had cameras on the audience and the performers at the same time." He goes on to say, "I think the initial break comes when the black people start to applaud."[24] In other words, the black audience members authorize the rest of the audience to enjoy freely the display of black subjection. The dynamic questions the utility of satire to critique antiblack racism. Not only does the audience look with pleasure, but the satire requires the black audience members-cum-surrogates to participate in making the degradation enjoyable.

Bamboozled depicts a television satire that is misunderstood, *and* it is itself a satire that is misunderstood. The persistent misreading of black bodies within filmic representation and American lived experience buttresses Eric Lott's assertion "that there is no way for black people to appear in public without being presented through this filter of blackface minstrelsy." He contends, "The ideological filter of blackface runs so deep that there may be no escaping."[25] In the film, the specter of minstrelsy looms large, even shadowing Junebug's performance, and it refers to a complicated tradition that encompasses both acts of degradation and dissent. In *Bamboozled*, the vexed viewing history of minstrelsy meets satire, a form predicated on misdirection. Glenda R. Carpio's *Laughing Fit to Kill* "investigates how 'black humor,'" or what she also calls "a kind of dark satire," "invoke[s] both the long tradition in African American culture of critiquing 'the vicissitudes of whiteness' and its 'relation to hallucinatory impressions of blackness' to explore how different generations of writers and artists improvise on that tradition as they symbolically create redress for slavery."[26] While Lott asserts that it is naïve to be surprised at the audience's response to Davidson and Glover in blackface, Carpio's definition illuminates how the audience's response highlights *Bamboozled*'s function as a kind of dark satire. Given satire's motivation to expose and critique the various manifestations of whiteness as they relate to "hallucinatory impressions of blackness," the unscripted outpouring of whiteness as a social regulatory force evidences the fulfillment of the film's promise; *Bamboozled* not only scripts a television satire but becomes a satire through its production.

Lee is not alone in his use of satire as a racialized device in the twenty-first century. It has become a signature device of black artists working in the post-soul era, emerging in George C. Wolfe's *The Colored Museum* (1986), Paul Beatty's *White Boy Shuffle* (1996) and *Slumberland* (2008), Dave Chappelle's *Chappelle's Show* (2003–2006); Lynn Nottages's *Fabulation, or the Re-Education of Undine* (2004) and *By the Way, Meet Vera Stark* (2011), Aaron McGruder's *The Boondocks* (first aired in 2005), and the visual art of Kara Walker.[27] Carpio explains how the attenuated hold of "political correctness" and the promise that satire would create redress for slavery informs the references to minstrelsy and use of racial stereotypes in current black cultural production.[28] Satire as a mechanism to call attention to ongoing racial inequality assumes that an audience will recognize black people as subjects worthy of social inclusion rather than as objects for another's entertainment. Instead of reveling in the dehumanization that *Mantan: The New Millennial Minstrel Show* produces, Delacroix assumes that his twenty-first-century audience, unlike its nineteenth-century counterpart, will be repulsed and revolted because they find themselves initially entertained and amused.

The audience's response exposes the power of constitutive narratives to override the function of genre, which solicits certain reactions. Satire requires an embrace of incorporation within the means of producing culture, but Jared Sexton argues for an oppositional approach to black cultural production in the post–civil rights era. In "People of Color Blindness," he charges that the equivalencies of colonialism and slavery are historically inaccurate and theoretically problematic. Calling attention to the unique historical trauma of slavery and its implications for ongoing social relationships, he explains that "freedom from the rule of slave law requires only that one be considered nonblack, whether that nonblack racial designation be 'white' or 'Indian' or, in the rare case, 'Oriental'— this despite the fact that each of these groups has at one point or another labored in conditions similar to or contiguous with enslaved African-derived groups. In other words, it is not *labor* relations, but *property* relations that are constitutive of slavery."[29] *Bamboozled* makes a similar point, one that not only informs this film but Lee's production company, 40 Acres and a Mule Filmworks, more generally. Its name memorializes a failed reparative act of Reconstruction and implies that the role of the company is to help finish the job.

Film scholar Kara Keeling's analysis of *Bamboozled* notes the oppositional perspective the film generates via its construction and depiction of blackness. Unlike Sexton, however, she sees the pervasiveness of commodity culture as a social commonality among various groups that theorists may understand by turning to black people's history as capital. The different conclusions that Sexton and Keeling draw suggest fundamental assumptions about the possibility of black social life within the frame of the film and simultaneously the afterlife of slavery. Like Keeling, I suggest that Lee makes the case for black social life within yet obscured by the camera frame.

Although I have argued that *Bamboozled* presents an oppositional point of view that enables a critique of cultural constitution predicated on abject blackness and the authoring of black social life, Shawn-Marie Garrett believes that it depicts an ambivalent relationship to black cultural production uncharacteristic of the filmmaker's usual biting approach in cultural critique: "Though Lee's point of view comes through clearly in the film's content, [he] hasn't shown such ambivalence in his manipulations of form since *Do the Right Thing*."[30] The crafting of human representations of black people inspires Lee's oeuvre; and while his treatment of certain modes of cultural production within the film may signal ambivalence, his signature use of panoramic tracking shots reinvigorates an oppositional point of view at the heart of black life in the afterlife of slavery. His film criticizes the use of satire because the device assumes black subjects no longer have to negotiate the position of being within and constitutive to the frame. *Bamboozled* alternatively suggests, as Sexton does, that the oppositional point of view needs reinvigorating in the twenty-first century because it is the only operable position of black social life in which individuals function formatively rather than instrumentally.

Whose "Look, a Negro"?

The original title of this book, *Do You Want to Be Well*, assumes certain givens about will, agency, individuality, and responsibility. How do such terms function in the afterlife of slavery? How does the desire for wellness cohere in a state constituted through black domination? What does it mean to be well in a context that thrives on one's abjection? The terms generatively coincide with some of the keywords of Saidiya Hartman's *Scenes of Subjection* (1997), which has reemerged as a primary text, alongside Frantz Fanon's *Black Skin,*

White Masks (1967), in the debates over black ontology, a central topic in twenty-first-century African American studies. Although often used to support Afro-pessimist claims for the impossibility of black ontology, *Scenes of Subjection* does not disallow black subjectivity. It does, however, call into question the nature of the black subject within the context of the brutal and quotidian terror of slavery. Hartman asserts, "The particular status of the slave as object and as subject requires a careful consideration of the notion of agency if one wants to do more than 'endow' the enslaved with agency as some sort of gift dispensed by historians and critics to the dispossessed."[31]

Fanon's text conversely establishes the impossibility of black subjectivity, asserting that "ontology—once it is finally admitted as leaving existence by the wayside—does not permit us to understand the being of the black man. For not only must the black man be black; he must be black in relation to the white man. Some critics will take it on themselves to remind us that this proposition has a converse. I say that this is false. The black man has no ontological resistance in the eyes of the white man."[32] Fanon's colonial perspective structures his analysis and prevents him from seeing any possible frame in which black ontology may appear. Black being amounts to the surrogation of colonial society in general and white ontology in particular. Black people exist only in service to white people but never for themselves, objects in the social drama but never subjects of it. And while this perspective may ring true to a certain Eurocentric readership, it does not constitute the definitive or final word on ontology itself.

This section of *Black Skin, White Masks* appears again and again in discussions of black ontology, as does consideration of Fanon's anecdotal description of alienation via his "corporeal schema." In response to the utterance of a child calling, "Look, a Negro!," Fanon examines how he comes to stand in for a transhistorical manifestation of blackness: "I was responsible at the same time for my body, for my race, for my ancestors." As he theorizes it, his blackness emerges in relation to the child's singling him out, noting his difference. The child reads onto his body desire for identification, which enables an understanding of, in Gina Dent's words, "the effects of that gaze."[33] In this now infamous moment of objectification, perhaps it is possible "to reckon with" what Anne Anlin Cheng calls "the collision between the violence of impersonality and the violence of personality."[34] Following Cheng, we can posit that Fanon's account teaches as much about ontology as it does about the violence that makes black being legible and recognizable to the white gaze.

The question of whether objects can resist their objectification animates Fred Moten's *In the Break* (2003) and his essay "The Case of Blackness" (2008). In that essay, he argues, "It seems to me that this special ontic-ontological fugitivity of/in the slave is what is revealed as the necessarily unaccounted for in Fanon. So that in contradistinction to Fanon's protest, the problem of the inadequacy of any ontology to blackness . . . must be understood in its relation to the inadequacy of calculation to being in general."[35] Moten reads imaginative possibility rather than foreclosure in Fanon's text. His interpretation reorients the conversation from the possibility or impossibility of black ontology to the contexts under which one may ascertain it. Moten's provocation reaffirms the importance of perspective in deciphering whether or not blackness can resist the annihilative violence of a Eurocentric ontology and the necessity of examining framing. The foreclosure of ontology precludes desire in general and the desire for wellness in particular. Just as the opening sequence of *Bamboozled* situates Delacroix within a frame and a predetermined order, Moten's analysis makes clear that colonial framing does not preclude but may occlude black social life.

The frame of *Bamboozled*, the mise-en-scène (in front of the camera), presents black subjection while the ontic-ontologies of the production (behind the camera) assert black social life. The different ontological positions of blackness established behind and in front of the camera place a premium on the doing rather than the perceiving of black life. Keeling explains how Lee's use of digital technologies enables a representation of the structures that challenge the appearance of black social life within the filmic or colonial frame (in front of the camera). In an overview of Manovich's *The Language of New Media*, she explains, "The filmic regime of the image claims to be an index of [what Manovich terms 'prefilmic reality'], thereby encouraging identification between the image and its presumed referent, while the digital complicates that schema of identification by calling into question the very notion of a 'prefilmic reality' to which the digital image might lay claim."[36] Keeling suggests that Lee's use of digital video introduces the concept of the simulacrum, a copy without an original, as the basis of black representation, positioning an absence at the sight of what film propagates as authentic blackness.[37] Attention to the means of producing visual representations arrests the representation of blackness as objecthood, distinguishing a phenomenological understanding of blackness from an ontic one.

The framing of *Bamboozled* renders the film ironic but does not belie the material consequences of the problematic representation of the main woman character, Sloan. As a critique of filmic representation, *Bamboozled* calls into question the ability of any film to index historical truths. Rather, it demonstrates cinema's ability to communicate national desires. Keeling explains, "To work with *Bamboozled* is to engage with the slippery, messy, and, often, repulsive racialized detritus of the American popular culture industry."[38] The film works in part to expose and reinforce racialized detritus across gender lines. As bell hooks and Victoria Piehowski have both argued, Lee's oeuvre consistently presents underdeveloped women characters that reinforce sexual and gender stereotypes.[39] In *Bamboozled*, Sloan functions in service of other characters' desires but not her own. Unlike the representation of all of the other central black characters, hers secures a social dynamic that excludes her from being imagined as a historically motivated, desiring subject. Given that the film's promise resides in disrupting and restructuring the position of subjects within the frame, her characterization is a significant missed opportunity. The film depicts her as a prop that secures gender hierarchies rather than a dynamic character who calls attention to the operation of the audience's desire.

The male characters better actualize the possibilities of the film in their mitigated pursuits of self-definition. *Bamboozled* does not spare its black characters from the lure of black objectification as an authentic form of blackness. In one scene, Sloan's brother (played by rapper and actor Mos Def) and leader of the pseudo-revolutionary group the Mau Maus, named after the Kenyan independence fighters, accuses her of being a house nigger and treating him like a field nigger. Given the spectrum of characterization, *Bamboozled*'s digital properties nevertheless call such essentialisms into question.[40] Keeling argues, "I find it significant that a movie shot largely on digital video and later released on film is a vehicle for one of the most far-reaching critiques of the racist imagery that has been a salient characteristic of American film and television throughout the 20th century."[41] If we accept her compelling reading of *The Language of New Media*, which suggests that the filmic indexes prefilmic reality, the digital might call into question the veracity of such representation. Keeling's analysis gives insight into the ways in which Lee's use of digital video reinforces Moten's theory of not being able to capture black life within the logics of western ontology. Fugitivity, and the justice that may adhere therein, belies capture.

Lee imagined *Bamboozled* as a retrospective of African Americans in film and therefore a referendum on American culture and the indexical nature of film:

> I think this film deals with our shared history. Earlier you [the interviewer] used the word "heritage." I mean, people can sing "Hooray for Hollywood" and talk about the "Golden Age of Television" all they want. But a large part of that stuff is what we put in the final montage of this film. . . . A lot of people don't want to deal with the images in this montage. But we're showing them. And we're showing that these images didn't just spring from the warped mind of D. W. Griffith, but reflected accepted behavior. Judy Garland, Mickey Rooney, Bing Crosby, they all did the black minstrel thing. This was accepted behavior. And people don't want to deal with this as part of the legacy of those two powerful mediums—television and film. In both people were doing this from the beginning—from the very beginning.[42]

Lee attempts to "change the joke and slip the yoke," to borrow a famous phrase from Ralph Ellison. His work challenges the indexical quality of film and reveals the filmic representation of black folk as cartoonish. *Bamboozled* creates a context in which film has the dynamic power to reveal the social positionings of the male characters who create misrepresentation. It intervenes in the representation of Delacroix, Manray, and Womack, disrupting the veracity of perceptions of historical pasts predicated solely on black suffering, offering insight into the figures being represented rather than those creating the images for consumption.

Lee's choice to shoot *Bamboozled* primarily in digital format has theoretical implications for the ways in which it may be understood to offer a sign of black social life, yet the choice also reflects the financial pressures of filmmaking. The market for *Bamboozled* excluded making the project with traditional film techniques: "We decided to shoot in DV [digital video] early on, as the script was written. . . . We knew that getting the film made would be a very hard task."[43] The economics of film production informs the formal attributes of the film and its themes. *Bamboozled* demonstrates that access to capital, whether in the case of Lee's production company or Delacroix's status as an executive for CNS, does not sever one's relationship to the past. At the same time, the film gives us the opportunity to remember and imagine futures in reparative ways.

Moving On Up

What is the relationship between wellness and exercises of power? The context of slavery creates one extreme power dynamic that severely circumscribes acts of will. To understand the cultural work of *Bamboozled,* one also has to consider how power operates in the global economy of twenty-first-century New York City and the production of a television show. Lee's film is set during the Rudolph Giuliani administration (1994–2001); and two scenes—the police raid of the squatter residence where Manray and Womack live and Manray's street performance outside of CNS headquarters—demonstrate that era's wealth disparity and the resulting regulation of populations.

In the era of YouTube (founded in 2005), a street act may qualify as an audition for superstardom. Gone are the days of Motown, when performers spent years being groomed, cultivated, and developed . In the new millennium, anyone with a camera has the potential to move instantly from obscurity to renown. Often a quick ascent matches the speed with which a cultural figure becomes irrelevant, but the transformation of the means of circulating cultural production particularizes the individual's relationship to distribution and therefore the means of production.

Bamboozled predates YouTube, but its use of digital technologies anticipates the potential for the democratization of distribution in online media. At the same time the temporal and geographical strictures of Manray's performance in front of the CNS building would qualify, during the Giuliani administration,

as nothing more than a public nuisance. For viewers in 2000, the scene may
have drawn them back in time as much as projected futurity. According to Lott,
"the first time you see the guys dancing on the sidewalk, they're on a shingle. . . .
Black slaves in lower New York back in the 19th century used to be confined to
this shingle by their masters when they danced, so if they strayed off, the master
could hear the feet not hitting the wood anymore."[44] The ongoing circulation
of the film along with the disruption of time in the opening scene (the hand of
the clock ticking backward as Delacroix circles his apartment) creates a multi-
temporal perspective, blending the past into an understanding of futurity.

Manray and Womack's performance outside CNS headquarters functions
as their first audition. It is here that Sloan discovers the duo and encourages
Delacroix to cast them in his show. Depicted near the beginning of the film,
the performance establishes the value of Manray's dancing as a thing in itself;
and Delacroix, the wealthy executive, gives the pair a ten-dollar tip. Later in
the film, when the performance becomes packaged as minstrelsy, the duo
earns enough money for Manray to rent a high-rise apartment in Manhattan.
Importantly the references to minstrelsy linger in the embodied movements
that Manray enacts. Delineating the different evaluations of his performance
in and out of blackface, the film aligns the heightened compensation with
degradation. It also admonishes against not remembering black performance
traditions in general.

But what do the shifting contexts of Manray's performance suggest
about the relationship between agency and systems of regulation? How might
Hartman's analysis of the performance practices of the enslaved in *Scenes of
Subjection* offer a theoretical paradigm for Manray's performances? Hartman
argues that "performance and other modes of practice are determined by,
exploit, and exceed the constraints of domination." Even though *Scenes of
Subjection* examines the conditions of the enslaved, the text serves as a touchstone for analyzing the persistently quotidian and juridically authorized violence that characterizes and threatens black life in the United States. Likewise,
to understand Manray's initial performance on the street, his role in the television show, and his final dance of death, one must consider how "institutions of
power condition the exercise of agency."[45]

Following the opening sequence in Delacroix's apartment, *Bamboozled*
cuts to the boarded-up and condemned tenement where Manray and Womack
live. The cut itself emphasizes the social stratifications of the characters:
ready for bed, Delacroix turns off the lights, and the darkness serves as a transition to Manray and Womack's home. The silence of Delacroix's residence
shifts to the chaotic sounds of the duo's domestic space, as helicopters and
a police bullhorn enforce the mayor's evacuation orders. Viewers see lights
flash, hear sirens blare, and watch occupants scurry away from police officers
with billy clubs.

The pair's living conditions emblematize precariousness. As Rebecca Schneider explains, "not only do the stateless or migrant or *sans papiers* exist precariously, but 'the public's' capacity to even 'apprehend' (which is not the same as recognize) these persons as live or as dead—as injurable—is also precarious."[46] One could argue that such precariousness renders Manray and Womack socially dead, bereft of the protections that belong to a member of the state. Social death, however, also denies Manray's street performance as an act of subject formation. Although their show has limited monetary value, Manray and Womack carve out public space in order to perform. The compensation is a form of social recognition, one that does not assume that capitalism produces subjectivity but that participates in the "violence of personality."[47] In the context of co-opting public space, the pallet that Manray uses as a surface to dance on is a necessary twenty-first-century prop rather than an extension of the social policing of nineteenth-century black bodies. Manray's and Womack's fugitive acts do not transform the juridical apparatus that renders their behavior criminal, but they do interfere with the regulation of space and the removal and redistribution of criminal populations. The film individualizes the disruption of criminalization, or what Ruth Wilson Gilmore depicts as a "geographical solution that purports to solve social problems."[48] The characters exercise their ability to willfully refuse, an act that is itself a sign of social life. Yet the film misses the opportunity to depict criminalization, as Gilmore and Caleb Smith argue, as a mechanism to manage populations through geographical displacement.[49]

During the Giuliani administration, New York City experienced an unprecedented decline in crime. Although this decrease has often been attributed to Giuliani and his police commissioner's "broken windows" theory of crime, the city had already begun to see a decline during the administration of the previous mayor, David Dinkins. According to Franklin E. Zimring's fine statistical analysis, "when the particular history of New York since 1990 is combined with other studies of police and crime, there are two strategies of policing on which the data don't produce plausible indications of value added in crime prevention—aggressive street intervention and 'quality of life' or 'broken windows' in New York City."[50] When Giuliani became mayor, he promised to equalize treatment of all New Yorkers with his "One City, One Standard" campaign. The result: a disproportionate policing of black and brown youth due to stop-and-frisk policies as well as a reallocation of resources from city agencies that had historically employed black people to ones that predominately employed white people. As the historian Jerald Podair explains, "Giuliani's budgetary measures were not explicitly designed to take power from African Americans, but reducing the city payroll, cutting welfare benefits, downsizing city-owned hospitals, and privatizing city services had the effect nonetheless."[51]

Even as New York became known as one of the safest cities in the country, its number of black and brown people with police records ballooned. Podair writes:

> [Giuliani's] aggressive policing policies targeted young black men, who were stopped and frisked at a rate disproportionately higher than whites. In one year, 1998, there were 27,000 police frisks in the city, only 5,000 of which resulted in arrests. This meant that 22,000 New Yorkers, a significant portion of whom were African American, were detained by police without cause. Even those few African Americans who were close to Giuliani were not immune. On two occasions, Rudy Washington, a black deputy mayor, was stopped in his car and harassed by overzealous officers. Floyd Flake, an African American congressman and Giuliani supporter, suffered a similar fate.[52]

Podair's anecdotal evidence suggests that economic and social status do not defend against what Frank B. Wilderson III describes as "blackness's grammar of suffering."[53]

Throughout the opening scenes of *Bamboozled,* the repeated juxtaposition of the characters' living conditions highlights how distinct social positions and access to wealth inform the ability to influence means of production. Delacroix proposes the show as a ruse, and Manray and Womack become pawns in his scheme to expose the racism of the television network, initially working for food and clothes. Yet by the end of the film, Delacroix and Manray suffer the same fates: communal alienation, self-loathing, and death. What, in fact, have Delacroix's access, wealth, and influence purchased? His ghostly voice comments at the end of the film, "As I bled to death, as my very life oozed out of me, all I could think of was something the great Negro James Baldwin had written. 'People pay for what they do, and still more for what they have allowed themselves to become. And they pay for it very simply; by the lives they lead.'"[54] The idea of living as a mode of repayment—what Harry J. Elam Jr. and Michele Elam call "payback"—gives more force to the importance of acknowledging the presence and persistence of black social life, even if the frame of the afterlife of slavery renders it at best obscured and at worst invisible.[55]

The film presents Junebug as *one* example of living well but does not champion his racial performance as the *only* acceptable form; such an essentialist idea would reinforce reductionist modes of black representation. Nevertheless, *it* mocks the appropriation of blackness made available through understandings of the racial designation as merely a performance. In the film, Dunwitty challenges Delacroix, saying, "I understand black culture. I grew up around black people all my life. If the truth be told I probably know 'niggers' better than you, Monsieur Delacroix. Please don't get offended by my use of the quote-unquote N word. I got a black wife and three biracial children, so I feel I have a right to use that word. I don't give a damn what Spike says, Tarantino is right. Nigger is just a word. If Dirty Ole Bastard can use it every other word so can I." Dunwitty authenticates his blackness via references to sports figures and hip hop, and he diminishes Delacroix's claim to the racialized identity: "You got your head stuck up your ass with your Harvard education and your pretentious ways. Brother man, I'm blacker than you." Delacroix sarcastically asks: "I'm an Oreo, a sell-out? Because I don't aspire to do *Homeboys from Out of Space, Secret Diary of Desmond Pfeiffer*, a *PJ's* or some, as you might put it, some 'nigger' show? I'm a Tom?"[56]

The lines of racial authenticity trace two trajectories: one of culture, the other one of class. According to Dunwitty, Delacroix's access to elite education and privilege alienates him from blackness. But one may reasonably assume that the two men share a similar class position. Therefore, Dunwitty's appropriation stems from an understanding of certain modes of cultural production that he perpetuates in his role as a television executive. The two lines of thought may seem at odds in determining the shifting position of blackness in the twenty-first century. As the cultural critic Vijay Prashad writes, "what the [civil rights] movement was able to gain was the power of people who had been treated as second class citizens to now occupy space in society, to go as they wanted, particularly in public space, . . . to vote, to have political rights. . . . These were substantial victories, but they were largely in legal, political, and to some extent in social domains."[57] According to his persuasive argument, the victories of the civil rights movement did not affect the economic structures of institutions. Therefore, although a few qualified non-Europeans were accepted into the institutions, nothing fundamentally changed about the institutions themselves. Yet I question the extent to which we can apply Prashad's claims to the media, an amorphous institution that not only produces but also traffics in culture. As Keeling makes clear, the logics of global capital inform all modes and means of production, including cultural ones. Cultural wars have an economic impact that asks us to consider how the properties of blackness inform making black property.

Dancing with Death

The filmic arc of Manray's performance demonstrates how contexts determine valuation and position informs an individual's ability to seek and enact redress. Manray is a virtuoso performer on the street, but he is only recognized as such by a mass audience when he wears blackface on a television show, where he participates in clownish depictions of blackness that render him foreign even to himself. On the night of the show's premiere, Manray, Womack, and Sloan gather to watch the episode, and Manray and Womack take offense at the intro's cartoon depictions of their characters. They complain about the animations' protruding lips, bulging eyes, and coal-black skin (fig. 7.4). Quickly, however, the team becomes more comfortable with the social advantages purchased through the abjection of blackness. They not only come to terms with their domination but also begin to participate in the domination of others.

In one scene, Womack sits in on one of Manray's rehearsals with the backup dancers. After listening to Manray lace his corrections with degrading comments, Womack questions the derisive pedagogy. Manray responds by accusing Womack of riding his coattails. Insulted, Womack leaves, never to return. *Mantan* continues, with a secondary character filling Womack's role in the show, until Manray's conscience finally refuses to allow him to perform in blackface. For the final episode of the show, he enters the studio, refuses to blacken up, takes his place on stage, and begins to dance. Although his dancing is identical to his style in other episodes, it is no longer performed with the trappings of degradation. Manray has refused to pay the price for black legibility in the public sphere, an act that now renders him extraneous. With the stunned response of the audience as a backdrop, security guards haul him off the stage and leave him in an alley.

In *Scenes of Subjection*, Hartman asks, "Does the captive's dance allay grief or articulate the fraught, compromised, and impossible character of agency? Or does it exemplify the use of the body as an instrument against the self?"[58] Manray's final performance on stage is a dance of death because it challenges

FIGURE 7.4. Screenshot of animated versions of Womack (Tommy Davidson, left) and Manray (Savion Glover, right) in blackface, from Spike Lee's *Bamboozled*, New Line Cinema/40 Acres and a Mule Filmworks, 2000.

the economies of legibility that make his movements commodifiable. Discarded like the trash, he is thrown back into the street from whence he came. His choice to reclaim his body calls attention to the life-and-death stakes of resistance to black subjection. In fact, "Dance of Death" is the title of the scene as it appears on the DVD version of the film. For as Manray has been undergoing this crisis, the Mau Maus have been plotting his death. Seeing him as a race traitor, they have devised a plan to execute him on live television, and they are waiting in the alley where the security guards leave him.

The Mau Maus' misplaced aggression mirrors the corrupted ideals of black nationalism and their anemic manifestation in the new millennium. In a bitter irony, a satirical representation of post–Black Power hip hop is policing Manray's own satirical performance of television as the continuation of minstrelsy. Thus, commodity culture evacuates the political possibility of hip hop as a social movement. The Mau Maus succeed in killing Manray before the police kill them in a shootout. Manray's death signals the cost of attempting to reanimate looking at the black subject without the minstrel mask. His dance attempts to make visible black social life. His final dance demonstrates performance's ability to trouble commodification and co-optation and to operate against time—to disrupt, dismantle, and perform dissent.[59] It serves as yet another technology for reimagining black representation untethered from perpetual death and suffering.

By creating diverse kinds of looking, *Bamboozled* asks us to consider what types of humanity, what ontologies and ways of living, are obscured by historical preconditions and their symbolic legacies. Satire attempts to slip the yoke and change the joke, and the performance of abject blackness may also enable a change of hand. In an often-analyzed scene from the film, the jolly-nigger bank, a minstrel figurine that Sloan gives to Delacroix, transforms into an animate object. To deposit coins, the owner manipulates the figurine's arm, and its wide mouth opens to receive the currency. Degradation results in monetary reward; and Delacroix, already suffering from guilt for creating the show, sees the bank begin to operate on its own.

While several critics have interpreted the animation as a comment on the inability to objectify blackness, Keeling argues that it calls attention to multiple temporalities as well as circuits of exchange: "*Bamboozled* frames a milieu in which black culture enters the circuits of mass mediation, a frame that allows it to ask crucial questions regarding 'how to renegotiate' social bonds 'corrupted by commercial relationships.' Interrogations into the possibilities for negotiating viable and life-sustaining social bonds in a milieu permeated by the terms of commerce are (or ought to be) fundamental to contemporary socio-political and/or cultural claims to 'the human.'"[60] Both lines of thought ask us to reexamine how the resistance of the object offers insight into the operation of the human.

The multiplicity of time, introduced in the opening scene and reinforced during Delacroix's ghost speech, calls attention to a metaphysical quality that the animation of the bank produces. Couched as Delacroix's mental instability, the animation may signal the life within entities that are presumed to be objects. Moten and Hartman locate signs of black social life but argue that the living itself disrupts the social order because it remains invisible, imperceptible, or unrecognizable. *Bamboozled* allows a gaze that produces representational blackness, a powerful force that mediates the ability of the individual to be well in a culture predicated on the regulatory power of looking. The film offers the audience a chance to see what it has done to and desires of new millennial blackness. It produces the dialogical quality of looking backward in order to look forward and looking inward in order to look outward. It thus arrests the apprehension of black ontology while making it possible within the frame of the afterlife of slavery.

NOTES

1. Saidiya Hartman, *Scenes of Subjection: Terror, Slavery, and Self-Making in Nineteenth-Century America* (Oxford: Oxford University Press, 1997), 116.

2. Stuart Hall, "What Is This 'Black' in Black Popular Culture?," in *Black Popular Culture*, ed. Gina Dent (New York: New Press, 1998), 33.

3. Hortense J. Spillers, "Mama's Baby, Papa's Maybe: An American Grammar Book," *Diacritics* 17 (summer 1987): 65.

4. Julia Kristeva, *Powers of Horror: An Essay on Abjection,* trans. Leon S. Roudiez (New York: Columbia University Press, 1982), 4.

5. Darieck Scott, *Extravagant Abjection: Blackness, Power, and Sexuality in the African American Literary Imagination* (New York: New York University Press, 2010), 17.

6. David Scott, "The Government of Freedom," in *New Caribbean Thought: A Reader*, ed. Brian Meeks and Folke Lindahl (Kingston, Jamaica: University of West Indies Press, 2001), 428–452.

7. Greg Tate, "*Bamboozled:* White Supremacy and a Black Way of Being Human," *Cineaste* 26 (March 2001): 15–16.

8. Jacques Lacan, *The Seminar of Jacques Lacan: The Four Fundamental Concepts of Psychoanalysis* (New York: Norton, 1998), 235.

9. W.J.T Mitchell reads the clock as a sign of automation while Susan Booker Morris argues that it participates in a parody of the documentary form. See Mitchell, "Living Color: Race, Stereotype, and the Animation in Spike Lee's *Bamboozled*," in *What Do Pictures Want? The Lives and Loves of Images* (Chicago: University of Chicago Press, 2005), 294–308; and Morris, "*Bamboozled:* Political Parodic Postmodernism," *West Virginia University Philological Papers* 49 (fall 2003): 67–76.

10. Lauren Berlant, *Cruel Optimism* (Durham, N.C.: Duke University Press, 2011), 2.

11. Stuart Hall, "Cultural Identity and Diaspora," in *Colonial Discourse and Postcolonial Theory: A Reader*, ed. Patrick Williams and Laura Chrisman (New York: Columbia University Press, 1994), 395.

12. Malcolm X quoted in Michael Sragow's "Black Like Spike," in *Spike Lee: Interviews,* ed. Cynthia Fuchs (Jackson: University Press of Mississippi, 2002), 190.

148

SOYICA DIGGS COLBERT

13. Paula J. Massood, "Introduction: We've Gotta Have It—Spike Lee, African American Film, and Cinema Studies," in *The Spike Lee Reader*, ed. Paula J. Massood (Philadelphia: Temple University Press, 2008), xv–xxviii, xxiv–xxv.

14. Sragow, "Black Like Spike," 191.

15. Toni Morrison, *Beloved* (New York: Vintage, 2004), 110.

16. Judith Butler, "Performative Acts and Gender Constitution: An Essay in Phenomenology and Feminist Theory," in *The Performance Studies Reader*, ed. Henry Bial (New York: Routledge, 2007), 160.

17. Ta-Nehisi Coates, "The Case for Reparations," *Atlantic*, May 21, 2014, http://www.theatlantic.com/features/archive/2014/05/the-case-for-reparations/361631/, accessed December 28, 2015.

18. Stephen Best and Saidiya Hartman, "Fugitive Justice," *Representations* 92 (autumn 2005): 5.

19. Ibid.

20. Joshua Chambers-Letson, "Reparative Feminisms, Repairing Feminism: Reparation, Postcolonial Violence, and Feminism," *Women and Performance* 16 (July 2006): 173.

21. Lev Manovich, *The Language of New Media* (Cambridge, Mass.: MIT Press, 2001), 298; Hartman, *Scenes of Subjection*, 7.

22. Greg Laski, "Falling Back into History: The Uncanny Trauma of Blackface Minstrelsy in Spike Lee's *Bamboozled*," *Callaloo* 33 (fall 2004): 1098.

23. *Bamboozled*, dir. Spike Lee (Burbank, Calif.: New Line Cinema/40 Acres and a Mule Filmworks, 2000), DVD.

24. Fuchs, *Spike Lee*, 194, 195.

25. Stanley Crouch, with Eric Lott, Margo Jefferson, and Michele Wallace, "Minding the Messenger: A Symposium on *Bamboozled*," *Black Renaissance* 3 (summer 2001): 3.

26. Glenda R. Carpio, *Laughing Fit to Kill: Black Humor in the Fictions of Slavery* (Oxford: Oxford University Press, 2008), 8.

27. For the original definition of *post-soul*, see Mark Anthony Neal, *Soul Babies: Black Popular Culture and the Post-Soul Aesthetic* (New York: Routledge, 2002), 3.

28. Carpio, *Laughing Fit to Kill*, 22, 23.

29. Jared Sexton, "People-of-Color-Blindness: Notes on the Afterlife of Slavery," *Social Text* 28 (summer 2010): 36.

30. Shawn-Marie Garrett, "Return of the Repressed," *Theater* 32 (summer 2002): 26–43.

31. Hartman, *Scenes of Subjection*, 54.

32. Frantz Fanon, *Black Skin, White Masks*, trans. Charles Markmann (New York: Grove, 1967), 110.

33. Gina Dent, "Black Pleasure, Black Joy: An Introduction," in *Black Popular Culture*, ed. Gina Dent (New York: New Press, 1998), 7.

34. Anne Anlin Cheng, "Shine: On Race, Glamour, and the Modern," *PMLA* 126 (October 2011): 1023.

35. Fred Moten, "The Case of Blackness," *Criticism* 50 (spring 2008): 187.

36. Kara Keeling, "Passing for Human: *Bamboozled* and Digital Humanism," *Women and Performance* 15 (June 2005): 238.

37. Daniel Morgan writes, "Cinema, Jean Luc Godard once remarked, is truth twenty-four times a second. Digital technologies, which allow for the almost total transformation

and creation of images by means of binary coding, are thought to undermine the claim for the truthfulness of photographic media. The classical theories now seem inadequate and irrelevant." Although he goes on to trouble the dichotomy between cinema and digital technologies, his essay establishes the long-held belief of cinema as indexical. See "Rethinking Bazin: Ontology and Realist Aesthetics," *Critical Inquiry* 32 (spring 2006): 443–481.

38. Keeling, "Passing for Human," 243.

39. See bell hooks, "Male Heroes and Female Sex Objects: Sexism in Spike Lee's *Malcolm X*," *Cineaste* 19, no. 4 (1992): 13–15; and Victoria Piehowski, "'Business as Usual': Sex, Race, and Work in Spike Lee's *Bamboozled*," *Frontiers* 33 (November 2012): 1–23.

40. For a linguistic analysis of the real versus the fake, see Phil Chidester, Shannon Campbell, and Jamel Bell, "'Black Is Blak': *Bamboozled* and the Crisis of a Postmodern Racial Identity," *Howard Journal of Communications* 17 (2006): 289.

41. Keeling, "Passing for Human," 238.

42. Fuchs, *Spike Lee*, 196.

43. Ibid., 184.

44. Crouch et al., "Minding the Messenger," 3.

45. Hartman, *Scenes of Subjection*, 54.

46. Rebecca Schneider, "It Seems As If . . . I Am Dead: Zombie Capitalism and Theatrical Labor," *TDR* 56 (winter 2012): 152.

47. Cheng, "Shine," 1023.

48. Ruth Wilson Gilmore, *Golden Gulag: Prisons, Surplus, Crisis, and Opposition in Globalizing California* (Berkeley: University of California Press, 2007), 14.

49. Ibid.; Caleb Smith, *The Prison and the American Imagination* (New Haven, Conn.: Yale University Press, 2009).

50. Franklin E. Zimring, *The City That Became Safe: New York's Lessons for Urban Crime and Its Control* (Oxford: Oxford University Press, 2011), 144.

51. Jerald Podair, "'One City, One Standard': The Struggle for Equality in Rudolph Giuliani's New York," in *Civil Rights in New York City: From World War II to the Giuliani Era* (New York: Fordham University Press, 2011), 215.

52. Ibid., 212.

53. Frank B. Wilderson III, *Red, White, and Black: Cinema and the Structure of U.S. Antagonisms* (Durham, N.C.: Duke University Press, 2010), 37.

54. *Bamboozled*, dir. Spike Lee.

55. Harry J. Elam Jr. and Michele Elam, "Blood Debt: Reparations in Langston Hughes's *Mulatto*," *Theater Journal* 61 (March 2009): 85–103.

56. *Bamboozled*.

57. Aziz Rana, "Break the Silence," *Asian American Writers Workshop*, http://aaww.org/break-the-silence-vijay-prashad/, accessed June 25, 2014.

58. Hartman, *Scenes of Subjection*, 22.

59. Daphne Brooks, *Bodies in Dissent: Spectacular Performances of Race and Freedom, 1850–1910* (Durham, N.C.: Duke University Press, 2006).

60. Keeling, "Passing for Human," 247.

8

Laughing to Keep from Crying

Dave Chappelle's Self-Exploration with "The Nigger Pixie"

BRANDON J. MANNING

Most important, enjoyment defined the relation of the dominant race to
the enslaved. In other words, the nefarious uses of chattel licensed by the
legal and social relations of slavery articulated the nexus of pleasure and
possession and bespoke the critical role of diversion in securing the relations of bondage. In this way, enjoyment disclosed the sentiments and
expectations of the "peculiar institution."[1]

–Saidiya Hartman

Slavery created a legacy of trauma that has regulated black joy and merriment for centuries in the Americas, and Saidiya Hartman's words remind us
that society has made a collective effort to diminish the hardships of slavery by
contorting black affect. In antebellum America, whites regularly co-opted black
merriment to create the veneer that blacks were happy in their subjugated
roles. Yet as Paul Lawrence Dunbar's poem "We Wear the Mask" reveals, black
people have devised opaque modes of expression to challenge these images.
Lines such as "With torn and bleeding hearts we smile" illustrate the ubiquity
of black people's intentional obfuscation of their anger, sadness, and joy, a
means of surviving in the harsh landscape of American racism. When Dunbar
asks, "Why should the world be over-wise," he also suggests that emotional
sharing would be ineffective because of the impossibility of white empathy for
black affect.[2]

Within the antebellum context, such forced duplicity ensured that both
black suffering and black merriment were unreliable signifiers when serving
white supremacist structures. While there were spaces where black emotionality could thrive, the coerced utility of masking demonstrated how practitioners
of slavery contorted and dismissed black affect. In the twentieth century, this

practice of co-optation was evidenced by the popularity of stage minstrelsy, a performance in which the "socially aware edge of slave comedy was nearly always distorted or excised by the white entertainers who mimicked blacks on stage."[3] By the late twentieth century, the masking of the early twentieth century had transformed into satire, which also uses inversion to give voice to black suffering.

Slave comedy and its legacy in minstrelsy are fertile ground for exploring the shifting power dynamics that shape black humor. Although they did not make Zora Neale Hurston's list, they certainly fit the tone of her essay "Characteristics of Negro Expression."[4] Black expressions of joy through laughter emerged in early African American texts and have continued through the twenty-first century, and attending to them can help suture the rupture actuated by New World slavery. As Jessie Fauset has asserted, laughter can be an "emotional salvation" for black Americans.[5] In *Laughing Fit to Kill*, Glenda R. Carpio extends Fauset's sentiment, arguing that contemporary black humor as embodied in the work of Richard Pryor and others attempts to redress the historical fissure that slavery created. Carpio analyzes Pryor's 1976 comedy album *Bicentennial Nigger*, the "short but potent history of the Middle Passage and slavery, told from the perspective of a 'two-hundred-year-old' 'nigger in blackface' . . . with stars and stripes on his forehead." Pryor's minstrelsy is central to her theorization of the potential and impossibility of redress: "In adopting the tone of celebration to recount a captive's survival through dispossession and enslavement, [he] reenacts part of the violence of slavery, which entailed the forced performance of gaiety, while also restaging the impact of that violence on black performance."[6]

Although Carpio acknowledges the importance of minstrelsy in Pryor's subversion of stereotypes, she does not specifically examine the interstices of black laughter and minstrelsy and the psychological toll of attempted redress. Nevertheless, because of its appropriation of black emotionality during slavery, minstrelsy has become central to other contemporary attempts at redress. Eric Lott asserts, "While [minstrelsy] was organized around the quite explicit 'borrowing' of black cultural materials for white dissemination, a borrowing that ultimately depended on the material relations of slavery, the minstrel show obscured these relations by pretending that slavery was amusing, right, and natural."[7] Similarly, Michael Rogin states, "Democratized from the court and the plantation, minstrelsy enacted the urban white desire to acquire African American expressive power and supposed emotional freedom without actually freeing the slaves."[8] Contemporary black comedians who use minstrelsy as a site of redress set out to undermine the co-optation of African American expressive power while drawing similarities between the peculiar institution and current spaces that seek to police black emotionality. Carpio sees Dave Chappelle as Pryor's comedic heir, and she acknowledges their similarities and their shared investment in redressing slavery when she highlights his portrayal of slavery in the comedy sketches of *Chappelle's Show*. As with her discussion of Pryor, she does not address the issue of minstrelsy in Chappelle's work or the psychological and emotional cost of redress at this site of masking. Yet in certain ways, Chappelle's countercultural aspects are reminiscent of Pryor's activities in Berkeley, California, during the late 1960s and early 1970s, a period when he befriended the political activist Huey P. Newton and began attracting "younger African Americans who were also inspired by the Black Power movement."9

Continuing the tradition of *The Richard Pryor Show* (1977), *In Living Color* (1990–1994), and, to a lesser extent, *The Chris Rock Show* (1997–2000), *Chappelle's Show* (2003–2006) features a highly visible young black man who is a humorous interlocutor in national conversations about race and racism. Comedy Central's website still touts it as a "social phenomenon."10 Like his predecessors, Chappelle came to sketch comedy by way of a successful standup career as well as through his cult classic film *Half Baked* (1998). However, he did not become a juggernaut of black popular culture until he performed black authenticity in more legibly "cool" ways—what scholar Bambi Haggins terms the "multiple levels of 'down-ness.'"11

Taped in front of a studio audience, the sketches for *Chappelle's Show* were prerecorded and then replayed in a lounge-like atmosphere. With an average of more than 3 million viewers each episode, the show became a television event. People all around the country were talking and laughing about race. Yet Comedy Central's ability to monetize Chappelle's biting critiques of American racism and to thereby reproduce a system of control that his satire sought to expose complicated the comedian's relationship to his work. His last sketch on the show, "The Nigger Pixie," is a particularly powerful illustration of how the psychological, emotional, and economic roles of redress mediated Chappelle's artistic freedom and his ability to critique racism.

Post-Soul Laughter

In 2006, as part of the Sundance Institute's interview series, *Iconoclast*, Dave Chappelle spoke with Maya Angelou. Explaining that his satirical work is personal and, "when done well, cathartic," he said he relies on audience engagement to produce a collective acknowledgment of the everyday intricacies of race and racism in the lives of black Americans.12 In his view, they also demand a level of emotional vulnerability, so he uses his corporeal body and emotive life as the sites of this community building. Chappelle's remarks demonstrate how vulnerable his comedic process is, and they make clear that his vulnerability inadvertently set the terms for the premature end of his wildly successful television show. "With laughter when I'm at my best I'm not looking for it. But you kind of get sensitive about how people laugh. When I left my show it was because I did this sketch ["The Nigger Pixie"] and I knew what I intended but somebody laughs differently than I intended—and I caught it. It was painful."

Chappelle's embrace of emotional vulnerability reflects his role as a post-soul satirist. Coined by Nelson George, the term *post-soul* points to the contemporary moment in which black cultural producers, especially satirists, attain a discursive space in which they may subvert, challenge, and laugh about representations of black Americans.[13] They have been afforded this space by the repeal of de jure segregation, the unprecedented socioeconomic advancement of a small subset of African Americans, and widespread popular claims of a postracial cultural-political sphere. Mark Anthony Neal asserts that it is the potential of the post-soul aesthetic to radically reimagine "the contemporary African American experience, attempting to liberate contemporary interpretations of that experience from sensibilities that were formalized and institutionalized during earlier social paradigms."[14] A post-soul aesthetic fits well with the kind of satirical freedoms that *Chappelle's Show* was celebrated for, such as the popular sketch "Frontline," featuring Clayton Bigsby, played by Chappelle. Bigsby is a blind orphan whose upbringing in the rural South has given him the unique ability to become the leader of a white supremacist group. In previous generations, black vanguards suppressed stereotypical images and racial epithets about black people. They likely would have frowned on the sketch's copious use of the N-word and racist stereotypes. In an introduction to the sketch, Chappelle himself has said, "I showed it to a black friend of mine and he looked at me like I had set black people back with a comedy sketch . . . sorry."[15] But as the audience's laughter confirms, post-soul can depart from sanctimonious images of racial uplift and shift toward irreverence about racially sensitive material.

For black satirists, the concept of laughter is complicated. On the one hand, they hope that audience laughter acknowledges both the ironies and absurdities of living as a person of color in a country that proclaims freedom and democracy yet has unequal access and protections for people of color. Such laughter of resistance recognizes the fortitude of these people as they negotiate the ever-evolving American racial landscape. On the other hand, white supremacist sensibilities may invade a space intended for communal catharsis, thus leaving a satirist vulnerable to misunderstanding and to a barbed, racist laughter that reifies hegemonic power and racist ideologies. Satire is a multivalent, duplicitous form that laces acerbic wit with digestible amounts of laughter, and it is aimed at audiences who approach the material with varying levels of cultural, historical, and political knowledge. Such entanglements produce layered laughter, the byproduct of a collective meaning-making process wherein multiple sites of laughter create multiple meanings. While some comedians attempt to corral these meanings in longer satires, the brevity of sketch comedy shortens their ability to frame their message. Chappelle's solution was to introduce his prerecorded sketches in front of a live viewing audience, an attempt to mediate viewers' laughter and their meaning-making processes.

As psychoanalysts, sociologists, and humorists have noted, societal rules and norms mediate the physical and psychological process of laughing. "Only jokes that have a purpose," Sigmund Freud has written, "run the risk of meeting with people who do not want to listen to them."[16] The interplay of intent and reception is key in post-soul exchanges of laughter. In *Laughter and Ridicule*, Michael Billig asserts, "Some acts of humor might appear rebellious to the participants, those who laugh might imagine that they are daringly challenging the status quo or transgressing stuffy codes of behavior. . . . However, the consequences of such humour might be conformist rather than radical, disciplinary not rebellious."[17] In other words, as Rebecca Krefting clarifies, "even if stereotypes are introduced as cultural myths we cannot say with certainty that viewers will not misinterpret performances to fulfill rather than challenge existing beliefs, to reinforce rather than raze stereotypes."[18] For Freud, Billig, and Krefting, the intent of laughter does not always translate into the right kind of laughter. While the intrinsic ambivalence of post-soul laughter is supposed to jettison any discrepancies between a cultural producer's intent and his or her reception, the peculiarity of minstrelsy, as a performance tradition, has complicated this process for Chappelle. The urge that postmodern black satirists have to represent scenes of bondage acknowledges the impact of slavery on conceptions of blackness and the impossibility of a realistic representation of slavery in the contemporary moment.

Conventional scholarship on humor is overwhelmingly concerned with the audience's perception and consumption of the humor and thus tends to undervalue what Ralph Ellison has called "the sheer joy of the joke." According to him, "the Negro's masking" is often "motivated not so much by fear as by a profound rejection of the image created to usurp his identity. Sometimes it is for the sheer joy of the joke; sometimes to challenge those who presume across the psychological distance created by race manners, to know his identity. Nonetheless, it is in the American grain."[19] Ellison redirects our attention to the pleasure of producing this type of humor. Chappelle's joy is the catharsis he experiences when he laughs and makes others laugh. By centering his satirical voice and perspective on race, he demonstrates his self-care as he joyfully makes sense of the world around him—a move that usurps historical discourse that positions black comedy as a site of white consumption.

Chappelle's stage is the primary site of his comedic catharsis; it re-creates the standup stage and allows him both to be physically close to his audience and to perform the desired response for that audience (fig. 8.1). His singular stage presence foregrounds his physiognomy and laughter, allowing them to serve as a hermeneutic for interpreting the psychology of his unique style of satire. In the DVD audio commentary for season 1, Chappelle and his longtime writing partner

FIGURE 8.1. Screenshot of *Chappelle's Show* set, season 1, episode 1, Comedy Central, 2012.

and friend, Neal Brennan, discuss the stage and the improvisation that the comedian uses to connect with the audience. As he explains, his standup roots helped him foster a relationship with his audience, so he has difficulty focusing on the camera. Thus, in *Chappelle's Show*, the stage privileges his laughter over the audience's; in contrast to the video approach in other sites of racially charged humor, the camera rarely pans to the laughing audience to show their tacit acceptance of the joke. There are a few memorable moments in which Chappelle laughs within the narrative scope of a sketch—for instance, at the end of "The Niggar Family," when he says, "This racism is killing me inside," and when he plays a cocaine-fueled Rick James in "Charlie Murphy's True Hollywood Stories: Rick James." Yet these moments fall outside the rubric of catharsis because they do not include the audience's shared understanding. Mutuality is key if the performance is to function as a potential occasion for redress.

In his conversation with Angelou, Chappelle mentions a moment when a white crewmember "laugh[ed] differently than I intended and [he] caught it."[20] This person's "particularly loud and long" laughter did not register as solidarity, and Chappelle's recognition of this difference may allow us to reshape popular interpretations of his abrupt departure.[21] Articles and interviews in *Time* and *Newsweek* suggest that drugs, partying, and mental health contributed to his decision to stop the show and also indicate the influence of misunderstandings and racial paranoia. However, Chappelle's "I caught it" remark illustrates his ability to exert power over laughter that is meant to diminish him. He walked away from the show as an agent who knew the possibilities and limitations of his cultural impact.

Pixie Problems

"The Nigger Pixie" sketch begins with Dave Chappelle sitting in a first-class airplane seat as a white flight attendant approaches him. She greets him as "Mr. Chappelle" and asks whether he wants chicken or fish for his meal.[22] Chappelle is the only person of color in this scene and the only one who is visibly uncomfortable. As he listens to the flight attendant, a pixie appears on the back of the seat in front of him. This pixie is a technologically altered miniature of Chappelle in blackface acting in the traditional minstrel role, speaking broken English, and using exaggerated bodily gestures. Like *Pinocchio*'s Jiminy Cricket, the figure is a racially stereotyped, visual representation of the comedian's subconscious. The pixie says to Chappelle, "I just heard the magic word, chicken. Go on ahead and order you a big bucket, nigger, and take a bite. . . . Black motherfucker." Then it begins to tap dance (fig. 8.2). Chappelle wants the chicken, as his inner pixie demonstrates, but worries about how whites around him will interpret his blackness if he succumbs to the stereotype.

FIGURE 8.2. Screenshot of a scene in "The Nigger Pixie," from *Chappelle's Show*, season 3, episode 2, Comedy Central, 2012.

He irritably says to the flight attendant, "I'll have the fish thank you very much." The repartee becomes more hostile when the frustrated pixie says, "You son of a bitch, you don't want no fish." The sketch succeeds in trivializing the decision, especially after the pixie taunts, "Maybe it's catfish."[23] At the same time, it successfully demonstrates that there are both internal and external stakes in how one publicly performs blackness in the post–civil rights era.

Throughout the sketch, Chappelle remains preoccupied with verbally one-upping the pixie. His investment in winning grows as he tries different ways to eat the fish. The pixie is the object against which he can gauge his own "progress," and their repartee demonstrates his ambivalent attachment to an idea of blackness that has been forged through a history of dehumanization, the production of a robust, attendant discourse, and the cultivation of community, culture, and positive self-identification. Furthermore, although the pixie is an antagonistic entity bent on dehumanizing him, it also represents Chappelle's internal strife. It personifies his anxieties about belonging in the predominately white, affluent space of first class. He needs to dominate these anxieties, yet the pixie's catfish taunt demonstrates the impossibility of achieving a subjectivity that is wholly detached from stereotype. At the end of the scene, Chappelle finally gets up from his seat to escape the harassment. Yet there is nowhere else to go on a plane; and because the pixie is embedded in his subconscious, it would follow him anyway. The sketch is a visual reminder of the legacy of slavery and the way in which it envelops the mundane moments of black life, even something as trivial as choosing an inflight meal.[24]

In the initial airing, the segment included Chappelle's friend, the rapper Yassin Bey, then known as Mos Def. He was a pixie sidekick, playing banjo music so that Chappelle's blackface pixie could danced minstrel-show jigs. But both the online and DVD versions removed Bey from the sketch, and Comedy Central changed key details to mitigate any backlash from Bey's caricature. For instance, it archived the sketch on its website as "The Stereotype Pixie" rather than "The Nigger Pixie."

A brief clip follows "The Nigger Pixie" in which Chappelle's black pixie comments on the Ying Yang Twins' *MTV Cribs* episode.[25] "I never thought I'd say this but I'm embarrassed," the pixie says, commenting on a scene in which the rap duo picks up a wooden monkey statue and performs an emphatic monkey call. Now the pixie is no longer manifesting Chappelle's racial anxiety but gauging whether black cultural production advances stereotypical images of blackness. The segment illustrates Chappelle's perception that certain black artists are enacting something worse than minstrelsy—unabashed black buffoonery. It also legitimizes the pixie's cultural authority from the perspective of respectability politics because his embarrassment represents a cultural logic that disavows such buffoonery.

The two sketches reveal Chappelle's cognitive dissonance about issues of black authenticity and authority. On the one hand, he demonstrates his commitment to representing nuanced black life by disrupting monolithic notions of blackness and black masculinity with sketches such as "When Keeping It Real Goes Wrong" in which black men and women are portrayed as uncool and physically and emotionally vulnerable to racial ideologies of blackness. On the other, as the second nigger pixie sketch shows, his relationship to neo-soul and hip hop points to his belief in the cultural, political, and moral grounding of blackness.

Pixies appear in other sketches in the same episode of *Chappelle's Show*, illustrating the pernicious effect that stereotypes have on all Americans. A Latino pixie tempts a Latino man (Guillermo Díaz) to buy stolen automotive seat covers, and an Asian pixie tries to convince an Asian man (Yoshio Mita) to mispronounce television personality Lala Anthony's name. Two sketches feature white pixies, whom Donnell Rawlings introduces by exclaiming, "This is for all the crackers that ain't here." In these sketches, Chappelle, in his popular whiteface, tempts a white man to not dance with Latinas and not to look down when standing at a urinal next to a black man.

At the end of the episode, Donnell Rawlings and Charlie Murphy explain in a prerecorded segment that Chappelle left the show because of the "The Nigger Pixie" sketches. As evidence, they highlight excerpts from his interview with *Time* and conclude, "At the taping, he wondered if the new season of his show had gone from sending up stereotypes to reinforcing them."[26] The highlighted quotations do not include the comedian's complaint that "one spectator, a white man, laughed particularly loud and long" and Chappelle's admission that "it made me uncomfortable." Instead, the text intimates that his reservations about the direction of the show were unwarranted. The voiceover declares that Comedy Central is invested in creating a guilt-free laughing experience, unmediated by questions of propriety and racial guilt, for all audiences. It notes that the network's neoliberal investment in an amoral racial humor is supposed to evoke a narrative of racial progress. Yet the segment also demonstrates the psychic hold of slavery on both Chappelle and a large part of his viewership. As a close-up of Rawlings replaces the image of the *Time* article, he says, "We didn't know if we should air the sketch or not, so we asked the audience." In other words, would re-creating the types of conversations about race that the show was famous for assuage the tension of airing episodes that Chappelle had said he did not want to air?

The subsequent conversation with the audience was somewhat one-sided, with most of the speakers expressing their love for the show and downplaying the charged humor in the episode. Yet one audience member said, "I feel like [the pixies are] derogatory to black and Spanish people but [play] on the good stereotypes of white people," and another said, "I thought the sketch was cool.

The only problem is . . . the white race is seen as the generic race." Both dissenting audience members were black, and both implied that there is no comparable situation in which a white racial performance will produce a similar level of anxiety and stereotypical imagery. Their comments reinforced the potentially offensive nature of the episode and clarified why Chappelle might have had reservations about letting his audience view it. During the conversation with the audience, Rawlings and Murphy frequently returned to the racial diversity of the pixies to legitimize the episode's production and airing. They also kept mentioning the white pixie to mitigate issues of representation.

Minstrel Musings

Minstrelsy, which dates back to the mid-nineteenth century, grew out of a white working-class vaudeville tradition.[27] Initially, white working-class actors would blacken their faces with burnt cork and dance and sing for white audiences throughout the North and the South. The productions popularized stock caricatures of black Americans as lethargic, simple-minded, and happily subservient and set the standard for their later representation in theater, television, and film. Thomas Rice's "Jumping Jim Crow" minstrel routine became so associated with black life and culture that it reappeared in the moniker *Jim Crow laws*, the codes that enforced southern segregation and inequality well into the mid-twentieth century.

According to Daphne Brooks, pre–Civil War white minstrelsy was praised for its skill and attention to detail; but by the late nineteenth century, most members of the public believed that the black minstrels who stepped into this premade entertainment were better able to tap into the black American experience.[28] Thus, the minstrel is the first widely acknowledged artificial racial representation that has ironically produced a narrative of authenticity. This ironic legacy set the terms for Chappelle's "The Nigger Pixie" and the type of laughter he hoped to receive, even as he playfully referred to himself as "a real live coon" to a *Newsweek* reporter on set.[29] His pixie represents the extent to which racial stereotypes are dialectically illogical and artificial yet derived from actual desires and characteristics. Furthermore, it emphasizes the greater stakes for this contradiction as it ensnares people of color.

The cultural labor of white laughter in the minstrel tradition, "in which blackface comic and white spectator shared jokes about an absent third party, usually resolved to a configuration of two people, the joker personifying the person being joked about." The suggestion was that this simple-mindedness produced an unintentional buffoon, who, when juxtaposed with the ideals of white masculinity, created a sense of innate backwardness, thus producing comedy. At the peak of minstrelsy's popularity, its cultural logic was a repressive communal laughter that maintained racial markers of whiteness and blackness as the concepts of freedom and enslavement shifted. Thus, the "racist pleasure" embedded in the visual consumption of blackface "was converted through laughter and humor into a beloved and reassuring fetish."[30]

Chappelle grappled with this legacy when he heard someone laugh longer and louder than he expected during the taping of "The Nigger Pixie." But what kind of laughter did he intend to provoke? Viewers of the prerecorded show hear laughter from the studio audience after examples of minstrel-like humor. Chappelle's intent was to represent the anxiety all people feel when stereotypes and lived experiences intersect; as Charlie Murphy asks in the intro, "Have you ever been in a situation where you feel racially insecure?" Murphy is referring to the moment in which racial ideologies converge on an individual's existential will. In Chappelle's multiple pixie sketches, these convergences range from the dismissive white man who does not follow his white pixie's dancing advice to the temporary madness of black and Latino men whose pixies force them to try to escape. Yet the audience's laughter suggests that Chappelle's performance as a blackface minstrel is the defining characteristic of the sketch. Audience members laugh when the pixie's behavior is at its most racist.

Nonetheless, Chappelle's emphasis on racial insecurity and anxiety shifts the original joking formula of the minstrel stage. Originally, performers were able to create laughter from what Lott describes as the "oscillation between currency and counterfeit," or the interplay of authenticity and artificiality—a kind of reductive and often fictitious mimetic humor that invited audiences into the black experience.[31] However, the interior nature of Chappelle's pixie, coupled with its direct hostility toward Chappelle, create a markedly different type of comedic engagement. As Chappelle's pixie argues with a black man who is not in blackface, the sketch captures the tension between artifice and authenticity in a black modern context.

The pixie wears a porter costume that subtly conjures a legacy of black labor and mobility. This legacy is particularly fraught in the first-class section of an airplane, where the terms of servitude have shifted: Chappelle is the passenger, and a white woman is the flight attendant. The symbolic class markings of the black porter remind us that black men's relationship to transportation is tied to a history of labor and lack of access. Like Aunt Jemima, the black chef on the Cream of Wheat box, and the black lawn jockey figurine, the notion of a black porter carrying luggage through a train triggers a national nostalgia.[32] On the minstrel stage and in early cinema, performers purposefully evoked this nostalgia by wearing porters' costumes. In fact, in 1831, minstrel Thomas Rice borrowed one from a black man named Cuff to wear when he performed an early version of his Jim Crow routine.[33] Chappelle's use of the porter iconography juxtaposes that history with the dynamic of sitting in the first-class section of the airplane. The pairing suggests that, if a comedic redress is going to be successful, it has to be coupled with images of financial success.

To that end, *Chappelle's Show* couples other images of slavery with financial success. In "Time Haters: Great Misses," for instance, a group of player haters assembled in a previous episode exhibits the clothes and dispositions of stereotypical pimps. The sketch's concept is borrowed from the Players' Ball, an annual gathering of pimps. Here, the characters travel back in time to "hate," or play the dozens on people. In one outtake, they travel back to antebellum America so that the leader of the group, Silky (played by Chappelle), can call a slave owner a cracker. The sketch ends with Silky shooting the slave owner dead. In his remarks after the sketch, Chappelle says, "Apparently shooting a slave master isn't funny to anybody but me and Neil. If I could, I'd do it every episode."[34] Writing about this scene, Carpio argues:

> The fantasy of retribution finds violent, although also symbolic, outlet while the object of that violence is not, as in Pryor's scene of introjection, the black body. Yet its redirection to the white body of the master depends on simplified notions of retribution (and race) in which the crimes of slavery, enormous as they are, would find some kind of redress in the shooting of a white man. Still, the fact that the skit provides cathartic release—both in the form of the light humor that precedes the violent act and the violent act itself—is important given the need for the redress of slavery even when if only symbolically, that Pryor's, as well Rock's and Chappelle's, work make clear.[35]

The player haters' ostentatious fashion sense creates a narrative of financial success that is imbricated in Chappelle's meaning-making process of redress and catharsis. As Buc Nasty (played by Charlie Murphy) states, "You better watch your mouth, white boy, before I put these gaiters up your ass and show your insides some style."[36] Furthermore, because the sketch is presented as a flawed outtake, the act of screening it for an audience is itself a defiance in which the comedian privileges himself in these comedic and meaning-making exchanges.

Like the porter costume, the centrality of chicken in "The Nigger Pixie" evokes a specific image—in this case, the Zip Coon stereotype and the cultural logic of disempowering black masculine aspirations. In *Building Houses out of Chicken Legs*, Psyche A. Williams-Forson writes, "The images of African American men, portrayed in the likeness of Zip Coon in compromising positions with chicken, are perverse and overwhelming." She demonstrates that, in the dominant popular culture of the late nineteenth century, such images helped to inscribe black people, particularly black men, with an animalistic quality. This move, like many of the other caricatures of black people in post–Civil War America, was intended to undermine their newfound citizenship. From Ralph Ellison's yam-eating *Invisible Man* to Chappelle's chicken-eating pixie, the inclusion of food in creative scenes has been a way to represent black Americans' negotiation of "how power can be present in even the most mundane objects of our material lives."[37] Again, the enduring threat of dehumanization helps to create the racial anxiety that Chappelle captures in the sketch.

"The Nigger Pixie" echoes an earlier bit in Chappelle's standup routine, *Killin' Them Softly*, in which he recalls doing a show in Mississippi and afterward going to a restaurant where the white server tells him that he wants chicken. When Chappelle asks how the waiter knows what he wants, the waiter replies, "It is no secret down here that blacks and chickens are quite fond of one another." Chappelle responds, "I'm genetically predisposed to liking chicken. I've got no say in the matter . . . [but] now I'm scared to eat it in public."[38] As the server's assumption and rationale demonstrate, the stereotype continues to animalize black people. Thus, the minstrel complexities that Chappelle evokes create a palimpsest of meanings for his audience and their laughter.

Chappelle is optimistic about creating a collective laughter and meaning-making practice that acknowledges and celebrates black subjectivity. Yet he left *Chappelle's Show* in the middle of taping the episode that includes "The Nigger Pixie," thus forfeiting his 50-million-dollar contract. For contemporary African American satirists, the impasse of the current moment is a continued preoccupation with the power appropriated to race. Although we are living in a post–civil rights era, we are not living in a post-racial era; and Chappelle's unraveling both inside and outside the sketch marks how he and other satirists have been unable to move past this conclusion. The pixie is a supernatural being beyond the passenger's control, and Chappelle's decision to use it as a character has given him a way to creatively articulate the forced suturing of black people's psychic selves to a derisively stereotyped history of racial injury.

Chappelle's appropriation of blackface minstrelsy also manifests his personal turmoil. The passenger's phantasmagoric engagements with the pixie bespeak an inner competing consciousness and contributed to the comedian's "clumsy dismount" from *Chappelle's Show*. Chappelle later said, "It had a little psychological element to it. I have trust issues, things like that. I saw some stuff in myself that I just didn't dig." Neal Brennan elaborated on Chappelle's psychological state: "He would come with an idea, or I would come with an idea, pitch it to him, and he'd say that's funny. And from there we'd write it. He'd love it, say, 'I can't wait to do it.' We'd shoot it, and then at some point he'd start saying, 'This sketch is racist, and I don't want this on the air.' . . . There was this confusing contradictory thing: he was calling his own writing racist."[39] Chappelle's reactions suggest that something about the television frame was divorcing the final product from his original meaning. Perhaps, during the conceptualization phase, he had imagined an audience poised to participate in a cathartic response, but he later adopted a dominant gaze when producing and viewing the sketch. Indeed, as the crewmember's unexpected laughter affirmed, there is a disconnect between Chappelle's intent and the visual reception of his work. Whereas "white people, white artists, are allowed to be individuals," he declares, this is a "dilemma" for black cultural producers, who have to be more critical about the images they create for popular consumption and the lasting effects they have on black Americans.[40] In chapter 1, Robert J. Patterson drives home this point: "The assumed realness of negative and stereotypical representations of black subjects and black life has had real (that is, meaningful, substantive, and material) consequences for black people and thus contextualizes why representation has been an important force for the making of black cultural politics."

In the DVD's audio commentary for the episode, Brennan, Rawlings, and Murphy reveal both their collective fatigue as well as their deep, lingering confusion about the sketch and its aftermath. Brennan says, "Being responsible was never a concern of the show until . . . it gets popular, then it's like, I guess." As the three try to contextualize the audience members' problems with the white pixie, he eventually states, "It didn't make a difference that we had two white pixies and we peed on them because it still doesn't undo all the awful shit white people have done in the history of the world." Murphy argues, "But that's not what that sketch was about," and Neal replies, "The sketch stopped being what the sketch was about a long time ago."[41]

Subverting the Marketplace Value of Satire

During an interview with James Lipton, Chappelle said, "When art and corporate interest meet just prepare to have your heart broken."[42] His comment suggests that misplaced laughter was not his only reason for leaving *Chappelle's Show*. Rather, he realized that Comedy Central was economizing racial progress through his racial humor and the show's television ratings, co-opting his message and causing him to doubt his ability to make subversive critiques of large power structures. When designing the show, Chappelle had assumed that America would not be willing to take "a tour through a young black man's subconscious" and the show would be canceled quickly.[43] Throughout much of the first season, he noted on air that the show had not been canceled yet, perhaps referring tacitly to the short run of *The Richard Pryor Show*. At the same time, he intentionally distanced his show from *The Chris Rock Show*—notably, with a fifteen-second clip during the pilot that announces, "It's not HBO. It's just regular ass TV."[44] This early posturing shifted at the end of the second season, when he was engaged in contract negotiations. He understood how power breathes life into structural forms of racism, and this prompted him to be more self-reflexive about the show's politics or its lack thereof: "Fifty million dollars is a lot of money. And what I'm learning is I am surprised at what I would do for $50 million. I am surprised at what people around me would do for me to have $50 million."[45]

Chappelle's awareness of his economic value to the network has been stressful. For instance, when Comedy Central featured him on a panel discussion of the N-word, he knew the goal was to market his brand. Although Brennan asserts, "There is no one from the network sitting on his head. Dave is in charge of his own world," Chappelle often feels otherwise.[46] In an interview with Oprah Winfrey, he said, "When you're a guy that generates money, people have a vested interest in controlling you. And I feel like the people that were trying to control me were putting me through stressful situations."[47] When addressing hints that drug use and insanity had influenced his premature departure from the show, he said, "Maybe corporate America fucks with human beings like they're products and investments."[48] His word choice evokes the long history of economized black existence. This shift in language, from the nineteenth century's *property* to the twenty-first century's *product and investment*, substantiates the expansion of capital in black cultural production and links black cultural producers to what Houston Baker refers to as the economics of slavery and blacks' ability to appraise themselves in this economic landscape.[49] As Chappelle's father told him early in his career, "name your price before you get there. And if you ever find it's more expensive than what you're prepared to give, then get out."[50]

The logo of Pilot Boy Productions, aired at the end of every episode of *Chappelle's Show*, illustrates the tensions among financial success, neoliberalism, and an attempt at redress and catharsis. The image shows a shirtless, shackled Chappelle holding handfuls of money. In the accompanying voiceover, Rawlings shouts, "I'm rich, bitch!" The voiceover is from "Reparations 2003," a sketch that, in Carpio's words, pushes the stereotypical "carrying out [of] white fantasies about race to their most absurd levels."[51] Yet even as Carpio acknowledges the importance of the reparation sketches, she quickly bypasses the Pilot Boy Production image. It, like the sketches I have discussed, is both a site of attempted redress and a precursor of the issues that would arise between Chappelle and Comedy Central. Chappelle's depiction as both enslaved and rich reifies his position to the network. His expression is cautious; his face is slightly tilted away from the camera, his eyes glance sideways, and his pursed lips are solemn. Rawlings's voiceover creates figurative reparations for viewers, but Chappelle's static image suggests that this reparation comes at a cost to himself. He does not look happy.

In the years since the end of *Chappelle's Show*, the Internet has shifted the terms of satirical production and post-soul laughter, giving creators space to subvert the demands and capital of network television. As Richard Iton writes, "On the technological front, digital media and the Internet enabled consumers to create their own scripts: to rearrange or anarrange [*sic*] recorded or video product as they saw fit."[52] This shift has also given satirists more distance from corporate interests. Websites such as YouTube and other user-generated content sites have made possible a do-it-yourself production that is the primary avenue of today's black satirical visual culture. Web series such as Issa Rae's *The Misadventures of Awkward Black Girl* demonstrate that satirical and comedic cultural creators no longer have to depend on television networks to share their art.

Within these digital enclaves, there is continued interest in engaging the site of slavery in this post-Obama moment. On *Ask a Slave*, for instance, actress Azie Mira Dungey discusses her role as the enslaved fictional character, Lizzie Mae, which she played as part of an interactive tour of Mount Vernon, the home of President George Washington. In various episodes, she recounts some of the absurd questions tourists have asked her. The biographical section of the website explains that Dungey began playing enslaved black women during the rise in racist vitriol that accompanied Obama's terms in office. "Though this is a comedy, it is my hope to honor the memory of those people who struggled and survived through their uncanny intelligence, their strength, their love, and . . . laughter."[53] Shows such as Dungey's demonstrate that, while laughter is still a sought-after way of sharing people's limited understanding of the institution of slavery, it is not always directly shared— and often does not go beyond the comments section of a video.

As for Chappelle, his attempt to redress slavery through minstrelsy, laughter, and money took a psychological toll that prevented his work from being cathartic. Much of the commentary on the last days of *Chappelle's Show* mark his departure as a passive form of escapism; sites such as *Time* and *Newsweek* have failed to consider his critique of capitalist excess or to see his moral adherence to an emotional and cultural logic as an act of agency. For while the immediacy of the Internet now provides a platform for circumventing the monetizing effects of network television, these visual texts will always produce a layered laughter that engages in a meaning-making process that has multiple outcomes.

NOTES

1. Saidiya Hartman, *Scenes of Subjection: Terror, Slavery, and Self-Making in Nineteenth-Century America* (Oxford: Oxford University Press, 1997), 23.

2. Paul Laurence Dunbar, *The Collected Poetry of Paul Laurence Dunbar*, ed. Joanne M. Braxton (Charlottesville: University of Virginia Press, 1993), 71.

3. Mel Watkins, *African American Humor: The Best Black Comedy from Slavery to Today* (Chicago: Chicago Review Press, 2002), xvii.

4. Zora Neale Hurston, "Characteristics of Negro Expression," in *Within the Circle: An Anthology of African American Literary Criticism from the Harlem Renaissance to the Present*, ed. Angelyn Mitchell (Durham, N.C.: Duke University Press, 1994), 79–94.

5. Jessie Fauset, "The Gift of Laughter," in *The New Negro*, ed. Alain Locke (New York: Boni, 1925), 166.

6. Glenda R. Carpio, *Laughing Fit to Kill: Black Humor in the Fictions of Slavery* (Oxford: Oxford University Press, 2008), 74–75, 77.

7. Eric Lott, *Love and Theft: Blackface Minstrelsy and the American Working Class* (Oxford: Oxford University Press, 1993), 3–4.

8. Michael Rogin, *Blackface, White Noise: Jewish Immigrants in the Hollywood Melting Pot* (Berkeley: University of California Press, 1998), 22.

9. Carpio, *Laughing Fit to Kill*, 147.

10. Comedy Central, http://www.cc.com/shows/chappelle-s-show, accessed January 8, 2016.

11. Bambi Haggins, "In the Wake of 'The Nigger Pixie,'" in *Satire TV: Politics and Comedy in the Post-Network Era*, ed. Jonathan Gray and Jeffrey Jones (New York: New York University Press, 2009), 207. Haggins convincingly locates Chappelle's "downness," or coolness, as the primary factor in his rise to fame. Thus, her articulation deconstructs Comedy Central's continuing claim that *Chappelle's Show* is a "social phenomenon."

12. "Dave Chappelle and Maya Angelou," *Iconoclasts*, dir. Joe Berlinger (New York: Sundance Institute, 2006), television series: episode 6.

13. Nelson George, *Hip Hop America* (New York: Penguin, 1998).

14. Mark Anthony Neal, *Soul Babies: Black Popular Culture and the Post-Soul Aesthetic* (New York: Routledge, 2002), 3.

15. In the DVD audio commentary, Chappelle explains that his black friend is Cey Adams, a hip hop visual artist who created many of Def Jam's early album covers. During the conversation, Brennan quotes Adams as later saying, "People will laugh at anything." Chappelle also mentions that the idea for the sketch came from his grandfather, a blind man who was either white or light enough to pass but was raised black in Washington, D.C. The anecdote is another example of Chappelle's tendency to make himself vulnerable by sharing personal experiences with his viewers.

16. Sigmund Freud, *Jokes and Their Relation to the Unconscious* (New York: Norton, 1960), 107.

17. Michael Billig, *Laughter and Ridicule: Towards a Social Critique of Humour* (London: Sage, 2005), 211.

18. Rebecca Krefting, *All Joking Aside: American Humor and Its Discontents* (Baltimore: Johns Hopkins University Press, 2014), 180.

19. Ralph Ellison, "Change the Joke and Slip the Yoke," *Partisan Review* 25, no. 2 (1958): 55.

20. "Dave Chappelle and Maya Angelou."

21. Christopher Farley, "Dave Speaks," *Time*, May 14, 2005, http://content.time.com/time/magazine/article/0,9171,1061512,00.html, accessed December 30, 2015.

22. In many ways the scene echoes the two jive-talking black men in the 1980 film *Airplane!* When the flight attendant asks what they want for their inflight meal, they respond by speaking jive as if it were a separate language. The move seemingly embraces stereotypical representations of black men as the epitome of cool.

23. Dave Chappelle, *Chappelle's Show* (New York: Comedy Central, 2003–2006), DVD: season 3, episode 2.

24. Hartman, *Scenes of Subjection*.

25. *MTV Cribs* is a television show about prominent young artists, athletes, other celebrities who give tours of their homes and other assets. The show began airing in 2000.

26. Chappelle, *Chappelle's Show*, season 3, episode 2.

27. Lott, *Love and Theft.*

28. Daphne Brooks, *Bodies in Dissent: Spectacular Performances of Race and Freedom, 1850–1910* (Durham, N.C.: Duke University Press, 2006), 63.

29. Devin Gordon and Allison Samuels, "Dave Chappelle: Fears of a Clown," *Newsweek*, May 16, 2005, 60.

30. Lott, *Love and Theft*, 142.

31. Ibid., 20.

32. Maurice Manring, *Slave in a Box: The Strange Career of Aunt Jemima* (Charlottesville: University of Virginia Press, 1998).

33. Robert Nevin, "Stephen C. Foster and Negro Minstrelsy," *Atlantic* 20 (November 1867), 605–616.

34. Chappelle, *Chappelle's Show*, season 2, episode 11.

35. Carpio, *Laughing Fit to Kill*, 114.

36. Chappelle, *Chappelle's Show*, season 2, episode 11.

37. Psyche Williams-Forson, *Building Houses out of Chicken Legs: Black Women, Food, and Power* (Chapel Hill: University of North Carolina Press, 2006), 38, 49.

38. Dave Chappelle, *Killin' Them Softly*, dir. Stan Lathan (New York: Home Box Office, 2000), DVD.

39. Christopher Farley, "Dave Speaks," *Time*, May 14, 2005, p. 68.

40. Kevin Powell, "Heaven Hell Dave Chappelle: The Agonizing Return of the Funniest Man in America." *Esquire*, April 29, 2006, http://www.esquire.com/entertainment/movies/a1122/esq0506chappelle-92/, accessed December 30, 2015.

41. Chappelle, *Chappelle's Show*, season 3, episode 2.

42. James Lipton, "Dave Chappelle," *Inside the Actor's Studio* (New York: Actor's Studio, 2006), DVD: season 12, episode 11.

43. Powell, "Heaven Hell Dave Chappelle," 148.

44. Chappelle, *Chappelle's Show*, season 1, episode 1.

45. Farley, "Dave Speaks."

46. Ibid.

47. Oprah Winfrey, "Chappelle's Story," *The Oprah Winfrey Show*, dir. Joseph C. Terry (Chicago: Harpo Productions, 2006), http://www.oprah.com/oprahshow/Chappelles-Story, accessed December 30, 2015.

48. "Dave Chappelle and Maya Angelou."

49. Houston Baker, *Blues, Ideology, and Afro-American Literature: A Vernacular Theory* (Chicago: University of Chicago Press, 1987).

50. Farley, "Dave Speaks," 73.

51. Carpio, *Laughing Fit to Kill*, 111.

52. Richard Iton, *In Search of the Black Fantastic: Politics and Popular Culture in the Post–Civil Rights Era* (New York: Oxford University Press, 2008), 112.

53. "Lizzie Mae," *Ask a Slave*, dir. Jordan Black, web series, http://www.askaslave.com/lizzie-mae.html, accessed December 3, 2015.

9

The Cartoonal Slave

MICHAEL CHANEY

> I wanted to be proved wrong. I wanted to imagine a present not tethered
> to a long history of defeat, but this was difficult to do with Elmina Castle
> dominating the shoreline. It entailed a great effort to remind myself that
> the destruction of the holding cell hadn't been absolute and that I was
> part of what had lived on. Ghana was as good a place as any other to
> think about the afterlife of slavery and the future of the ex-slave. Secretly
> I hoped that it wasn't too late to believe in freedom dreams.[1]
>
> —Saidiya Hartman

According to the principle of *Bilderverbot*, the ban on images related to the
Shoah, prohibition functions as a means to commemorate, if not acknowledge,
the gravity of the event; that is, an ethics of silence insulates historical trauma.
The filmmaker Claude Lanzmann famously extended the discourse of idolatry
associated with the second commandment to representations of the Holocaust,
which he sees as "unique in that it builds around itself, in a circle of flame,
the limit that cannot be transgressed because a certain absolute of horror is
intransmissible. To pretend to be able to do so is to make oneself culpable of
the most serious transgression."[2] Perhaps cartoons' generic affinity with the
grotesque and caricature enabled Art Spiegelman to create his graphic novel
Maus (1986), with its elaborately masked animal metaphors, to bypass these
iconophobic prohibitions. For Marianne Hirsch, *Maus*'s embedded photographs
and illustrated photos of lost loved ones not only precipitate memory but also
generate a tension of realism that is typical of graphic novels. The photographs
"connect the two levels of Spiegelman's text, the past and the present, the
story of the father and the story of the son, because these family photographs
are documents both of memory (the survivor's) and the 'postmemory' (that of
the child of survivors). As such, the photographs included in the text of *Maus*,
and, through them, *Maus* itself, become sites of remembrance."[3] Likewise,
Andreas Huyssen claims that *Maus*'s sophisticated image-text strategies and its
psychodynamic projections of victims and survivors allow it to escape a more

paralyzing form of mimesis: "Spiegelman did need a different, more estrang-
ing mode of narrative and figurative representation in order to overcome the
paralyzing effects of a mimesis of memory-terror. . . . Drawing the story of his
parents and the Holocaust as an animal comic is the Odyssean cunning that
allows Spiegelman to escape from the terror of memory—even 'postmemory'
in Marianne Hirsch's terms—while mimetically reenacting it."[4]

What is the semiotic architecture of critical illustration that buttresses
recent representations of the African American slave? Insofar as contemporary African American graphic storytellers are concerned, figuring the slave in
cartoonal drawings rather than in media with presumptively stronger claims
to objectivity or verisimilitude gives artists a measure of distance from the
prohibitions, interdictions, and martyrlogical sanctities of the slave. In other
words, the graphic novel relies on its implicit and explicit claims to stylistic
antirealism to negotiate slavery's ineluctable unspeakability as both a historical and psycho-traumatic site of rupture, one that also signifies as a structural
continuity. As I will show in this chapter, the resulting contradictions play out
in a range of visual media.

Constitutively styled, the comics' version of atrocity, however traumatic,
always comes with palliating touches of the surreal. So does their built-in
historical irreverence or their proclivity for the ludic explain their recent
forays into the traumatic slave past? What is it about the cartoonal, the mode
of representational exaggeration that pressed offended Muslim extremists
to target the satirical magazine *Charlie Hebdo*, that both recapitulates and
revises our ordinary suspicions of the visual field? How are obviously drawn
(and thus to some extent anti- or unrealistic) renderings of historical trauma
different from more photorealistic depictions in the visual field? And in view
of the concerns raised by Robert J. Patterson in his critique of the political
ineffectuality of certain films (see chapter 1), are cartoonal images (that is to
say, recognizably hand-drawn images) of slavery or scenes of historical black
subjection any more effective at circumventing the dangerous political work
that such imagery does in the contemporary United States? In the context
of startling diachronic oppression in black communities around the nation,
do comics normalize longstanding American popular cultural associations
between state-sanctioned violence and the black body?

In *Sites of Slavery*, Salamishah Tillet identifies a trend among contemporary
black artists to combine postmodernist aesthetic practices with a "preoccupation with the antebellum past to work through discourses of citizenship,
democracy, and African American political identity in the present."[5] The
past becomes an ideal site, according to Tillet, for the performance of "critical patriotism"—rehabilitated by an aura of antebellum American sincerity
(both white and black) for national principles never justly available to African
Americans. Lisa Woolfork, who explores immersive re-creations of slavery in

literature, film, and art installations, suggests that artists such as Carrie Mae Weems and Kara Walker may be motivated as well by the recalibration of Freudian trauma. "In their representation of the slave past as insoluble," these representations provide "an alternative to the predominant mode of trauma theory that defines trauma as elusive and unknowable."[6] It is the *back-then*-ness of simplistic conceptions of trauma that many African American representations radically eschew. Who, for instance, would discount the pressing urgency of racial violence and injustice in view of so many recent and fatal incidents of racial profiling? Like the fatality of blackness, slavery's trauma is only historical if one is to accept as logical the untenable severance of these contemporary traumas from the *longue durée* of structural oppression that entwines both. As Patterson cogently argues in chapter 1, contemporary cinematic representations of slavery often fail to clarify the structural alignment between American slavery and a host of contemporary oppressions, from police brutality to the systematic economic disenfranchisement of people of color across the globe. For him, such representations reinforce (perhaps unwillingly or unconsciously) the inequalities they may have intended to expose and dispel. They examine "slavery's intricacies and legacies" without examining "how ideas about capitalism, the nuclear family, hetero-patriarchy, masculinity, and femininity intersect with racist, sexist, and heterosexist ideologies to further contextualize the wide reach of slavery's arm."

The salutary psychic benefits of experiencing historical trauma as suddenly and uncannily knowable surely may factor into the success of cultural texts that revisit or review antebellum slavery. Examples include the films *Django Unchained* (2012) and *12 Years a Slave* (2013); the TV series *Black Sails* (2014); Kyle Baker's graphic novel *Nat Turner* (2005, 2008); and two books about South Carolina artist and slave Dave the Potter—Leonard Todd's biography *Carolina Clay* (2008) and Laban Carrack Hill and Bryan Collier's award-winning picture book *Dave the Potter: Artist, Poet, Slave* (2010). How much further outside "the circle" of slavery are these African American artists than Frederick Douglass was, who in his 1845 *Narrative,* considers the complex limit of experience, memory, and ontology that prevents him from speaking for his own former slave self—those years when he was "within the circle; so that I neither saw nor heard as those without might see and hear"?[7] How do these texts negotiate the solemnity of unspeakability that has become a critical commonplace in literary studies of slavery, at least since the canonization of Toni Morrison's *Beloved* in 1988? Perhaps it is only in the blithely postmodern oeuvre of a Quentin Tarantino that an Afrocentric revenge fantasy reminiscent of Ishmael Reed can so easily follow up an alternative history of Nazi assassination worthy of Michael Chabon or Philip Roth. Like Robert S. Levine, I am convinced that "alternative histories are always immanent in particular cultural moments," yet I hesitate to claim the present to be another of the slave's recurring moments of significance in the American imaginary.[8] When represented in graphic novels, the slave shares company with other formative icons of traumatic race history. The result of such a semiotic affiliation disrupts the central hold that slavery may have as the discursive limit of meaning for any representation of it as comic art. The trauma on display is thus untethered from a purely historical reading, the kind that mollifies racial anxieties about the present by divorcing it from the terrifying politics of slavery. Leaving aside for the moment the larger question of whether any form of cultural production or visual representation may be politically effectual, I note that comics not only operate according to different semiotic and material modes than cinema does but often traffic in far more marginal affiliations, associations, and unruly representations. For obvious budgetary reasons, films must anticipate and appeal to the ideologically normative "discursive audience," to borrow Dwight McBride's phrase.[9] Graphic novels and illustrated books, which are independently produced and financed, do not face the same pressure.

The political effectiveness of the comics form depends upon its ambivalence, its facility for acute fluidity when making visual connections between the past and the present—a precondition, one might argue, for a historically materialist view of the world rather than the falsely conscious vision routinely sold to Hollywood's "discursive audiences." For example, according to Qiana J. Whitted, Jeremy Love's representation of the Golliwog in his graphic novel *Bayou* (2009) proves that "the postmodern narrative's struggle to reclaim the past, to explore the turmoil between the Self and the Other, and to unveil the deep consequences of an interdependent world are given new life in horror and fantasy comics."[10] Similar goals underwrite Mat Johnson and Warren Pleece's depiction of the lynched body in *Incognegro: A Graphic Mystery* (2008) and Ho Che Anderson's brief treatment of the infamous 1955 photograph of Emmett Till's mangled face in *King* (2005). Each graphic novel conveys its epochal injustices without arousing too many countervailing suspicions of the image as idolatry or sacrilege. This is because the form and style of the comics have historically congealed around a prevailing antirealism—an effect that Huyssen and others have pointed to in Spiegelman's *Maus*, whose style holds out the possibility of disavowing the text's own mimetic aims. The formal simultaneity that the comics structure affords—by which I mean the possibility of reading two sequential images as narratively related, contiguous yet logically separate—intensifies the particular treachery of images that graphic novels induce. Like *Maus*, both *Nat Turner* and *Incognegro* proclaim their characters as being history's survivors as well as brazen fictions. The fiction seems to be a precondition for an exercise in trauma history that the exculpatory antirealism of drawing permits and pans by turns. And this capacity for a simultaneous display of the both-and relationship, side by side, endows the comics form and associated still images (hand-drawn, painted, penned, collaged, and so on) with a facility that cinema as a medium generally lacks.

Needless to say, cinema is not an inherently lesser form, despite its greater global capital. Indeed, graphic novels and illustrations share with film a preoccupation with extroversion as a tactic for metaphorizing complexities of history, culture, and power. If the novel has been hailed as a crucial technology for voicing the bourgeois individual whose private interiorities are converted into public textual effects, comics and graphic novels have been noted for loading up the personae they simulate with iconic primacy—an investment in visual exteriorization that concomitantly extols optic forms of knowledge and experience and often normalizes, as in the case of conventional graphic memoir or autobiography, the mediational construct of third-person narration. Indeed, even when telling his own story or retrieving his father's Holocaust experience, Spiegelman draws himself as a character, a deliberate mask, who exists in a world populated with harrowingly moving masks, all taking part in an elaborate autobiographical historical fiction.

None of the authorial protagonists of the most celebrated graphic novels (many of which are also autobiographies: *Blankets, Persepolis, Fun Home, 100 Demons, Epileptic, Stitches*) present the world as it is seen. All use a third-party extroverted vantage point to show themselves and the world through which they move. The content of that world may be purely conceptual so long as it signifies visually, a condition that lends a quality of stasis, frieze, or suspension to the pictorial information conveyed by any comic. Like religious icons, they rely on visual repetition and ritual to convoke a community.

In an American context, few figures of injustice match the iconic primacy of the whipped slave, a fleeting but constitutive traumatic origin that engenders and is critically and creatively sustained by an African American historical community of recovery and redress. Evidence of such a relationship appears in the critical reception of the film *12 Years a Slave*, which consciously and necessarily collapses and individualizes the long history of slavery and thereby inevitably takes part in minimizing that history. For instance, consider the film's use of the temporal freeze during the thwarted lynching of Solomon. Tied to a tree by a sadistic overseer, he is "rescued" by another overseer, who leaves him to hang there for many more seconds. With little else happening in the foreground, the typical viewer is liable to respond with an affective surge proper to the sequence. In other words, the scene stalls the film's narrative momentum, freezing the scene into a tableau and turning the moment into a monument. We may read such stretched-out, uncut scenes of black mortification as symptomatic of a larger oceanic suspension that Hortense Spillers and others have associated with Middle Passage remembrance and diasporic consciousness.[11] Yet following Spillers, Patterson, Hartman, and others, we must also always respond to the ways in which these scenes are implicated in a contemporary politics of oppression. If no cultural production can ever rise to the level of a material political action (a poem is neither a revolution nor a ballot), artworks can at least be the means of political action, of raising consciousness, or of making viewers (as *12 Years a Slave* may do) uncomfortably aware of an otherwise subtler politics of voyeurism and temporality at work in this or any film.

Just as the protracted camera gaze of *12 Years a Slave* seems to deliberately violate conventions about showing uncomfortable things on screen for too long (in filmic salute to the greater violations it analogizes), the camera gaze, so to speak, of Johnson and Pleece's *Incognegro* (2008) likewise plays tricks with perspective when illustrating its historical image-object: lynching. Zane Pinchback, a hero in the vein of NAACP leader Walter White, is a passer in the 1930s and a top-notch antilynching journalist. Resembling the classic repertoire of lynching photography (both show mobs gathered around a tree and a tortured victim), Pleece's illustrations are so starkly monochromatic that they do not distinguish skin-tone differences. Hence, many viewers have difficulty discerning the tortured *black* body in the midst of the bacchanalian mobs. In most of the book's scenes, the punctumous lynch victim is present but not automatically visible. While two of the book's three lynching scenes bolster voyeuristic viewing practices by obscuring the detail of the wounds, the final scene brings the victim up close. But even then, the encounter remains overdetermined due to the design impositions of what we might refer to as the *monstrator*. In his essay "The Monstrator, the Recitant, and the Shadow of the Narrator," Thierry Groensteen posits that the authorial personae of the *recitant*, which is "the authority responsible for enunciation" in comics, narrates certain propositions that are radically revised by its corresponding but in no way subordinate personae of the *monstrator*, the one "responsible for the *putting into drawing (mise en dessin)* of the story."[12] The monstrator is thus another type of author, one who uses pictures according to a logic that is not always congruent with the words in a comic.

In one example, two extra panels of Pinchback's face break up an otherwise direct approach to representing trauma in this final display (fig. 9.1). The panels reverberate with Pinchback's "Nooo!!!" so that the close-ups of his horrified face compete with the lynching—the sacred abjection to be witnessed—for representational space and signifying primacy. How can witnessing happen here when our affective response has already been performed for us? By fiat of the panel arrangement, Pinchback is made to do our witnessing for us. Elements in the panels have the potential of linking back and forth, making them the emblem of one view of African American history and suggesting that all efforts to psychically recover it are a tragic echo chamber of negation in relay.

Despite their differences, both *12 Years a Slave* and *Incognegro* manage their grievous historical sights in ways geared to disturb and frustrate viewers. Their violations of viewing norms reveal their ethical burdens of historical

FIGURE 9.1. Illustration from *Incognegro* by Mat Johnson and Warren Pleece. Copyright © Warren Pleece and Mat Johnson. Reprinted with permission.

representation. By turning voyeurism into a form of minor torture, they allow viewers to suffer a token penitence for a historical trauma they can neither claim nor rightly witness. Nonetheless, as Rebecca Wanzo explains, the cartoonal is a somewhat unlikely medium of witnessing for African American artists: "The phenotypic excesses of caricature produce challenges for creators of black characters, who recognize that blacks are always already stereotyped when their bodies are represented."[13] Pleece bypasses the problematic non-neutrality of blackness in the visual field by portraying the lynched body in the earliest scenes with as much chromatic whiteness as the surrounding torturers possess. Indeed, the viewer who seeks psychic redress through brutal representations of race history will be thwarted by *Incognegro*, a text that exemplifies even as it agrees with Douglas A. Jones Jr.'s critique of similar recovery projects—"for such repair is impossible" (see chapter 2). *Incognegro* suggests that repair is possible in scenes that replay iconic spectacles of subjection with pernicious repetition, but it revokes that suggestion in its final frieze of negation. There, multiplicity and ambivalence disrupt the narrative of sympathy simultaneously on view in the same large panel. Pinchback is shown occupying two visual locations at once. On the one hand, he is the close-up face that utters "Nooo!!!" in response to the horror, an exclamation that seems to posit a desire for a historical past that can be reconstituted in a visual medium, drawn up again in order to be soundly denounced once and for all. The shrieking sympathetic hero stands for redress, or what Jones or Stephen Best would refer to as his embodiment of "Morrisonian poetics" or "melancholic historiography."[14] He makes utterances in the present that were never allowed to be uttered in their own time. Fulfilling sacrificial and ghostly debts to the dead happens to be another unusual skill that the character of Pinchback, also known as Incognegro, possesses: he sees murder scenes in reverse at various crime scenes in the book. This suggests an interesting congruity between the character and his mythopoetic type.

But the hero of sympathy is not the only one represented in this panel. There is also the tiny silhouette in the wagon passing along the horizon. That is the real Incognegro. Once again he has magically outpaced yet another lynching—this time, his own. The sidekick interposes, sacrificing himself—as all sidekicks inevitably do—so that the hero may live on. The sidekick has lied to the lynchers, proclaiming himself to be the antilynching journalist-avenger, the one and only noir-style superhero, Incognegro. Here is where the ludic tips its hat: the text's hybridizations and surpluses undermine the psychic redress its sympathetic hero seems to seek. He is not just any hero, after all, but an unkillable superhero, par excellence, a genre to which Pinchback explicitly alludes when he announces his alias to himself in front of a mirror. Incognegro will be his secret identity as an undercover detective and journalist; his superpower is being able to pass. Thus, in a genre predicated on hyperbole, the pathos the sympathetic hero enacts in the two panels of the final lynching scene is ironic because it is juxtaposed against the notion of a superhero who cannot be killed, a characteristic so unfairly withheld from every other character in his universe.

Like most superheroes, Incognegro is a titular *Übermensch*, an autocratic, antihistorical fiction. Therefore, if we are to identify with his face in order to heap salvific denunciations onto past unspoken injuries, then our sympathy must come with a dose of ambivalence. Sympathy, however suspicious we may be of it, is additive, extolling logics of inclusion, whereas the superhero is the metonym for a principle of impermeability, of substitution and logics of exclusivity. Each is the antipode of the other. Taken together, the two faces of *Incognegro*'s polysemous protagonist emblematize the way in which the text as a whole tempers its psycho-historical and photo-archival engagements with concomitant investments in fantasy, genre, fictionality, and even ambivalence itself.

Because of its fluency in ambivalence, the comics form is uniquely able to represent processes of history and memory—a capacity that Derek McCulloch recognizes in his graphic novel *Stagger Lee* (2006), published with illustrator Shepherd Hendrix. Frederick Luis Aldama writes, "The comic book medium [is] particularly suited to alternating between a 'comparatively conventional fictional narrative and a pseudo-scholarly examination of the story's progression into folklore.'"[15] Comics have a critical facility, which both McCulloch and Spiegelman depend on for a ludic access to trauma. As John Berger reminds us, "drawing works to abolish the principle of disappearance, but it never can and instead it turns appearance and disappearance 'into a game,' [which] can never be won or wholly controlled, or adequately understood."[16] For African American artists, that limit of intelligibility also subtends the politics of appearance and invisibility. These key terms of embodiment are never simply political in the purest sense; they encompass ontology as well and thus hearken back to the horrors of the not-yet Americanization experience of the Middle Passage. One may recognize the felicitous aptitude drawing seems to possess for *speaking* slavery, yet the comics as a style and a form readily connote other violations as well. Not just a genre but a mode of antirealism, the cartoonal routinely produces visual traversals of the human, telling stories about rupture and conveying all manner of conceptual schisms—of temporality and ethics, justice and history—and it does so using primarily visual effects.

In *Laughing Fit to Kill*, Glenda R. Carpio acknowledges the ludic tendencies of the cartoonal in her interpretation of Kara Walker's Topsy silhouettes, writing that Walker "suspends direct references and clear connections" to elicit in viewers a "disconcerting effect"—"her images haunt the imagination because they are often, in various degrees, partly familiar, partly bizarre. Sometimes, too, . . . they are also disarmingly humorous."[17] Whimsical, macabre, and profuse, Walker's oeuvre has inspired various critical claims—for instance, Gwendolyn DuBois Shaw's argument that it "revokes the sexual power of the white male body" and Roger Winter's remark that its crisp cut-paper outline has "such amazing grace that we may miss at first glance her edgy narratives."[18]

Whatever their critical orientation, critics often push their own descriptive limits to convey the scope of Walker's inimitable cast of characters. For instance, Joan Copjec writes, "Hottentot harlots, sambos, mandigos [sic], Uncle Toms, churls, and scallywags of every sort engage nonchalantly in violent and licentious acts of parturition, sodomy, cannibalism, and coprophany, as well as in other acts we have no idea how to name."[19]

In some ways, the cartoonal's startling range reflects the wider field of reference that any drawing generates. But whether through the antihistorical ambivalence of the superheroic (*Incognegro*) or the materiality of the form (Walker), graphical translations of historical trauma tend to rely upon topoi of ambiguity to commemorate whatever mars remembrance, making a spectacle of mnemonic interference. The result reveals the comic form's aptitude for play. For Jones, ludic artworks offer an "irreverent and ironic treatment of slave history," striving "to encourage new conceptual horizons with which to reconceive and thus inhabit our post-slavery present—and such openings, it seems, might be the best we can hope for."

Huey Copeland (and many other critics) have adopted a psychoanalytical lexicon in their discussions of the psychic variables of African Americans' visual representations of slavery. Speaking of Walker, he writes, "by exploiting silhouette's defined edges and amorphous centers, she carves out images capable of physically and psychically unmooring both place and racial identity, everywhere confronting her audience."[20] Wanzo applies Anne Anlin Cheng's notion of racial melancholia to diagnose a similar psychic sensibility in Kyle Baker and Robert Morales's graphic novel *Truth: Red, White, and Black* (2003).[21] *Truth* rewrites the origins of Captain America to jibe with the grim historical verities of the Tuskegee experiments, imagining Marvel Comic's first supersoldier not as the white Steve Rogers but as the black Isaiah Bradley. Baker's melancholic drawings evince cartoonal vacillations of style and position themselves at a traumatic distance from the American Dream. Nevertheless, Wanzo notes that this "skilled illustrator [is also] capable of more complex renderings of black characters—perhaps most evident in his award winning graphic novel *Nat Turner*—[where] Baker chooses to visually tell the story by blending the cartoonish and the tragic."[22] Thus, if *Truth* and Walker's more grotesque silhouettes represent one end of an aesthetics of slave representation (call it a diasporic bathos, whereby the mimetic slippages endemic to hand-drawn or hand-cut artworks excuse departures from real and imaginary protocols of solemnity), Baker's *Nat Turner* and Tom Feelings's *Middle Passage: White Ships/Black Cargo* epitomize a diasporic pathos. That is, these works, as Wanzo writes, contain "more complex renderings of black characters."[23] Their style of remembrance favors a more realistic composition, focusing not on the "cartoonish and the tragic" but on the tragic—though sometimes *by way of* the cartoonish.

If we think of the cartoonal as opposing political and aesthetic regimes of realism, we might begin to notice that Feelings's surreal black slave figures, whose bodies stretch beyond the limited perspective of their placement in the transport ships, are surreal in the truest etymological sense of the term. That is, rather than exaggerating the perceptual real, they reflect far more profound though perceptually untraceable hyper-realities. Indeed, the illustrations in his chimerical picture book defy monolithic definitions and figurations. Starkly shaded and wispily plastic in form and expression, his cartoonal slaves literalize in style what they connote as subjects. They are ghosts and abstractions, signs and smears, marks and cuts, life and cargo all at once—and Feelings has composed them in just such a protean way (fig. 9.2). The medium of drawing becomes a cartoonal force of permissive and articulate distortion, which, like classic literary romances, benefits from a certain haziness. Unfortunately for those who insist on a sacral Middle Passage remembrance, haziness takes all comers. To be sure, one could as easily use the horrifying figures in Feelings's text to equate diaspora to trauma and thereby squelch anything that could be described as a race consciousness. Fear of the drawings' indiscriminate capacity for reference, of the possibilities of co-optation, presses Vivian Yenika-Agbaw to exhort that Feelings's imagery "demands that we rise and reclaim our rightful place in the world as heroes" and to declare that *The Middle Passage* is "a story of trauma from which we can learn tremendously about our racialized history."[24]

FIGURE 9.2. Illustration from *The Middle Passage: White Ships/Black Cargo* by Tom Feelings. From *The Middle Passage: White Ships/Black Cargo* by Tom Feelings, copyright © 1995 by Tom Feelings. Used by permission of Dial Books for Young Readers, an imprint of Penguin Young Readers Group, a division of Penguin Random House LLC.

For Walker, Feelings, Baker and their reader-viewers, the cartoonal slave becomes a catalyst for the aesthetic, racial, and historical condition that Daphne Brooks dubs "Afro-alienation," which takes "the traumas of self-fragmentation resulting from centuries of captivity and subjugation" as fuel for engaging in "counter-normative tactics" that "turn the horrific historical memory . . . into a critical form of dissonantly enlightened performance."[25] The cultural work of the visual text is both mnemonic and psycho-ethnic—that is, related to the tension between collective and private intensities that any use of the historic and imagined slave may conjure. Baker's audience may expect his text to provide the same crucial working through of diaspora found in the work of Feelings and Walker, and in truth his graphic and hypermasculine rendition of Nat Turner's uprising is just as transferential. As if to function better as a fantasy of return, *Nat Turner* repudiates words altogether, manifesting its antebellum and Middle Passage scenes via font styles and textual structures that mirror those of the nineteenth century. As Andrew Kunka has pointed out, "Baker's illustrated narrative contains almost no conventional verbal elements, such as word balloons or caption boxes, with the exception of a few sound effects." Even so, it brokers a robust intertextual dialogue with *The Confessions of Nat Turner*, edited by Thomas Gray in 1831, the year of Turner's Southampton, Virginia, uprising. With a style that "suspend[s] closure on the Nat Turner story and leave[s] in play multiple Nat Turners," Baker's text, as Kunka succinctly observes, "exploits the graphic narrative's potential to visualize historical trauma."[26] Whitted comments on the metonymic associations with books that reappear throughout the graphic novel, which "allow Baker to (re)assemble [. . . Turner] as an embodied visual text." Thus, Baker wrests Turner and his legacy from Gray's competing account with a ferocity so palpable that it imbues Gray's final confrontation with Turner. There, Baker characterizes Gray as not only stupefied in the presence of the slave's unaccountable intelligence (which has been written out of the historical record) but also temporarily deprived of literacy himself when his pen breaks under what appears to be the duress of a shocking recognition. As Whitted puts it, "the broken pen renders the page before Gray inadequate to the task of ventriloquizing the full picture of Turner's subjectivity." Ultimately, for her, the image of Gray's broken pen "open[s] up a gap that Baker hopes to close with his art—an image of Turner that begins where words fail."[27]

In one scene of *Nat Turner*, when a corpse is thrown from a slave ship, Baker's volatile text explicitly enacts the protocols of slave remembrance that Whitted notes at the end of the book, when a slave youth steals away with a copy of Turner's confessions. In that moment, according to Whitted, "Nat Turner reconstitutes the enslaved martyr's broken body in her hands (and in ours) as image/text."[28] As I argued in an earlier essay on the subject, such a reconstitution through iconicity is effected by the image of the discarded slave, which is strangely accompanied by another image of a dead slave in the form of what appears to be a speech balloon. Thrillingly, troublingly, the corpse seems to speak its own name via the balloon that identifies an otherwise anonymous body as the same dead slave seen a few pages earlier in the ship's hold. By attaching the identifying image to the slave body at the very moment it threatens to ossify into an iconic acme of historical detritus, Baker arranges this panel—as tragically flat and provocatively edged as any of Walker's silhouettes—to signify both retroactively (linking back to the previous image) and proleptically (linking forward to the African baby that will soon be thrown overboard by an angry but proud father). That iconic infanticide will reappear in a speech balloon of information that a preadolescent Turner is telling to young revolutionaries. All of this pictorial and visionary dialogue suggests that "history is best experienced not in academic, lexical, or verbal terms but in soteriological terms, as icons and idols; not as some past event reprised through narration, but as vision, immediate and materially present."[29]

While I still believe the soteriological to be a viable lens for seeing the wounds (and possible futures) of race history as Baker mediates them, this belief rests on one seemingly trivial and assuredly minute editorial change made between the mass market omnibus edition of *Nat Turner* (2008) and the earliest comic book edition (2005) and rarer Encore edition (2006). This fact has further focused my thoughts about the diacritical function of the speech balloon. Aurally pictorial and vocative, the panel permits its subject, the martyrological personification of the Middle Passage, to speak, particularly for those affective reading and viewing audiences seeking wellness through such a graphic representation of slavery, that mythical epicenter of distinctly American forms of unwellness. Baker's text visualizes radical forms of black historical community and in the process both resists and revisits the slave of representation that is expressible only in terms of invisibility. But there is much more to his depicted slave, a figure whose strange ability to speak though dead (twice dead, in fact) and brutally forgotten iconicizes the Middle Passage as a traumatic origin. It is fitting, then, that this origin be itself unwell—if unitary rather than multiplex compositions are the symptom of unwellness. For, as it turns out, there is not one version of this panel but two.

The differences are simple enough to observe; their implications, less so. The speech balloon I dissected in my earlier essay was from the more popular 2008 edition, where the tail of the balloon looks no different structurally from any other speech balloon meant to index the speaker of the balloon's content (fig. 9.3).[30] In the 2006 edition, however, this tail is clearly an arrow (fig. 9.4). It frames the inset image, setting it up to function not so much as a pictorial speech act but as an exploded view—a pictorial mode of amplification or elaboration that takes no lexical marker for its refashioned rhetorical basis. With an arrow, the image is less obviously in a state of communicative equivalence with all those other images in *Nat Turner*; that is, it is not necessarily a prior

FIGURE 9.3. Illustration from the 2008 edition of *Nat Turner* by Kyle Baker. *Nat Turner* written and illustrated by Kyle Baker. Copyright © 2008. Used by permission of Abrams Books, an imprint of Harry N. Abrams, Inc., New York. All rights reserved.

narrative scene becoming embedded visual speech. Creating a nested discourse of pictorial storytelling as a form of reading and prophetic retelling, this soteriological dialogue between picture stories in *Nat Turner* energizes the image-within-an-image of the cast-off slave and the baby deposited into the shark's maw, which is replayed as the iconic speech young Nat is shown delivering to horrified listeners—our doubles.

With an arrow, that dialogue is muffled. The arrow seems to specifically delimit what cannot be pointed to, a subject or site that is anything but simple to apprehend or locate. With a conventional speech balloon tail, however, the "pictorial aurality addresses more than the tragic moribundity of the Middle Passage"; it leads us to "dismiss any urge to explain away the tail of the speech balloon as exclusively designative, accepting it as a sign that forges an unlikely relationship between speech and death."[31] Yet in this context, there is nothing unlikely about unspeakability, which is another way of articulating the convergence of speech and death, or the nullifications to speech symbolized by death and its historical agents—the Middle Passage and slavery.

The arrow and the speech balloon tail invoke very different reception communities. Through aesthetic experience, re-memory, or performance, one strand of a large and varied tradition of African American reading practices seeks to produce catharsis and cathexis in relation to slavery. The endeavor often involves poetry and the funereal, as in Lucille Clifton's poem "at the cemetery, walnut grove plantation, south carolina, 1989," which seeks materially affective connections to ancestry at the skeletal level—where "your silence" is vitally transmuted into the "drumming in my bones" that demands address: "tell me your names."[32] The deceptively small distinction between the arrow of 2006 and the tail of 2008 spans more than the difference between showing and telling. It also measures the impossible space of address animating Clifton's poem, the space between the mute and univocal finality of death as mere designation and the possibility of *eidolopoeia*—death as enunciation. The arrow is diacritically mimetic, spatially contextual, and relationally indexical. The tail tells its bone-drumming names pictorially.

Both versions of this panel seek, as I have written elsewhere, "to obviate the representation of the slave body as so much erased and forgotten evidence," not only by repurposing conventional comics devices but by short-circuiting the logic that relies solely on verbal or pictorial authority. They emphasize a "deathly circular logic" that sustains the "discursive void that . . . bears the possibility of forging new relationships with history, memory, and performance."[33] Yet we require only an instant to contrast their differences: one balloon with an arrow, one with a tail; one with a black border, one without a border; one pinpointing the corpse's thigh, the other aimed at his groin.[34] The heavy border of the arrowed balloon transforms the image into more of a bubble than a balloon and thus quarantines it from its pictorial environs. Without the border, later printings lessen the stark spatial and narratological divisions between the detailed cameo portrait of the slave and its placement as an inset inside another image. The change disrupts the assumed cause-effect temporality of the emanation within the balloon and its source in the image of the corpse because the two images seem to arise together as one disjointed set of parts.

The collaging of the slave body that results from this interplay between panels and printings reveals the discursive circulation of diaspora as a morbidly recursive atomization. Yet there is a sequential, internal coherence to these images, especially in the second printing, in which the slave corpse as oceanic refuse and the slave corpse as repellent death's-head warning seem phantasmatically coterminous. Their weird epiphenomenal relationship is not possible in the arrow panel, which insistently maintains its pictorial divisions. That panel's bordered image functions as an inset or an incrustation; it is not part of the pictorial world it overlays. As opposed to the more unsettling simultaneity of the tail panel, it offers a message of elaboration and explanation to a world onto which it rhetorically intrudes. That incrustation may also be comprehended as a label, one asking viewers to imagine an equals sign between the falling corpse and the inset visual information.

In contrast, the tail balloon operates as quotation marks. It moves speech from a presumptively subjective interior into the world where it is transacted. That the tail pinpoints the corpse's groin only accentuates what the composition already suggests: the panel occasions a paradoxically generative emanation, the self-naming of an entity without a self.[35] The act is libidinal insofar as the slave body is always the locus of inoperable political and natural rights. The iconic slave is a body bereft of pleasures in the self or the possession of the self as more than a body of parts, and its negated intellection by fiat of de jure interdictions against literacy and education leaves only flesh. As such, it is infinitely fungible, symbolizing an extroversion of surplus and hence an obscene embodiment. In other words, if the slave body cannot be a body for itself, then it must be one for others. If we follow that slavocratic logic, we automatically notice an anxiety of desacralization at the very moment the text wavers over assigning transactional speech to its cartoonal slave. To be sure, as an icon of unspeakability, Baker's illustrated slave expresses its subalternity poignantly in the fact that we have two major versions of this panel to mull over. It is not the slave, after all, but Baker's text that wavers over this radical moment of speech; and this is one of the few places in the narrative (which elsewhere depicts the rebels' gruesome killing of cherubic white infants) that pulsates with the historical and traumatic stakes of proclaiming a sacrificial slave who speaks his own name in death. The fact that this slave cannot speak so boldly does little to diminish Baker's vision of diasporic trauma. We should be cautious, then, not to view the two panel variations as having a solely positive evolution, or *telos*. Instead of traducing their difference narratively, as a

FIGURE 9.4. Illustration from the 2005 and 2006 editions of *Nat Turner* by Kyle Baker. *Nat Turner* written and illustrated by Kyle Baker. Copyright © 2005 and 2006. Used by permission of Abrams Books, an imprint of Harry N. Abrams, Inc., New York. All rights reserved.

development from one iteration (the arrow) to a more effective one (the tail), we should read them as serial incident reports about the visual traffic of slave representation.[36] Neither is more apt or accurate; it is their plenary undecidability that matters.

With its flickering, funerary dialogue, *Nat Turner* bespeaks trauma's circularity in its refusal of what comics aficionados refer to as *closure:* the process by which reader-viewers rationalize the relationship between any two contiguous panels. Yet the term has other meanings—among them, the emotional closure of psychological discourse that seals hurt feelings and brings about resolution. From one angle, we might conclude that there is very little of either type of closure in any of *Nat Turner*'s editions. With its carefully wordless structure, antebellum stylistic imitations, and subordination of Gray's authorship, *the book's* dialogism frustrates easy correspondences between images and meanings. Moreover, the recurring circularity of the image utterances highlight the way in which trauma is encircled, as Lanzmann muses, with a "limit that cannot be transgressed."[37]

The limit here has to do with the addressability of the abused and subjectless figure of history—what it says and what seems to be said on its behalf. Here, we see the substantial thematic overlap between Baker's pictorial text and narrative returns to slavery told in traditional print forms. Openness to indeterminacy, narrative and epistemological circularity, destabilizations of identity: the critical epithets apply to Baker's text as easily as they do to Morrison's or Ishmael Reed's. What, finally, does the primarily visual text of the cartoonal slave do that traditional literary evocations do not? The answer returns us to the importance of those small diacritical marks that attach their enclosed visual content to the figure depicted in the panel. These marks are visual prepositions, no doubt intended to carry on the conceptual work of propinquity. That is the work, after all, that any pictorial sign does with greater force than any printed word or set of words; it maps the proximities of subjects in time and space. Thus, the issue here is rather more prepositional than pictorial, for the preposition is untransmissible in Baker's nearly exclusively pictorial medium. What matters is not *what* the falling slave means but rather *toward what* and *by whom*.

Prepositions provide us with a grammar of relationality. They require that the locational relations they name be orderly and legible, stipulations that the conditions and legacy of diaspora deny. Whether the text merely indicates the figure as the slave from before (a literal *prioriti*zation) or shows the figure making that announcement of its own accord and seeming to puncture the impossible limit of death in doing so, ambivalence about that limit is finally what remains stable in *Nat Turner*. We come to know Baker's text as we do the hero of *Incognegro* as neither fixed nor prepositionally determinative but as a series of variegated encounters. At stake in the superficially minute visual difference of arrow and tail are the terms of fact and fiction, history and imagination, which unravel in the traumatic slave's cartoonal reconfiguration.

The Collage of Dave the Potter

Dave the Potter was a slave in South Carolina who etched poetic couplets and signatures into the large storage vessels he made. On the heels of Leonard Todd's biography of the artist, *Carolina Clay*, white poet Laban Carrick Hill and black illustrator Bryan Collier published *Dave the Potter: Artist, Poet, Slave,* a children's picture book that later won the Coretta Scott King Award. In Baker's text, both the arrow and the tail place the slave at the epicenter of racial identity, whether denied or attributed; but Hill and Collier's book does different work. As Hill's poetry casts Dave as the catalyzing slave manqué who is really a Romantic artist par excellence, Collier represents the slave within a network of diasporic relations. Collier's implied matrices of connection stymie any facile perpetuation of the fantasy of a slave that is somehow bigger than slavery— a fantasy that Patterson, in chapter 1, would classify as behaviorist discourse. Such discourse underwrites numerous versions of the story of Dave "The Slave" Potter—the name that many twentieth-century curators and collectors have given to him.

Even though Dave's face is included in a number of the images in the book, the illustrated slave is not necessarily Collier's focal point. Rather, he focuses on the arboreal (filial, lineal) relations that the slave subtends. So networked, the slave is reducible neither to equivalence nor quotation. Nor is the slave's reconstitution based upon the metaphorics of the mirror and the lamp. In Collier's hands, slave representation is a matter of dispersal. It is comparable grammatically to the function of parenthesis: a capacity for inventorying nonspecific relationalities positions the slave as part of a larger diasporic set of experiences.

In an extraordinary collage of a tree, for example, Collier incorporates distinctly African American faces along the branches (fig. 9.5). By posing Dave's face against these others that fuse with the tree, the artist identifies Dave through his arboreal affiliation rather than through his signature or his pots, as in other illustrations. The result is a shift from the celebration of Dave's writing (mentioned in the poetry) and the wonder of his oddly namable slave status, the twin foci of many contemporary retellings, including nonfictional ones. Collier's de-emphasis of the priority of identity is, I argue, an implicit criticism. To expect the historic slave, no matter how skilled or privileged, to exhibit strains of selfhood consonant with dominant Euro-American conventions (as with ex-fugitives such as Douglass or William Wells Brown, who used their narratives in part to prove their successful transformation through bourgeois acquisition and assimilation) is to endorse a fundamentally Romantic conceptualization of history and identity. This conception is so culturally durable that it seeks to attach signatorial traces to an author who remains transcendently mediated in his creations and was himself an owned thing. In contrast to those Romantic conventions of personhood, Collier's images relentlessly reposition

FIGURE 9.5. Illustration from *Dave the Potter: Artist, Poet, Slave* by Laban Carrick Hill and Bryan Collier. From *Dave the Potter: Artist, Poet, Slave* by Laban Carrick Hill, with illustrations by Bryan Collier. Text copyright © 2010 by Laban Carrick Hill. Illustrations copyright © 2010 by Bryan Collier. Reprinted by permission of Little, Brown Books for Young Readers.

Dave amid the plantation's arboreal relations of diaspora and dispersal, while everywhere crediting labor as an alternate field of potentially collectivity.

The arboreal image appears in the middle of the book after a series of close-ups on Dave's hands molding clay on a wheel. One page features a foldout that materially performs a Romantic magic ascribed to Dave, who "pulled out the shape of a jar. Like a magician pulling a rabbit out of a hat"; another places Dave's face next to the "walls of the jar . . . like a robin's puffed breast."[38] But in the arboreal illustration, Dave's eyes are closed, and his open arms visually echo the tree behind him. On one level, this composition seems to reflect the descriptive grandiosity in Hill's accompanying lines:

> The jar grew so large
> Dave could no longer
> wrap his strong arms around it.
> If he climbed into the jar
> and curled into a ball,
> he would have been embraced.

Here, the *topos* of large things made small so that children can identify with them bodily aligns the slave with the child. Hill's emphasis on bodies and their dimensions within containment ingeniously connects contemporary children and historic slaves, but the gesture toward enclosure as an analogue for the child's presumed filial love clashes with the slave's assumed natal alienation and slavery's associational ties to spaces of enclosure such as the tight packing of slave ships—the murderous habitat of Baker's ur-slave of trauma. Beyond the pressures of literary identification (or the immeasurable corporate and industry protocols of children's bookselling), there is another conceptual pressure exerted in the poetry to yield the fatalistic and temporally fixed slave, who exists only in the grammatical past, unlike his jars, which continue to demand recognition. That this figure needs an embrace, despite his "strong arms," is a problem for the book's past tense to deal with—as long as we confine our understanding of "book" to mean only the text of *Dave the Potter*. For in Collier's visuals, a slightly different picture emerges, one that assigns an alternate valence to the tensions between words and image.

Take the image of Dave the Potter at his wheel, spinning like a "wheel of fortune" (fig. 9.6). Hill's metaphor denotes the aleatory forces of chance and providence familiar to diasporic narratives of souls flung adrift from home cultures or filial relations. Significantly, Dave has his back to us. He is absorbed in his work, the magnificent products of which line the background walls. If we look more deliberately at them, we might catch Collier using the artwork he has been commissioned to create in the vein of Dave the Potter's as the ground for a field of communication that potentially is not only beyond what has been "authorized" but opposed to it as well. We begin to detect the traces of such an under-language in the particulars that lie beyond the foreground, which induces a roaming, scrutinizing gaze.

Dave has his back turned to us, frustrating his conversion into spectacle. No unfettered gaze captures him; hence, the image may be seen as a form of anti-portraiture, which Huey Copeland, citing Lauri Firstenberg, ascribes to contemporary site-installation artists such as Lorna Simpson and Glenn Ligon:

> Although there is affect aplenty in these works, the primary impact is not of a replaying of the trauma of slavery, which would imply that repressed horrors have somehow been recovered or bubbled up from a temporal interregnum. Rather, in marking and metonymically conjuring the enslaved, these installations can be considered modes of "antiportraiture." . . . The artist's frequent deployment of turned-back figures, [Firstenberg] argues, is meant to refuse the gaze, to deny any presumed access to the sitter's personality, and to refute both the classificatory drives and emotional projections typically satisfied by photographic portraiture of black subjects.[39]

FIGURE 9.6. Illustration from *Dave the Potter: Artist, Poet, Slave* by Laban Carrick Hill and Bryan Collier. From *Dave the Potter: Artist, Poet, Slave* by Laban Carrick Hill, with illustrations by Bryan Collier. Text copyright © 2010 by Laban Carrick Hill. Illustrations copyright © 2010 by Bryan Collier. Reprinted by permission of Little, Brown Books for Young Readers.

Moreover, the pose recalls Gertrude Stein's ventriloquism of Alice B. Toklas at the dawn of cubist and collage aesthetics, in which she admits that she likes a painting best when she sits with her back to it. Such a position encourages viewers to look for its faces elsewhere. That gesture of refusal simultaneously indicates the extent to which wellness depends upon encounters with and the eventual acceptance of the unknowable. In Collier's illustration, we may soon descry collaged writing at the top left corner of the background wall, snatches of correspondence printed on ochre paper in a ruddy shade of period script. Upside down, cut up, and disconnected, the words of Collier's anti-portrait conjure one of Dave the Potter's most moving couplets, which he inscribed on a storage jar with two slab handles and dated August 16, 1857:

> I wonder where is all my relation
> friendship to all—and, every nation

As the detail emphasizes, the cubist poem takes shape through the subtractive processes of collage (fig. 9.7).

FIGURE 9.7. Detail of illustration from *Dave the Potter: Artist, Poet, Slave* by Laban Carrick Hill and Bryan Collier. From *Dave the Potter: Artist, Poet, Slave* by Laban Carrick Hill, with illustrations by Bryan Collier. Text copyright © 2010 by Laban Carrick Hill. Illustrations copyright © 2010 by Bryan Collier. Reprinted by permission of Little, Brown Books for Young Readers.

> . . . change
> Friends meeting
> Ne'er to
> Yet friend
> Token given that
> Them never forget

The resulting erasure poem expresses its textual lyricisms as an effect of occlusion. Because the shackles obstruct the words, violating their integrity with its own, we are unable to distinguish the coherence of the "original" and simultaneously experience that elision as poetry. Of course, repackaging Collier's words apart from their visual context is as artificial a rendition of them as every transcription of Dave's inscriptions are of his original writing. Extirpated from its ceramic ground, the graphological materiality of his scriptive incisions vanishes when transferred to the page or screen. Collier's imaged writing is just as inimical to fungibility. Indeed, there is no keystroke with which to make slave shackles the negative space of the hidden, upside-down poetry of Collier's antiportrait even when *transcribing* the most celebrated slave imaginable.

The mnemonic ("never forget") and the material ("token," the shackles) urgencies endemic to African American artists' slave representations permeate Collier's vision of Dave the Potter. As a mnemonic intertext, the illustrations at times vie with Hill's poetry to make assigning a face to the historical slave figure less of a priority than putting that face in relation to the historical slave figure. The affiliative matrices outlined in the illustrations support Tillet's observation that the antebellum past has become an ideal site for processing "discourses of citizenship," for the pages of the children's book dramatize a democratic mélange of views of Dave: there are Hill's, Collier's, and a third that belongs to neither but grows out of their sometimes uneasy partnership.[40] Moreover, Collier's preference for collage lends his illustration textures and edges, a physicality that corresponds with the emphasis on experiencing trauma as bodily rather than as "elusive and unknowable," which Woolfork finds in many African American revisitations of slavery.[41] In particular, his representation of shackles as part of the disoriented writing on the wall for his un-presented (un-presenced) slave figure theorizes the symbolization of slavery as an image-word tension. Shackles and chains transform from "horrific historical memory" into the same "dissonantly enlightened performance" Brooks ascribes to all incidents of Afro-alienation, which this illustration certainly exemplifies. The illustration suggests that, while words may slip the yoke of historical slavery's physical mortifications, they can never obliterate the unyielding artifactuality of the shackles.[42] In fact, the obdurate frontality of the shackles fashions the negative space necessary for us to create opportune distances that we as viewer-readers feel compelled to close—accomplishing the work of closure central to any comics viewing, in which proximate but disconnected units of potential meaning are resolved typically in narrative meaning.

But the resolution on offer here is not narratological. As with Copeland's description of the "unmooring" effects of Walker's silhouette, Collier's chain-haunted collage suspends from within his book's presumed cultural project to resurrect a salvific myth of the subaltern who not only speaks but shouts his own name.[43] Though tucked away in a corner of a single interventionary image, the shackles function in some ways like Baker's uncertain diacritical mark. Both hang fire in an authorial space of remembrance. Both momentarily disrupt the forward momentum of the narratives they provide and prevent by turns. Both acknowledge the limit that Lanzmann and others have observed with regard to the trauma of witnessing. They show narrative to be part of the problem, seeking as it does to eliminate gaps and disconnection in favor of formal unities of time, character, and event. Narrative presumes a story to tell or a name to announce, assign, or inherit; it proposes a face to view or pity, to love or abhor. All of these urgencies are storytelling's attendant fictions, vaunted as premises; and when applied to diasporic trauma they always return us to Dave the Potter's insurrectionary question of 1857 (this time, un-narrativized from its concessional final couplet): "I wonder where is all my relation"? In this formulation, social and historical contexts of place (of "where") move beyond the more narratival concerns of identity (the vexatious "who" of historical trauma). As we have seen, the word-image tensions in African American artists' recent visual narratives of slavery prove the endurance of that model of trauma that prioritizes a recurrent breaching of the symbolic order.

NOTES

1. Saidiya Hartman, *Lose Your Mother: A Journey along the Atlantic Slave Route* (New York: Farrar, Straus, and Giroux, 2007). 107.

2. Quoted in Margaret Olin, "Graven Images on Video? The Second Commandment and Jewish Identity," in *Complex Identities: Jewish Consciousness and Modern Art*, ed. Matthew Baigell and Milly Heyd (New Brunswick, N.J.: Rutgers University Press, 2000), 40.

3. Marianne Hirsch, "Mourning and Postmemory," in *Graphic Subjects: Critical Essays on Autobiography and Graphic Novels*, ed. Michael A. Chaney (Madison: University of Wisconsin Press, 2011), 21–22.

4. Andreas Huyssen, *Present Pasts: Urban Palimpsests and the Politics of Memory* (Stanford, Calif.: Stanford University Press, 2003), 128.

5. Salamishah Tillet, *Sites of Slavery: Citizenship and Racial Democracy in the Post–Civil Rights Imagination* (Durham, N.C.: Duke University Press, 2012), 14.

6. Lisa Woolfork, *Embodying American Slavery in Contemporary Culture* (Urbana: University of Illinois Press, 2009), 99. Woolfork argues that such a model of trauma "reinforces the mind-body split" and discovers a countervailing model in African American specular fictions that go back to the slave past, in which "bodily epistemology can be considered a form of black vernacular trauma theory" (6, 9). Though I approach the problematic of trauma, representation, and slavery differently, I share her implied mandate to read the comics' vernacularity as theoretical trauma work.

7. Frederick Douglass, *Narrative of the Life of Frederick Douglass, an American Slave, Written by Himself* (Boston: Anti-Slavery Office, 1845), 243.

8. Robert S. Levine, *Dislocating Race and Nation: Episodes in Nineteenth-Century American Literary Nationalism* (Chapel Hill: University of North Carolina Press, 2008), 12.

9. Dwight McBride, *Impossible Witnesses: Truth, Abolitionism, and Slave Testimony* (New York: New York University Press, 2002).

10. Qiana J. Whitted, "Of Slaves and Other Swamp Things: Black Southern History As Comic Book Horror," in *Comics and the U.S. South*, ed. Qiana J. Whitted and Brannon Costello (Jackson: University of Mississippi Press, 2012), 209.

11. Hortense Spillers writes: "Those African persons in Middle Passage were literally suspended in the 'oceanic.' . . . Removed from the indigenous land and culture, and not-yet 'American' either, these captive persons, without names that their captors would recognize, were in movement across the Atlantic, but they were also nowhere at all" ("Mama's Baby, Papa's Maybe: An American Grammar Book," *Diacritics* 17 [summer 1987]: 72).

12. Thierry Groensteen, "The Monstrator, the Recitant, and the Shadow of the Narrator," *European Comic Art* 3, no. 1 (2010): 7, 4.

13. Rebecca Wanzo, "Black Nationalism, Bunrako, and Beyond: Articulating Black Heroism through Cultural Fusion and Comics," in *Multicultural Comics: From Zap to Blue Beetle*, ed. Frederick Luis Aldama (Austin: University of Texas Press, 2010), 97.

14. Stephen Best, "On Failing to Make the Past Present," *Modern Language Quarterly* 73 (September 2012): 460.

15. Aldama, "Introduction," in *Multicultural Comics*, 13.

16. John Berger, *Berger on Drawing* (Aghabullogue, Ireland: Occasional Press, 2005), 112.

17. Glenda R. Carpio, *Laughing Fit to Kill: Black Humor in the Fictions of Slavery* (Oxford: Oxford University Press, 2008), 174.

18. Gwendolyn DuBois Shaw, *Seeing the Unspeakable: The Art of Kara Walker* (Durham, N.C.: Duke University Press, 2004), 83; Roger Winter, *On Drawing* (New York: Rowman and Littlefield, 2008), 27.

19. Joan Copjec, *Imagine There's No Woman: Ethics and Sublimation* (Cambridge, Mass.: MIT Press, 2002), 84.

20. Huey Copeland, *Bound to Appear: Art, Slavery, and the Site of Blackness in Multicultural America* (Chicago: University of Chicago Press, 2013), 197.

21. Anne Anlin Cheng, *The Melancholy of Race: Psychoanalysis, Assimilation and Hidden Grief* (New York: Oxford University Press, 2001), 3–30.

22. Rebecca Wanzo, "Wearing Hero-Face: Black Citizens and Melancholic Patriotism in *Truth: Red, White, and Black,*" *Journal of Popular Culture* 42, no. 2 (2009): 347, 345.

23. Another example of diasporic bathos worth mentioning is Stacey "Blackstar" Robinson and John Jennings's Black Kirby project, a ludic, Afro-futuristic reimagining of famed Marvel illustrator Jack Kirby's characterological universe. In one image, Malcolm X is wearing Magneto's helmet. When asked in a recent interview about the possible contradictions involved in a futurist project reaching back to Kirby's dominant vision of 1960s superheroism, Jennings responds in a way that one could easily imagine Kyle Baker agreeing with: "I think that Afrofuturism has always been about the idea of 'sankofa'; reaching back and getting the past and bringing it forward. The very idea of that is magical or sci-fi" (Julian Chambliss, "Black Kirby NOW: An Interview with John Jennings," *Pop Matters*, February 20, 2014, http://www.popmatters .com/feature/179294-black-kirby-now-an-interview-with-john-jennings/, accessed December 28, 2015).

24. Vivian Yenika-Agbaw, *Representing Africa in Children's Literature: Old and New Ways of Seeing* (London: Routledge, 2007), 87.

25. Daphne Brooks, *Bodies in Dissent: Spectacular Performances of Race and Freedom, 1850–1910* (Durham, N.C.: Duke University Press, 2006), 5.

26. Andrew Kunka, "Intertextuality and the Historical Graphic Narrative: Kyle Baker's *Nat Turner* and the Styron Controversy," *College Literature* 38, no. 3 (2011): 170, 187, 170.

27. Qiana J. Whitted, "'And the Negro Thinks in Hieroglyphics': Comics, Visual Metonymy, and the Spectacle of Blackness," *Journal of Graphic Novels and Comics* 5, no. 1 (2014): 81, 89.

28. Ibid., 92.

29. Michael A. Chaney, "Slave Memory without Words in Kyle Baker's *Nat Turner,*" *Callaloo* 36, no. 2 (2013): 289.

30. According to the noted art historian David Carrier, the speech balloon is productive of the comics' "word/image binary opposition"; no speech balloon is "entirely within the picture space nor outside it." As with treatments of phylactery in classical paintings, interpretations of depicted speech that want to pose the written text embedded within a painted one as a pure expression of the lexical fall prey to the duplicitous ubiquity of the visual. Even more complicated because of their intrinsically hybrid status, speech balloons cannot wholly be seen as occupying depictive space. As Carrier says, "they have no position in space" (30). Baker's vacillation between

arrow and tail may be seen as a hectic performance of the always unsettled territory of speech within comics more generally (*The Aesthetics of Comics* [University Park: Pennsylvania State University Press, 2000], 29, 30).

31. Chaney, "Slave Memory," 291.

32. Lucille Clifton, "at the cemetery, walnut grove plantation, south carolina, 1989," in *Quilting: Poems, 1987–1990* (Rochester, N.Y.: BOA Editions, 1990), 11.

33. Ibid., 292.

34. Thought of only as a visual difference, the arrow-tail divide is minute, just a mark, merely a diacritical line. Such reductivism only intensifies the formal self-reflexivity of their serial totality—that is, as drawings more concerned with drawing than we might at first surmise. As Deanna Petherbridge avers, the line is one of western art's most notorious artificers, particularly in light of its naturalization among those who would praise representational drawing for its resemblances to perceivable phenomena: "Line itself does *not* exist in the observable world. Line is a representational convention." *Nat Turner*'s wavering over the arrow and tail demonstrates a restless dissatisfaction with the representational conventions governing the slave's iconic nonexistence (*The Primacy of Drawing: Histories and Theories of Practice* [New Haven, Conn.: Yale University Press, 2010], 90).

35. My use of the word *emanation* is a nod to Hillary Chute, who pointed me to Mort Walker's use of *emanata* to describe the perplexing physics by which comics speech balloons do and do not occupy visual space within the panels they acoustically (and sometimes affectively) mediate. See Mort Walker, *The Lexicon of Comicana* (Bloomington, Ind.: Comicana Books, 1980).

36. While distinguishing between fine art drawing and mechanical illustration, Patrick Maynard bemoans the fallacious practice of dismissing constructional drawings that may have been an essential part of the process of art making despite being absent in the final product. Along the way, he offers us what may be the key to understanding Baker's diacritical vacillation: "we can better understand what some modern artists are doing in otherwise puzzling productions, if we see them as 'thematizing' constructional drawing activities" (*Drawing Distinctions: The Varieties of Graphic Expression* [Ithaca, N.Y.: Cornell University Press, 2002], 10).

37. Quoted in Olin, "Graven Images on Video?," 40.

38. Laban Carrick Hill and Bryan Collier, *Dave the Potter: Artist, Poet, Slave* (New York: Little, Brown, 2010). The book is unpaginated, so all quoted material will henceforth appear without citation.

39. Copeland, *Bound to Appear*, 9.

40. Tillet, *Sites of Slavery*, 14.

41. Woolfork, *Embodying American Slavery*, 99.

42. Brooks, *Bodies in Dissent*, 5.

43. Copeland, *Bound to Appear*, 197.

10

Trauma and the Historical Turn in Black Literary Discourse

AIDA LEVY-HUSSEN

So what does History look like if it can neither remember well enough nor move on?[1]

–Anne Anlin Cheng

How does one reconceptualize, through the critical lens of trauma theory, recent impassioned debates about the psychological, moral, and political value of cultivating affective ties to the African American slave past? Prominently staged in twenty-first-century black literary discourse, these debates turn on a presumed dichotomy: that imaginative reanimations of slavery, epitomized by the genre of the contemporary narrative of slavery, will be redemptive or nefarious. Either they will provide an opportunity for articulating and working through our relationship to a traumatic past, or they will tether us to an irreparable history of injury and grievance, inhibiting black thriving in the present. Forestalling both conclusions, I want to shift critical attention from the question of what we *should* do (remember, forget) to how and why writers, readers, and critics come to long for memory or forgetting in the first place. What kinds of desire and what unconscious prohibitions prefigure literary and critical narratives about the dangers or rewards of intergenerational racial memory? What *psychic forms* inhabit and give shape to the *rhetorical forms* of the fantasy of historical return and its inverse, the fantasy of an unencumbered present?

Trauma theory is instructive for readings of the contemporary narrative of slavery and its surrounding criticism, not only for the obvious reason that slavery was traumatic but because it joins the psychic structure of trauma to an epistemological critique of conventional modes of historical representation. By describing historical catastrophe's disorienting effects on how we give and receive accounts of the past, it offers unique insight into the psychic forces that compel the structure and style of the late modern African Americanist discourse on slavery. The ostensibly incompatible critical fantasies of memory and forgetting are in fact underwritten by a shared psychic grammar of trauma. Yet the concept of trauma implicitly undermines the very fantasies of teleological redemption or severance that it produces. Indeed, what trauma theory reveals in black historical fiction is nothing so certain as a strategy for healing, be it through the rupture or restoration of historical continuity. Its revelation is more modest and more intricate, consisting in the structure and mechanisms of a contemporary psychic predicament marked by insufficient yet ineradicable ties to historical devastation. Tracing trauma theory's routes through today's black literary discourse may help us to construct a more comprehensive, textured, and self-reflexive portrait of African American literary studies' historical turn, one that displaces this book's inaugural question, "Do you want to be well?," with a more fundamental question about how injury prefigures the contours of desire.

Contemporary humanistic trauma theorists widely agree that the fundamental effect of trauma is the profound disruption of the "narrative unity of life."[2] In general terms, their conceptualization of what constitutes trauma and the structure of its disruption goes like this: Human life is made intelligible and thus meaningful through temporally organized, cohesive stories that we tell about ourselves and, through this process, master. A person's sense of self and of her place in history and the world is determined in large part by her grasp of her story—the degree to which she achieves a sense of narrative continuity in and authority over her life. Traumatic events interrupt the stories we tell about history and identity by introducing cognitively inassimilable circumstances of grand-scale horror or loss. Confronted by the unimaginable within the domain of the real, the traumatized subject becomes unable to wield history in the service of self-story; she can no longer tell a coherent story about her life because the crisis event renders her life incoherent to her. Thus, as opposed to the normative pattern in which people appropriate and arrange historical facts to tell their stories, the trauma victim becomes, in Cathy Caruth's phrase, "possessed by history," haunted and claimed by a past that breaks from existing narratives of self and moreover appears to foreclose on the terms of conventional narrativity, such as chronology, self-consistency, and causality.[3]

Extrapolating from this model of individual psychopathology, a number of contemporary cultural theorists of trauma have proposed that the psychic effects of certain watershed crises in history eclipse the scale of the individual, ensnaring and warping modern consciousness itself.[4] Consequently, they argue, theories of trauma become the interpretive key to an irrevocably altered world that eludes existing approaches to self-knowledge. As Shoshana Felman and Dori Laub put it, in the wake of historical crises, "our cultural frames of reference and our preexisting categories which delimit and determine our perception of reality have failed . . . both to contain, and to account for, the scale of what has happened in . . . history."[5] In other words, at stake for today's trauma theorists is an understanding not only of psychic suffering but of epistemology itself. Their invocations of trauma include radical critiques of traditional methods of historiographical study and the disciplinary ideal of dispassionate objectivism as well as a moralizing call for new approaches to knowledge that grapple with the psychic devastation through which modern consciousness is forged.[6] Propelling a powerful cross-disciplinary phenomenon that Andreas Huyssen describes as a "turn against history" under an "avalanche of memory discourses," this prominent strain of trauma theory wishes to reveal a reality made incomprehensible by the unending fact of trauma and a modern condition that speaks in a "voicelessness no voice can represent."[7]

Collectively known for its immersive explorations of what Toni Morrison has called the "unwritten interior life" of the slave, the ever-proliferating archive of contemporary narratives of slavery often performs a companionate labor to trauma theory's critique of conservative historiographical methods.[8] As Ashraf H. A. Rushdy has famously shown, African American literature's historical turn has been preceded and inspired by a revolution in accepted historiographical practices in which a "second wave of New Left [historians]" displaced purportedly objectivist perspectives on the slave past, exposing the partiality of documentary evidence left by the planter class and lending scholarly authorization to the retrieved testimonies of slaves and abolitionists.[9] This epistemological reorientation has made the subject of the slave past speakable in different ways and has catalyzed a broader cultural interest in historical narratives that were once dismissed as incredible, immaterial, or otherwise unrepresentable. Alongside and following from a proliferating revisionist historiography, literary writers in growing numbers have expressed an urgent desire to open the traumatic slave past to moral, political, and psychic excavation.

Furthermore, the contemporary narrative of slavery keeps faith with trauma theory in a way that historiography, as it is generally understood, cannot because its counter-narrative of the traumatic past is characteristically conveyed through personal, interiorized, and affectively saturated accounts of unredeemed historical injury. (There are, of course, noteworthy exceptions, although even comedic novels about slavery are not necessarily exempt.) "I was trying to get people to *feel slavery*," Octavia Butler explains when asked about her approach to history in her 1979 novel *Kindred*.[10] Her implication is that feeling is an indispensable component of historical knowledge, particularly when traumatic events are involved, and that writers of contemporary narratives of slavery are charged with *producing feeling through narrative*. In such statements, we find a second way in which the contemporary narrative of slavery is akin to trauma theory: they share an elemental curiosity about how trauma disrupts and restructures narrative itself, locating in traumatic narrativity a mode of encountering history differently.

Nearly thirty years after its publication, Morrison's *Beloved* remains the best-known and best-selling example of an African American novel that takes trauma as its structural model. Much as humanistic trauma theorists have conceptualized trauma as an extraordinary and enduring disruption to the narrative unity of life, *Beloved* manifests what Roger Luckhurst names a "[disorder] of emplotment"; the novel "[mimics] the traumatic effect" through "formal [disturbances]" and "narrative [ruptures]."[11]

A brief review of Morrison's plot illustrates this concept. Although the premise from which the book derives is the historical figure's, Margaret Garner's, notorious act of infanticide in the panic of being pursued under the Fugitive Slave Law of 1850, the reader does not encounter this tragedy in real time. Rather, and as is characteristic of most accounts of post-traumatic memory, the reader realizes the catastrophe belatedly, partially, and in fragments. We encounter the protagonist, Sethe (whose past is modeled on Garner's) in 1873, seventeen years after she fled a Kentucky plantation, slit her daughter's throat, and bartered sex for a tombstone engraved with the word *Beloved*. Her experience of the present, metaphorized as the home she shares with her surviving daughter, Denver, is haunted first by an invisible, restless spirit and later by that spirit made flesh. In her human form, the ghost announces her claim to Sethe's past when she gives her name as Beloved.

Insatiable, compulsive, and bound to a history of devastation that defies comprehension, Beloved embodies Sethe's traumatic memory. The ghost's characterological core, and the core of Sethe's trauma, consists in the failure of maternal love against the assaults of slavery. Unable to assimilate this failure into a plausible narrative logic or meaning, Beloved obsessively mines Sethe's memory for a maternal response to a wish that has already been foreclosed—her wish for the saving grace of "enough" love. "She left me behind. By myself," Beloved's complaint goes. "She is the one I need." Or again, "She doesn't love me like I love her. I don't love nobody but her."[12]

Much as trauma is said to operate through "*possession* of the one who experiences it," Beloved threatens to consume Sethe, to overwhelm her day-to-day life with impossible, too-late demands to be remembered, loved, and saved in time.[13] Through the incessant force of the ghost's grievance, Sethe herself becomes obsessed with the task of satiating Beloved. The mother's psychic life comes to mirror Beloved's singularity of focus, excluding the social and the possibility of a livable present as an act of fidelity to a past that refuses to be forsaken. "There is no world outside my door," Sethe claims, as Beloved's hold on her approaches the absolute. "I only need to know one thing. How bad is the scar?"[14]

"The scar" at once represents the daughter's fatal wound and the aporetic core of maternal memory that that wound produces. Sethe cannot escape the gravitational pull of the horrific past, but neither can her memory articulate or fully confront the original traumatic event. Instead, she "[circles] the subject," "round and round, never changing direction."[15] The core of the "circle" that Sethe—and the text—asymptotically approach is, in Ann Snitow's words, "the vacuum, the absence" of "a gap in history, a blank in consciousness."[16] Felman's description of post-traumatic consciousness unintentionally elaborates on Snitow's characterization of Sethe's, and the text's predicament, for Felman writes of the event of trauma as "a missed encounter with reality, an encounter whose elusiveness cannot be owned and yet whose impact can no longer be erased, in taking hold of the [witness's] life which will henceforth, unwittingly, compulsively strive toward an impossible completion of the missed experience."[17] This is *Beloved*'s traumatic form: a propulsive pattern of fear and longing, re-experiencing but *never* remembering, that takes shape around the painful absence of memory.

In his 2012 essay, "On Failing to Make the Past Present," Stephen Best describes *Beloved* as the harbinger and the exemplar of contemporary African American studies' backward gaze. In his view, Morrison's powerful and acclaimed representation of a voracious, traumatic past demanding redress "[shaped] the way a generation of scholars conceived of its ethical relationship to the past." He argues that *Beloved* ushered in an era of dubious literary historicism, marked by the insatiable moralizing demand that we remember slavery. It reified a narrative of racial history as collective and continuous; presented slavery as the primary and overdetermining cause of the African American present; and elevated the evidentiary claims of affect by articulating an imperative that contemporary readers *feel*, with visceral immediacy, the impact of historical loss. Against this critical orientation, he wonders, "Why has the slave past had such enormous weight for an entire generation of thinkers? Why must we predicate having an ethical relation to the past on an assumed continuity between that past and our present and on the implicit consequence that to study that past is somehow to intervene in it? . . . And if we take slavery's dispossessions to live on into the twenty-first century, divesting history of movement and change, then what form can effective political agency take?"[18]

Best is not alone in identifying Morrison as the foremost purveyor of a fantasy in which the slave past refuses to release the present from its psychic grasp. In chapter 2, Douglas A. Jones Jr. articulates a similar view when he steps back from a "Morrisonian poetics" whose central aim is to "evince" for a modern public "the deepest truth of black/slave life." Similarly, Walter Benn Michaels derides *Beloved*'s "conversion of history into memory" as a dangerous sleight of hand, while Kenneth Warren enlists Michaels's case against *Beloved* to propel his own contention that African American literary studies' historical turn is a product of false consciousness that displaces and obscures the increasingly tenuous affiliative bonds of blackness.[19]

Despite significant differences among these thinkers, they tend in aggregate to affirm Best's qualified rehabilitation of one of black studies' most taboo terms, *post-racial*, "not as neoliberals tend to celebrate this condition (as a mark of the end of racism) but in the more analytically purposeful sense that the logic of racial slavery does not fully describe or capture racial injustice in the present. The past is here to be celebrated as a falling away—slavery to be appreciated in the failure to make its racial legacy present."[20] Together, these critics opine that the dominant literary and critical modes for engaging with the slave past rely on and reproduce a dangerous false consciousness by which the intergenerational past appears to the contemporary reader or critic as present, accessible, and ours. Rather, they argue that the slave past is radically inaccessible to contemporary consciousness, reject what Jones calls "narratives of historical continuity and temporal compression," and posit that the persistent popularity of black memory studies represents the field's misguided anachronism. "Simply put, the world *has* changed; thus, the conditions for black political belonging and the attendant terms of critical inquiry and imaginative narration, if they are to be efficacious, must change along with it."

Scholars writing against the historical turn are correct to cast their position as a minority view, although their claims, often articulated with polemical flair, have exerted a disproportionate impact on the field. (Warren in particular has summoned an extraordinarily prolific response.) The impressive reach of African American literary studies' historical turn is evident in any bibliography of post–civil rights fiction and criticism, and the present book is no exception. The authors represented here overwhelmingly endorse the study of historical memory as essential and central to contemporary African Americanist scholarship. For example, Régine Michelle Jean-Charles's chapter pushes back against the growing discourse on the value of forgetting the past to explore "what is lost by *not* reanimating the slave past." GerShun Avilez builds his argument on the assumption that "the experience of black embodiment can still be understood through [the] lens [of social death]," a theoretical construct that first emerged to describe black life under slavery. Soyica Diggs Colbert charts Spike Lee's filmic representation of a "new millennial blackness," whose relationship to slavery is not severed but repressed.

If the allegation against such projects, in brief, is that they are debilitated by false hope and "wounded attachments," then the opposing claim is that the unresolved, traumatic memory of enslavement persists as the insuppressible, haunting core of the African American cultural imagination.[21] Consequently, the proliferation of contemporary narratives of slavery, and of the African Americanist discourse on history and memory more generally, expresses an authentic orientation toward historical trauma that appears, for the present, to be a site of unresolved suffering and an object of reparative desire. To borrow Hortense Spillers's elegant phrase, black studies' historical turn is enlivened by the impossible moral task of returning to "the 'beginning,' which is really a rupture."[22] Best and Jones regard this constitutive compulsion to sit with the affective possibilities and remainders of the past as a kind of melancholia, while Margo Natalie Crawford, in chapter 4, proposes a radical redefinition of mourning and melancholia in light of the protracted course of African American history.

Yet one can make a case for trauma as the discourse's foundational psychic idiom. Mimicking trauma's peculiar negotiation of memory and forgetting, I walk a line between competing claims for and against the pursuit of memory in black literary studies. On the one hand, I readily accept Best's most basic post-racial premise, that we in the present are radically alienated from an irretrievable history of slavery's traumas. I share with him and others a substantive measure of incredulity about certain mystical strains of criticism, which hold that the "singular desire" of enslaved ancestors is to pierce and "author" contemporary lives.[23] I think critics are right to warn against the ethical and methodological pitfalls of transhistorical *over*identification with the enslaved, as Warren does when he cautions us against belief in "a dynamic relation between past and present that almost obliterates history, thereby casting the present-day historian in the role of potential hero, or even freedom fighter, on behalf of a past that almost magically becomes our contemporary in terms of what it needs or demands from us."[24] In my view, this line of critique upholds the theoretical relevance of trauma when it issues claims of radical difference from the past because trauma itself is constituted through an obsessive belatedness—what Felman calls the "missed encounter," and what Morrison describes as "circling the subject."[25] In contrast, scholarship on historical memory more frequently violates the traumatic paradigm in its understandable, if ultimately unpersuasive, eagerness to consummate reparative desire.

Here is where I part ways with the post-racial skeptics. From their perspective, African American literature's historical turn is a dubious academic and artistic trend because it imagines and prescribes the impossible: the contemporary memory of the slave past. But I am not convinced that the historical turn necessarily or universally conceives of historical memory as attainable. Although I am disinclined to put faith in literature's or criticism's capacity to facilitate a successful, reparative, historical return, I am at least as wary of the idea that historical desire has *no* place in black literary studies (to say nothing of my suspicion about a criticism that takes the feasibility of a literary plot as a measure of its value). Why does criticism of the historical turn so often issue its critique in the form of prohibition—"We have to put the past behind us"; we must admit that "the recognition of inequality makes the history of that inequality irrelevant"; we should "[replace] holding with letting go, clutching with disavowal"?[26] Why must the slave past, and the desire to clutch or hold it, be withheld from analysis, recanted, forsworn, or, in the mildest versions of this line of criticism, ironized? Aggregating this critical gesture under the name of *prohibitive reading*, I want to think about how trauma theory may help us, first, to rethink the problem of historical desire *in its painful impossibility* and, second, to contextualize prohibitive reading's extreme aversion to the historical turn.

So let us return to *Beloved*. From the perspective of prohibitive reading, the novel exemplifies black studies' historical turn insofar as it reifies and idealizes the notion of a past that does not end, is directly and eternally available to us, and beckons with demands for repair or redress. By contrast, prohibitive reading hinges on two assertions: first, that it is impossible to transmit memory, especially across intergenerational expanses; and, second, that the *claim* of intergenerationally transmitted memory is an insidious vehicle for the eternal reproduction of an unappeased political identity. According to Michaels, "if *Beloved*'s characters," enmeshed as they are in the real-time suffering of slavery and its aftermath, "want to forget something that happened to them, its readers—'black people,' 'white people,' Morrison herself—are supposed to remember something that didn't happen to them." Slavery, in this view, is "the thing they are supposed to remember," and the *idea* that its ancient, unappeased horror never dies is the force that consolidates black political identity as such.[27] In contrast, Michaels and Warren regard modern socioeconomic disparity as the dominant and reliable "real" of American life (though it is worth noting that neither Best nor Jones articulates a desire to replace race with class in cultural discourse).

Yet *Beloved* is a curious vehicle on which to launch prohibitive reading's condemnation of contemporary historical desire: its narrative action confines itself to the ante- and postbellum periods; and although its youngest character, Denver, never experiences enslavement first hand, she is born before Emancipation and under the threat of the Fugitive Slave Law. Therefore, the intergenerational and interpersonal transmissions of memory that Morrison stages are contained on a compact temporal stage. Strictly speaking, *Beloved* presents no technology for inserting the present into the past, as does, for example, Butler's *Kindred*, in which time travel recasts antebellum Maryland through the colonizing gaze of the late twentieth century. Why, then, *Beloved*? It seems that what proponents of prohibitive reading find objectionable, presentist, and uniquely illustrated in *Beloved* is the structure of memory through which Sethe describes her own and Denver's relationship to her past.

In a well-known scene, Morrison coins the term *rememory* to describe the properties of traumatic memories that appear to become permanent and fixed. If normative memory consists of a selective chain of recalled events, then traumatic rememory is beyond the scope of cognition. It is solid, inassimilable, unchanging, and unchangeable: "a picture floating around out there outside my head. I mean, even if I don't think it, even if I dies, the picture of what I did, or knew, or saw is still out there. Right in the place where it happened."

Furthermore, rememory is voraciously redundant and feared to be transmissible. Thus, Sethe tells Denver, "if you go there and stand in the place where it was, it will happen again; it will be there waiting for you."[28]

Presumably, this promise of eternal repetition is the curse that prohibitive reading wishes to dispel. For Best, the "historical ethics that underwrite 'rememory'" and the attendant, familiar "formation of history as memory" consist in Sethe's idea that "the slave past is 'never going away.'"[29] Similarly, for Michaels, the possibility that "Denver might bump into Sethe's rememory" is tantamount to the threat that—because "nothing ever dies"—contemporary blacks must live in fear of their enslaved ancestors' recurring pasts, which persist in their damning and unchanging exactitude.[30]

Yet as I read the novel, Morrison both depicts the trauma of enslavement with astonishing force *and* persistently undercuts the trauma victim's experiential impression of undifferentiated, intergenerationally transmissible, eternal suffering. Hence, there is dissonance between Sethe's rememory and Denver's life, which is colored by trauma but not mimetically so. What Denver feels most powerfully is in fact her *exclusion* from the slave past and its traumatic memory. For despite Sethe's fears, Denver cannot "bump into" her mother's rememory. Even when Sethe's past materializes in the form of Beloved, the ghost—though visible to Denver and an object of her desire—is interested only in Sethe: "The two of them cut Denver out of [their] games," writes Morrison. "[Denver] came to realize that her presence in that house had no influence on what either woman did. She kept them alive and they ignored her."[31] In short, the intergenerational transmission of trauma consists not in the literal return to an unchanging site of brutality but in the shadow of a parental past that colors the early development of the child's fears, desires, and identifications.

In fact, the novel's closest proxy for the contemporary reader is not Sethe, as prohibitive reading fears, but Denver, the surviving daughter. Born in the fugitive space of Sethe's northward escape from slavery and literally nursed on the blood of her sacrificed sister, Denver is profoundly marked by a past that she nevertheless cannot remember. Morrison characterizes her as "[stepping] into [a] told story" of dehumanization, fear, and murder; and she is haunted by "monstrous and unmanageable dreams about Sethe" that ultimately induce her own symptomatic deafness. At the same time, Denver is not a creature of the past. Instead, she despises the past, rejecting all stories that do not or cannot make a bridge to her future. "The present alone interested Denver," Morrison writes. "Denver hated the stories her mother told that did not concern herself." The past is a force that excludes Denver not only because she did not experience it but because she cannot feel it. "Closed off from the hurt of the hurt world," her affect and identifications are produced by a "[hungry] imagination" and a "loneliness" that "wore her out."[32]

Thus, *Beloved* self-consciously pairs the forceful desire for reparative return with the painful impossibility of that drive. Its past and present are not connected by a direct pipeline of timeless, affective immediacy, as proponents of prohibitive reading commonly suggest, but by a network of complex, non-mimetic psychic inheritances that closely approximate what trauma theorists have come to call, in the language of Marianne Hirsch, "postmemory." A sub-category of post-traumatic consciousness meant to describe the experientially unique trauma of the second generation (and often subsequent ones), post-memory is "defined through an identification with the victim or witness of trauma, *modulated by the unbridgeable distance that separates the participant from the one born after*."[33] It is, in other words, as much a product of the succeeding generations' absence of memory as it is a product of the powerful narratives of unmaking that preexist and interpellate the postmemorial subject. If, as prohibitive reading suggests, Sethe and Denver model the intergenerational transmission of trauma that is meant to extend further, to implicate the contemporary reader, then that model of transmission is far less fixed, transparent, or predictable than any of them acknowledge. For what Morrison and the concept of postmemory describe is not the immutable endurance of post-traumatic identity—or, as Michaels calls it, "the guarantee of identity" that trauma forges—but the ever-mutating force of history as it produces new subjects who are both constrained by and straining against the ascribed terms of their legibility.[34]

Let us consider prohibitive reading's criticism of *Beloved* from another angle. If one complaint is that the novel ensnares the present in the irredeemable suffering of the past, then another is that it enacts and encourages the manufacture of, in Jones's words, "imprecise if not wooly historiographies." Indeed, for each of the critics with whom this chapter engages, the repudiation of African American studies' historical turn is in some measure coextensive with a defense of conventional historiography. Best, for instance, sets up his argument against the development and sway of a contemporary historiography that is "recursive and generally athwart the established practice of writing history as a rational, developmental narrative."[35] Michaels is still more aggressive, asserting that, "where the conventional historian may be happy to settle for knowledge, Morrison . . . [is] more interested in experiencing the past (if only by talking to it) than [she is] in having true beliefs about it."[36] Warren specifies that what is at stake in the historical turn is the intellectual sanctity of a bounded and finite history that we can calendrically measure and record. Thus, he despairs that within contemporary African Americanist discourse "discrete periodizations" have been rendered "beside the point" and, more, have acquired a "taint of injustice." Affective attachments to the past may persist, the adherents of prohibitive reading seem to say, but they are beyond the rightful domain of academics or politics. They cloud and distort knowledge, obscuring what Warren perceives as the self-evident truth that, in order "to understand both past and present, we have to put the past behind us."[37]

But perhaps the truth of history is not so simple. If, as prohibitive reading would have it, "wounded attachments" to an injurious past form the psycho-affective scaffolding for black studies' historical turn, then what kinds of attachments structure the ostensibly opposite desires for a clearly demarcated, coherent, and self-separate past? Why should we consider it truer to read history as a containable object of knowledge than as an animating force that consists in *both* the events of the past and the desires—affective, narrative, political—that those events produce? My sense is that, for prohibitive reading, *Beloved* becomes an imprecise avatar for identity politics and its poisonous resuscitation of the past in large part because of a zealous, countervailing desire to secure the past as a fixed and detached object of study. *Beloved* in particular, and the ideas of trauma and postmemory more generally, provokes foundational anxieties of conventional knowledge projects that work in part through colonizing and taxonomizing time. I do not mean to diminish the value of periodization or "established [practices] of writing history" as modes of knowing and encountering the past.[38] Even as it has come radically into question, the idea of a future-oriented, progressive chronology certainly gets at an enduring and compelling sense of historical truth. But I am interested, too, in *how* and with what kinds of anxieties, desires, admissions, and foreclosures, conservative, objectivist historiographies assert their claims to truth.

Whereas *Beloved* depicts the transmission of traumatic memory within the temporal range of legal slavery and its immediate aftermath, David Bradley's novel *The Chaneysville Incident* extends its account of slavery's effects into the present. The novel was published in 1981, and its narrative present is 1979. Bradley's title refers to a fictional sequence of resonant, catastrophic events, for the titular incident is not an isolated act but an intergenerational series of traumatic historical events that the protagonist, John Washington, discovers to be his inheritance.

Recalling Sethe's idea of the spatial-temporal fixity of rememory, the setting, Chaneysville, Pennsylvania, is a site of repeated racial trauma that exceeds normative ideas of linear chronology. Here, John's father, Moses Washington, commits suicide in a cryptic reenactment of his grandfather's (John's great-grandfather's) death. Moses's ritualized suicide memorializes the tragic heroism of his forebear, a former slave turned liberator shot in the act of guiding smuggled slaves to freedom, but it does so by forsaking futurity for the moral righteousness of memory. What Moses leaves for his son is not a pathway to the future but a mysterious collection of clues leading back to the ghostly and aporetic origins of the Washington patrilineage. Willing his massive archive of family history to John, Moses dictates the following instructions: "The only restriction is that you [John] are not permitted to sell, bequeath, or otherwise divest yourself of their ownership until you have examined all volumes, including personal memoirs."[39]

But in spite of his portentous family history full of unassimilated feelings, John is a professional historian of Revolutionary America who adheres to a conservative, documentary model of historiography; nearly all of *Chaneysville*'s readers have remarked on its protagonist's obsessive habit of collecting and organizing facts in his attempt to capture a truth that inheres in the most basic articulation of what happened. Psychic experience and affective context are, for him, at best an unwelcome diversion. "There's no imagination in [historiography]," he tells his girlfriend, Judith. "You can't create facts." Here is how John describes his method:

> I went to work with my fountain pen and my india ink and my cards, going through the documents and leeching out single events, tearing them away from the other events that surrounded them, recording them in bare, simple, declarative form on the white lined cards, in a hand as precise and unemotional as I could make it. I dated each one carefully, as precisely as I could, with a string of digits—year, month, date—in the upper-left-hand corner. Then each one was an incident. A single event placed precisely in history, but apparently free of any cause. . . . The only truth—and that only a degree of truth—lies in the simple statement of the incident.[40]

A dramatic counterpoint to Sethe's mystical declaration of the permanence of the past, John's attachment to facticity and order is easily reconcilable with prohibitive reading's suspicion of the historical turn on the grounds that it is phantasmatic, narcissistic, or unprovable. In similar, if exaggerated, fashion, John posits that the sole route to historical truth consists in the sequential stringing together of unvarnished facts. This "true" history proceeds like an ordered stack of index cards: discrete, declarative, and decisive.

John attempts to exclude emotion from his research through a kind of numerical precision, yet his neurotic method ironically comes to bear a striking resemblance to a widely observed symptom of post-traumatic consciousness. Consider the striking similarity between his index-card method—which takes as its hallmark a stubborn literality effected through de-contextualization and rigorous detail—and Caruth's depiction of traumatic dreams and flashbacks. She writes, "Modern analysts . . . have remarked on the surprising literality and nonsymbolic nature of traumatic dreams and flashbacks, which resist cure to the extent that they remain, precisely, literal. It is this literality and its insistent return which constitutes trauma and points toward its enigmatic core: the delay or incompletion in knowing, or even in seeing, an overwhelming occurrence that then remains, in its insistent return, absolutely true to the event."[41]

Like Caruth's stipulated trauma survivor, John insistently favors a version of truth as the mimetic representation of the past. Moreover, both insist on the moral value of such truth. For the Caruthian trauma victim, "truth" disallows the production of meaning because traumatic experience does not surrender, in the process of happening, to comprehension. Thus, meaning can only be an amendment, a threat to the integrity of traumatic recollection. So, too, for John, the scene of archival discovery is "perfect" and vulnerable: "anything I did, one false step, would destroy that perfection, would probably obscure whatever message might be in the scene."[42] In both cases, "the simple statement of the incident" is the only gesture that can legitimately approach and approximate the truth of the past.

Unexpectedly, then, John reveals to the reader how the desire to periodize, to produce shape and certainty by putting the past behind us, mirrors the ostensibly opposite compulsion to *reexperience* the past—to go to the past, as Sethe does, and "stand in the place where it was, [where] it will happen again."[43] Like the traumatic flashback and Morrisonian rememory, those figurations that prohibitive readers cannot abide, objectivist documentary historiography—that method they so passionately defend—entails an impossible desire for exactitude, a compulsive and ever-unconsummated longing for mastery over the past.

Risking redundancy, let me restate my argument with an eye to the broader stakes of this essay. Trauma, as Caruth reminds us, is a dissociative disorder, defined, on the one hand, by the potent and compulsively reexperienced afterlife of unresolved, past injury (trauma's "insistent return") and, on the other hand, by presentist failures to assimilate that past into continuous self-story (trauma's "nonsymbolic" literality, its commitment to remaining "absolutely *true* to the event").[44] In parallel form, I have argued that one way in which the historical trauma of slavery manifests in contemporary black studies is through the literary and critical imagination of an unquiet, "intrusive past"; a second guise for trauma's impact on African Americanist scholarship consists in critical adherence to a code of stubborn literality and nonattachment to the painful past.[45] Historical altericism, a discrete and declarative style of historical narration, and the inflexible priority of fact over feeling: might we read these hallmarks of prohibitive reading as kindred of the inassimilable, mimetic materializations of traumatic flashbacks and dreams? Put another way, is it possible that trauma's effects are discernible not only when and as they announce themselves but also in a host of muted, unarticulated, or disavowed forms?

When I posit that prohibitive reading contains desires and mechanisms that are opaque to it, I am saying, in a sense, that it is like every other speech act; for at least insofar as psychoanalysis is concerned, there is no declaration that is not also a concealment. But I am wary of something central to prohibitive reading's attack on the historical turn—namely, critics' reluctance to frame their own desires as desire. Instead, they suggest, prohibitive reading is powered by positivism, antisentimentality, or common sense. This form of disavowal is most apparent in the work of Michaels and Warren, as when Michaels tells us that the singular value of historical knowledge lies in having "true beliefs" about the past or when Warren contends that fiction discredits itself when it "[forgets] the facts."[46] Without discounting certain merits of this brand of prohibitive reading, I believe that the will to eradicate affect from the domains of intellectual and political life is summoned by its own sirens, its own impossible desires. It is also important to recognize that prohibitive reading's foundational anxieties and desires—its will to self-containment and intellectual mastery, its aversion to dependence and susceptibility—reify a tacitly masculinist system of knowledge and value.[47]

It makes sense to parse the field of prohibitive reading more finely: although all of the critics gathered under this appellation move to discredit trauma's subversive take on historical narration, Best and Jones retreat from the counter-ideals of strict and progressive periodization (Warren) and unembellished factual truth (Michaels). In lieu of these idioms of detached mastery, Best and Jones circle back to the subject of slavery aslant, not to prohibit its consideration but to emphasize an unbridgeable affective distance that bars the readerly present from merging with the traumatic past. In this spirit, both model their proposed reading strategies on texts that retain a prominent interest in slavery. For Best, it is Morrison's most recent contemporary narrative of slavery, *A Mercy* (2008), about which he argues that the author contradicts *Beloved*'s influential epistemology by "[abandoning] us to a more baffled, cut-off, foreclosed position with regard to the slave past." For Jones, it is Terrance Hayes's "The Avocado" (2010), in which the poet's defamiliarizing "figuration of the slave-as-guacamole represents, in poetic form, the critical estimation of the impossibility of recovery and redemption of slavery's injuries: we can never make guacamole whole again, we can never restore it to its state as an avocado." Such readings are surprisingly proximate to my own interpretation of *Beloved*, in which the aim is not to collapse now into then or to "[promote] feeling to an axiom" but to index an unresolved yet nonmimetic course of intergenerational trauma as an underlying psycho-affective structure of contemporary African Americanist discourse.[48]

Whereas prohibitive reading has cast *Beloved*'s story of the reappearing past to the exclusion of the story of familial dis/continuity, the legacy of trauma always entails *both* the astonishing force of the desire to return to and rectify the past *and* the infuriating impossibility of that longing. Thus, Denver is desperate to feed and tend to Beloved but also rages against the stories that precede her existence or capacity to know. This is decidedly different from appropriation or incorporation of Sethe's trauma, even as Denver surely must forge a relationship to an intergenerational past to imagine a viable self that can step outside the haunted house. Like Hirsch's post-memorial subject, her identification with Sethe's past is ambivalent and partial, characterized by a sense of self-displacement that conjures both resentment and desire. If Denver symbolically resembles the contemporary reader/critic and an inherited trauma mediates her relationship to history, then we might deduce that for us, too, the past permeates the present by producing the formative conditions for our senses of agency and constraint, lack and longing, identity and anonymity. It establishes history as simultaneously continuous and discontinuous, as dialogic, and as both obscured and revealed by our projective investments in it.

NOTES

1. Anne Anlin Cheng, "Psychoanalysis without Symptoms," *differences* 20, no. 1 (2009): 98.

2. I borrow this elegant and economical phrase (and use it slightly out of context) from the moral philosopher Alasdair MacIntyre, who proposes that virtue itself depends on the possibility for imagining human life as a unity; see *After Virtue: A Study in Moral Theory* (Notre Dame, Ind.: University of Notre Dame Press, 2007), xi. For examples of theories that conceive of trauma as a disruption to self-story, see Cathy Caruth, ed., *Unclaimed Experience: Trauma, Narrative, and History* (Baltimore: Johns Hopkins University Press, 1996); Cathy Caruth, ed., *Trauma: Explorations in Memory* (Baltimore: Johns Hopkins University Press, 1995); and Shoshana Felman and Dori Laub, *Testimony: Crises of Witnessing in Literature, Psychoanalysis, and History* (New York: Routledge, 1992). For a vigorous critique of this formulation of trauma, see Ruth Leys, *Trauma: A Genealogy* (Chicago: University of Chicago Press, 2000).

3. Caruth, *Trauma*, 4.

4. According to Felman and Laub, the "historic trauma of the Second World War" comprises "a trauma we consider as the watershed of our times and which [our] book will come to view not as an event encapsulated in the past, but as a history which is essentially *not over*, a history whose repercussions are not simply omnipresent (whether consciously or not) in all our cultural activities, but whose traumatic consequences are still actively *evolving . . .* in today's political, historical, cultural, and artistic scene, the scene in which we read and psychoanalyze, and from within whose tumult and whose fluctuations we strive both to educate and write" (*Testimony*, xiv).

5. Ibid., xv. I have excised the word *contemporary* from the cited passage to avoid an explanatory digression. In brief, Felman and Laub cite the Holocaust as the singular crisis event that transforms modern consciousness, and thus regard epistemological failure as a contemporary phenomenon. African Americanist engagements with trauma often follow a similar model of crisis, disorientation, and epistemological failure but imagine a prolonged and continuous crisis event that can be traced as far back as the sixteenth century. For particularly successful African Americanist reworkings of this arm of trauma theory, see Michael Awkward, *Philadelphia Freedoms: Black American Trauma, Memory, and Culture after King* (Philadelphia: Temple University Press, 2013); and Ashraf H. A. Rushdy, *Remembering Generations: Race and Family in Contemporary African American Fiction* (Chapel Hill: University of North Carolina Press, 2001). Although it does not explicitly use the word *trauma*, Hortense Spillers's "Mama's Baby, Papa's Maybe: An American Grammar Book" is probably the most

powerful articulation of how historical rupture in the distant past of the Afro-European encounter underwrites the social and psychic grammars of contemporary life (*Diacritics* 17 [summer 1987]: 64–81).

6. For an excellent discussion of how trauma challenges the constitutive protocols of a "documentary or self-sufficient research model" for historiographical study, see Dominick La Capra, *Writing History, Writing Trauma* (Baltimore: Johns Hopkins University Press, 2001), 2.

7. To clarify, Huyssen is critical of this turn. See Andreas Huyssen, *Present Pasts: Urban Palimpsests and the Politics of Memory* (Stanford, Calif.: Stanford University Press, 2003), 5, 6; and Felman and Laub, *Testimony*, 197.

8. Toni Morrison, "The Site of Memory," in *Inventing the Truth: The Art and Craft of Memoir*, ed. William Zinsser and Russell Baker, 2nd ed. (Boston: Houghton Mifflin, 1995), 92.

9. Ashraf H. A. Rushdy, *Neo-Slave Narratives: Studies in the Social Logic of a Literary Form* (Oxford: Oxford University Press, 1999), 32.

10. John C. Snider, "Interview: Octavia E. Butler," in *Conversations with Octavia Butler*, ed. Consuela Francis (Jackson: University Press of Mississippi, 2010), 214.

11. Roger Luckhurst, *The Trauma Question* (New York: Routledge, 2008), 88, 89.

12. Toni Morrison, *Beloved* (New York: Vintage, 2004), 89.

13. Caruth, *Trauma*, 4.

14. Morrison, *Beloved*, 217.

15. Ibid., 189.

16. Ann Snitow, "Review of *Beloved* by Toni Morrison," in *Toni Morrison: Critical Perspectives Past and Present*, ed. Henry Louis Gates Jr. and Kwame Anthony Appiah (New York: Amistad, 1993), 26.

17. Shoshana Felman, "Camus," in Felman and Laub, *Testimony*, 167.

18. Stephen Best, "On Failing to Make the Past Present," *Modern Language Quarterly* 73 (September 2012): 459, 461, 454.

19. Walter Benn Michaels, *The Shape of the Signifier: 1967 to the End of History* (Princeton, N.J.: Princeton University Press, 2004), 136; Kenneth W. Warren, *What Was African American Literature?* (Cambridge, Mass.: Harvard University Press, 2011), 9.

20. Best, "On Failing to Make the Past Present," 474.

21. Wendy Brown uses "wounded attachments" to describe "the ways in which certain aspects of the specific genealogy of politicized identity are carried in the structure of its political articulation and demands, with consequences that include self-subversion" (*States of Injury: Power and Freedom in Late Modernity* [Princeton, N.J.: Princeton University Press, 1995], 55).

22. Spillers, "Mama's Baby, Papa's Maybe," 68.

23. M. Jacqui Alexander, *Pedagogies of Crossing: Meditations on Feminism, Sexual Politics, Memory, and the Sacred* (Durham, N.C.: Duke University Press, 2005), 315. The phrase I quote here is from the chapter "Dangerous Memory: Self through Spirit," which describes a reparative process through the summoned apparition of ancestral spirits. Although Alexander's monograph makes only passing reference to *Beloved*, Morrison's influence is palpable throughout the text, perhaps most explicitly in Alexander's frequent use of the Morrisonian neologism *rememory*.

24. Warren, *What Was*, 82.

25. Felman, "Camus," 167; Morrison, *Beloved*, 189.

26. Ibid., 84; Michaels, *Shape of the Signifier*, 166; Best, "On Failing to Make the Past Present," 456.

27. Michaels, *Shape of the Signifier*, 136.

28. Morrison, *Beloved*, 43, 44.

29. Best, "On Failing to Make the Past Present," 460.

30. Michaels, *Shape of the Signifier*, 136; Morrison, *Beloved*, 44.

31. Morrison, *Beloved*, 282, 296.

32. Ibid., 36, 121, 141, 74, 35.

33. Marianne Hirsch, "Surviving Images: Holocaust Photographs and the Work of Postmemory," *Yale Journal of Criticism* 14 (spring 2001): 11.

34. Michaels, *Shape of the Signifier*, 131.

35. Best, "On Failing to Make the Past Present," 457.

36. Michaels, *Shape of the Signifier*, 140.

37. Warren, *What Was*, 84.

38. Best, "On Failing to Make the Past Present," 457.

39. David Bradley, *The Chaneysville Incident* (New York: HarperCollins, 1981), 197.

40. Ibid., 268, 223.

41. Caruth, *Trauma*, 5.

42. Bradley, *Chaneysville*, 140.

43. Morrison, *Beloved*, 44.

44. Caruth, *Trauma*, 5.

45. Bessel A. Van der Kolk and Onno Van der Hart coin the phrase "the intrusive past" as a description of traumatic memory in "The Intrusive Past: The Flexibility of Memory and the Engraving of Trauma," in Caruth, *Trauma*, 158–182.

46. Michaels, *Shape of the Signifier*, 140. Warren's critique of the phrase "forget the facts" applies to his reading of *Chaneysville*; for over the course of the novel, John's objectivist approach to historiography is radically challenged. When John reaches an impasse in his efforts to accumulate sufficient documentary evidence, his girlfriend, a psychiatrist, recommends that he "forget the facts" (Bradley, *Chaneysville*, 391). In his analysis, Warren is unconcerned with the girlfriend's profession and its implications for the text's view of the nexus of history and psychology. Instead, he condemns the novel for straying from John's original epistemological orientation, finding in the protagonist's exploration of psychic life of history a "commitment to making the past present for us by any representational means necessary" (*What Was*, 99, 103).

47. On several occasions, colleagues have asked me to explain why prohibitive reading seems to appeal disproportionately—if not exclusively—to male scholars. My preliminary speculations are a first step in considering how this mode of thought implicitly upholds a model of selfhood that has been historically inaccessible to women. However, I instinctively recoil from any implication of an essential connection between a reader's gender and her or his critical orientation. My reaction is probably exaggerated, betraying my own powerful attraction to a number of the very "masculine" ideals that seem to power prohibitive reading, but I believe it carries a sound inference: that a compelling gendered exegesis of the African Americanist discourse on slavery would necessarily privilege a pliable, constructivist take on what it means to read through gender.

48. Best, "On Failing to Make the Past Present," 472, 464.

CONCLUSION

Black Lives Matter,
Except When They Don't

Why Slavery's Psychic Hold Matters

ROBERT J. PATTERSON

> To better understand contemporary racial dynamics, we must examine
> the connections among the histories of white supremacy, slavery, and
> other forms of chronic violence to which black people have been sub-
> jected. The ways in which the past informs the present can become
> obscured by the mythical face of narratives about racial progress.[1]
>
> –Paula Rothenberg

The project that led to this book, which we initially titled *Do You Want to Be
Well? The Psychic Hold of Slavery*, set out to investigate two related questions that
persist in popular conversation and scholarly inquiry. Why can't black people
get over slavery? And why don't black people *want* to get over slavery? Although
the phrase "getting over" remains fraught with psychological, epistemological,
and political complications, the first question turns our attention to a pervasive
(and, to me, curious) desire among Americans to once and for all close this
chapter of American history, forever relegating it and its legacies to a forgotten, unknowable, distant, irrelevant past. If black people simply would get over
slavery—stop remembering it, stop representing it, and stop discussing it—then
slavery and its legacies would cease to exist. To borrow the terminology of Toni
Morrison's *Beloved*, if black people would keep slavery out of their rememories,
America's racial relations could progress.[2] Aside from the fact that this logic
once again positions the onus of improving race relations on black people, it
ignores an argument that Soyica Diggs Colbert reminds us of in this book's introduction: slavery is only a part of a larger system of antiblack racism that governs
the modern period. Even if black people could get over slavery, that triumph
would not erase the antiblack epistemologies that continue to shape our epoch.

While the second question is equally pervasive (and, to me, equally curious), it leads to yet another question, one that we ultimately ended up investigating: what desires, investments, or identitarian logics account for our inability—or unwillingness—to get over slavery? In other words, although the project moved away from explicitly theorizing the issue of wellness, this book does think through the epistemological, political, and cultural stakes of situating slavery at the center of any discussion of black life and black politics in the late twentieth and early twenty-first centuries, particularly as black cultural producers explore blackness's multiple significations. Black people's inability to get over or (depending on whom you ask) move beyond slavery is tied to how slavery's overarching logics continue to structure black life. When Texas state trooper Brian Encinia tells the now deceased Sandra Bland, "I will light you up," careful listeners cannot ignore that this word choice conjures up a history of lynching, one in which white Americans used their unchecked authority to compel black people whom they thought had "gotten out of their place" to submit.

Adolph Reed Jr. and Kenneth Warren lament the tendency of black studies to treat "slavery as an a priori to account for, or insist upon, the essential distinctiveness of black Americans' political concerns and beliefs." They take exception to arguments that, in their view, "resolve down to an almost ritualistic assertion of familiar conclusions embedded in a pro forma narrative: that racism has been and remains a potent force constraining the black American experience, that black American agency has been propelled by pursuit of an ensemble of abstract goals such as autonomy, community, and family and performance of a comparably generic "resistance" to racial or other forms of oppression."[3] While their general claims are dubious, they are right to ask scholarship to provide more complex discussions of slavery, agency, and resistance. Each of the chapters in this book examines these issues with a deftness that demonstrates such necessary complexity. Building upon Saidiya Hartman's work, for example, both my own chapter and Colbert's demonstrate how the institution of slavery has complicated notions of agency, will, and resistance, thus debunking the idea, as Reed and Warren demand, that these notions manifested themselves as acts of radical rejection or dissent. That is, our analyses think through how and why enslaved Africans or otherwise disenfranchised African Americans engaged in particular behaviors that at times challenged systems of domination. Yet they do not presume unfettered agency or will that overstates the degree to which black people fought against the peculiar institution, or the consequence of those effects.

Our questions nonetheless begin with the premise that slavery was not simply a chapter in modernity but that modernity and slavery were coevals; that is, the (il)logics of the peculiar institution produced and continue to structure contemporary epistemologies about race in general and blackness in particular.

The reason, it seems, that black people cannot get over slavery is because some of the institution's economic, political, and social discourses continue to structure, if not haunt, many of the public and scholarly conversations surrounding race, race relations, access, equity, and social justice in the twenty-first century. On the one hand, we must hold in tension Calvin Warren's adept argument: the temporality of slavery is not simply confined to the historical period that demarcates its duration because this understanding of time reinforces the epistemological violence that historiography does to slavery in its attempt to confine this historical epoch to a beginning and end. On the other hand, we must consider Douglas A. Jones Jr.'s contention that the world has changed, that nineteenth-century chattel slavery no longer exists, and that black people enjoy many more privileges in this historical moment than they ever have. But I wonder if we sometimes overstate the degree to which black people—across socioeconomic classes, in particular—enjoy or have access to the privileges the modern civil rights movement has afforded. In the twenty-first century, it may be useful to remember Anna Julia Cooper's admonition at the turn of the twentieth century: we cannot use the progress that a small, *exceptional* population of the black race has made to represent the progress of the entire race.[4] This practice obfuscates the progress that has not yet been made.

Factually, Jones's argument is correct: the world has changed, the outlawing of Jim Crow segregation has facilitated black people's access to educational and employment opportunities that have increased their financial status, and the Voting Rights Act of 1965 has allowed black people to vote in unprecedented numbers and increased their access to and use of electoral power. Yet during this same era white and black wealth and income gaps have widened, the disparity between black and white educational attainment has increased, and black unemployment continues to outpace that of white people.[5] If these trends do not demonstrate an equity and access problem, recent events in American culture and politics—specifically, white police officers' continuing murder of unarmed black citizens—also have called into question the degree to which the world has changed for black people, demonstrating an increased skepticism toward the successes of the modern civil rights movement. In other words, statistics, experience, and conjecture converge to raise questions. To what degree has the theoretical promise of equality translated into actual equality of outcome? How can we maintain that the world has changed when many socioeconomic markers suggest that black people *continue* to lag behind in wealth and income? To what degree does the state protect or destroy black life, and how has the "justice" that the modern civil rights movement made possible under the law become obfuscated for black people through the law? Part of the answer to these questions lies in the antiblack sentiment that grew in the crucible of slavery and that increasingly has become entrenched in American institutions and discourses. As Colbert explains in the introduction of our book, this moment of post-blackness in the post–civil rights era makes these questions even more difficult to examine because the notion persists that the civil rights era has eradicated the legal barriers that prevented black people and black life from flourishing. There is no way, however, to talk about the civil rights moment without contextualizing its relationship to slavery.

The modern civil rights movement is at least discursively connected to chattel slavery because the discrimination Jim Crow segregation made legible was predicated on antiblack epistemologies that structured and buttressed slavery. Consequently, whenever we discuss civil rights, we also talk about slavery; whenever we discuss slavery, we also talk about civil rights. This argument, of course, acknowledges that each is necessarily understood through the other but does not suggest that slavery and civil rights are one and the same. Historians have demonstrated the links between the eras by employing a long teleology to explain that the modern civil rights movement was, in many ways, the culmination of several movements that began under slavery. Further, they show that contemporary issues of disenfranchisement are a part of an ongoing struggle that did not end during the 1950s and 1960s.[6] The title of my conclusion underscores this point, drawing attention to how twenty-first-century experiences of black disenfranchisement and state-sanctioned violence nominally *appear* to be connected to earlier historical antecedents. That is, when protestors chant, "Black lives matter," and wear t-shirts that assert the same claim, they respond to a longstanding notion that black lives are expendable to the state (necropolitics). From slavery, through Reconstruction, to the nadir of race relations, through World War I, World War II, the modern civil rights movement, and our putative post–civil rights era, ample evidence supports the claim that if the state does protect black people, it also endangers them.

While the specific facts of the recent cases involving white police officers shooting unarmed black people extend beyond the parameters of my discussion, the reaction—"Black lives matter"—taps into a history of racial tensions that remains largely connected to the antiblack epistemologies that continue to govern modern thought. In other words, contemporary reminders that black lives matter also invoke a historical past in which black lives did not matter, beyond their economic value. This parallel thus questions the degree to which the world, in fact, has changed. Slavery becomes the metonym for understanding blackness and inequality in the contemporary moment. Those making this argument insist that slavery, implicitly and explicitly, remains at the forefront of many understandings of blackness, race relations, and black political advancement, although they do not suggest that slavery is the *only* way to understand blackness. As the chapters in this book demonstrate, slavery remains at the forefront of black (and, more broadly, American) cultural production and has simultaneously become a major focal point in twenty-first-century black studies' scholarship and theorizations.

Reparations Revisited?

Despite calls for us to end our discussions of slavery and to create, in the words of Charles Johnson, "new and better stories, new concepts, and new vocabularies and grammar based not on the past but on the dangerous, exciting, and unexplored present," the fascination with slavery continues largely because, critically, it remains an underexplored aspect of American life insofar as the national conscience continues to repress the peculiar institution (as the post-racial, post-slavery, post–civil rights era philosophies propagate).[7] This repression is apparent not only in debates about reparations for the descendants of formerly enslaved Africans but also in the belatedness of the government's apology for slavery. In "The Accursed Share," Robert Wesley cogently demonstrates how the legal concepts of time and standing thwart the possibility of economic reparations for the descendants of formerly enslaved African Americans.[8] Notwithstanding the legal impasses to black reparation movements, the ethical bases are important for a movement that would dismantle the white privilege that embeds itself within American law:

> Beyond payment of an overdue debt that can never be fully repaid, or acknowledgment of historical injustices that can never be undone, there is white privilege and the question of its undoing. To rebuild bonds of broken relationships and broken communities, it is first necessary to have a frank confrontation with the infamy of white privilege and its entwinement in the law, especially the law that governs whether Black reparations will receive merit-based adjudication in the courts.[9]

That the debt can never be repaid suggests that slavery's injuries extend beyond the economic values that enslaved African Americans provided to the country. For Wesley, confronting white privilege also means attending to how American law has imprinted slavery's hold on the nation's psyche, culture, history, and ethics. "Contemporary claims for Black reparations pose a threat to white privilege by articulating a counterhegemonic narrative of self and community and, on that basis, by demanding redress of historical injustices that continue to skew social and economic value in favor of white privilege."[10]

While the United States may be interested in apologizing for the legacy of slavery, it has demonstrated its unwillingness to engage in conversations about black reparations. As I argue in *Exodus Politics*, the House of Representatives' apology for slavery acknowledges the peculiar institution's pernicious effects while absolving itself of financial responsibility for slavery. On the one hand, Congress's apology acknowledges slavery's psychic and material holds:

> Whereas millions of Africans and their descendants were enslaved; . . .
>
> Whereas Africans forced into slavery were brutalized, humiliated, dehumanized, and subjected to the indignity of being stripped of their names and heritage; . . .

Whereas after emancipation from 246 years of slavery, African Americans soon saw the fleeting political, social, and economic gains they made during Reconstruction eviscerated by virulent racism, lynchings, disenfranchisement, Black Codes, and racial segregation laws that imposed a rigid system of officially sanctioned racial segregation in virtually all areas of life; . . .

Whereas an apology for centuries of brutal dehumanization and injustices cannot erase the past, but confession of the wrongs committed and a formal apology to African Americans will help bind the wounds of the nation that are rooted in slavery and can speed racial healing and reconciliation and help the people of the United States understand the past and honor the history of all people of the United States; . . .

. . . The Congress—. . .

. . . apologizes to African Americans on behalf of the people of the United States, for wrongs committed against them and their ancestors who suffered under slavery and Jim Crow laws.[11]

On the other hand, the use of passive voice throughout the apology tellingly never holds any specific individuals or groups responsible for the "atrocities committed." That is, in as much as African Americans' ancestors were enslaved, somebody's ancestors did the enslaving. Congress then adds an appendix to this apology, clarifying that it cannot be used as admission of wrongdoing for any reparations suits and thus reinforcing the idea that the government does not intend to hold anyone financially or morally responsible for slavery. In many ways, the appendix exemplifies why the black reparations movement, whose logic and long history Randall Robinson and Ta-Nehisi Coates have robustly synthesized, has stalled.[12]

The desire to repress slavery stems from, as Angelyn Mitchell writes, how "systematically pervasive the infinite pain and shame of slavery remain in the American consciousness."[13] As the chapters in this book suggest, the post–civil rights era, when the legal barriers to black enfranchisement presumably no longer exist, shifts the discursive terrain, changing how we are able to understand how black people both experience disenfranchisement and respond to the legacies of slavery. At the same time, the chapters emphasize that a relationship to this past still exists, as Brandon J. Manning demonstrates when he asserts that Dave Chappelle's inability to detach "The Nigger Pixie" from the minstrelsy tradition shows how stereotyping continues to circumscribe black people's behaviors. That is, one effect of the psychic hold of slavery is that it tethers contemporary subjects to a traumatic history of racialization and political disenfranchisement that perpetually haunts them. Michael Awkward uses the phrase "traumatized black subjectivity" as "a way to conceptualize post–civil rights performances of identity that reflect both the complexities of the black American present and its relationship to the 'past of rope, fire and murder.'"

Clarifying the relationship between the past and present, he explains, "This concept encourages attentiveness to a pain-filled history, certainly, as well as to the largely still-deferred American Dream despite its availability to a supremely talented, industrious, or exceptionally lucky few."[14] While Awkward's discussion of the black traumatized subject focuses specifically on the aftermath of Martin Luther King Jr.'s assassination, his idea that black subjects attend to, or are reminded of and circumscribed by, the painful history of black disenfranchisement provides a useful way for thinking about the longer history of black political activity from which the modern civil rights movement grew: the tradition of abolitionism forged in slavery.

Whereas Awkward's notion of traumatized black subjectivity implicitly binds black subject formation to the slave past, Christina Sharpe explicitly makes this connection by arguing that slavery's discursive paradigms shape *all* modern subjects in general and black modern subjects in particular. "That is, while all modern subjects are post-slavery subjects fully constituted by the discursive codes of slavery and post-slavery, post-slavery subjectivity is largely borne by and readable on the (New World) *black* subject." Investigating how these discursive codes are read on (and onto) black bodies "means examining those subjectivities constituted from transatlantic slavery onward and connected, then as now, by the everyday mundane horrors that aren't acknowledged to be horrors."[15] Sharpe's insights are instructive because they acknowledge slavery's ubiquitous impact on all subjects while clarifying that its legibility manifests itself in specific ways for black subjects. For these subjects, whose traumatized black subjectivity bears the marks of slavery, the impossibility of getting over slavery lies in the fact that slavery's legacies are buried deep within them and constantly return. Black people invoke the systematic "everyday mundane horrors that aren't acknowledged to be horrors" when they remind the state, and each other, that black lives matter.

Where Do We Go from Here?

An episode in Gayl Jones's novel *Corregidora* (1975) grapples with what, to me, are many of the issues at stake in *The Psychic Hold of Slavery*, preceding and perhaps anticipating the post-neo-slave narrative genre that Margo Natalie Crawford thoughtfully considers in chapter 4. Set in post–World War II Kentucky, *Corregidora* charts the story of Ursa Corregidora, a contemporary traumatized black subject, who, like her foremothers, holds the responsibility of remembering and recounting how Old Man Corregidora, a Portuguese slave owner and breeder, raped their ancestors. This slave past haunts Ursa because her grandmother, Great Gram, has instructed her descendants to make generations—that is, to give birth to female children who will bear witness to this history of rape and exploitation. Because the Brazilian government has destroyed the evidence incriminating itself and plantation owners for these crimes against humanity, the imperative "to make generations" becomes a way to record this history (and perhaps hold the government accountable at some point). As many scholars have explained, *Corregidora* demonstrates how Ursa moves beyond "traumatized black subjectivity" by finding a way to recount this history without the repetitions that reinforce the original trauma. Her ability "to make generations" through the blues is important, not only because a hysterectomy has made it impossible for her to reproduce but also because the weight of historical trauma, her inability to get over slavery, would have remained intricately bound to the repetition of the traumatic history. Ursa never gets over slavery, though her transformed understanding of it does allow her a sense of psychic healing that was unavailable to her foremothers and that prevented them from developing close interpersonal heterosexual relationships.

Like several of the artists examined in *The Psychic Hold of Slavery*, Jones is invested in representing ways to deal with the burden of slavery, of acknowledging its significance and legacies while showing the *personal* and *political* stakes of failing to do so or of overstating a relationship to that historical past. She explains her perspective on how history—including collective histories—shape the contemporary subject:

> History affects Ursa's personality—the history of the women before her—their conflicts, frustrations, etc. She wants to make sense of that history in terms of her own life. She doesn't want to be "bound" by that history, but she recognizes it as important; and she accepts it as an aspect of her own character, identity, and present history. However, she doesn't want to be told by those women and their Corregidora stories how she must feel about that past. Her story is connected to theirs but she also wants her own choices and acts of imagination and will—most of which come through singing her own songs.[16]

Jones's statement usefully captures the argumentative stakes in *The Psychic Hold of Slavery*. First, it acknowledges history and historical forces as important factors that shape contemporary subjects' understanding and experiences of their historical epoch. Although Ursa does not want to be bound by that history, it still affects her. History is not easily detached from the present and consigned to an unknowable and unusable past. Second, while the past cannot be ignored, we also cannot overstate how it affects the present or easily attribute present conditions to the past without delineating specific ways (which may be discursive) that the past informs the present. Acknowledged or not, slavery matters, as does its psychic hold. It is also true that black lives matter—except when they don't, an exception that emerges all too frequently.

NOTES

1. Paula Rothenberg, *White Privilege: Essential Readings on the Other Side of Racism* (New York: Worth, 2016), 3.

2. Toni Morrison's meditations on what she calls *rememory* clarify the ways in which memories become collective and how they exist even when not consciously remembered. I borrow the term as a way to think through how slavery's collective trauma, as experienced or imagined, informs a black critical, political, and cultural conscience. See *Beloved* (New York: Vintage, 2004), especially 36–37.

3. Adolph Reed Jr. and Kenneth Warren, "Introduction," in *Renewing Black Intellectual History: The Ideological and Material Foundations of African American Thought*, ed. Adolph Reed Jr. and Kenneth Warren (Boulder, Colo.: Paradigm, 2010), viii.

4. Anna Julia Cooper, "Womanhood a Vital Element in the Regeneration and Progress of a Race," in *A Voice from the South* (New York: Oxford University Press, 1998), 9–47.

5. Melvin Oliver and Robert Shapiro, *Black Wealth, White Wealth: A New Perspective on Racial Inequality* (New York: Routledge, 2006).

6. Jacquelyn Dowd Hall notes that the *Brown v. Board of Education* case (1954) typically marks the beginning of the modern civil rights movement and King's assassination in 1968 marks its end. This periodization, she argues, obscures how movements before the mid-twentieth century fed into the civil rights movement as well as how those after 1968 connect with it. A longer periodization would demonstrate how the mid-twentieth-century movement that aimed to dismantle legal segregation connects with earlier movements and make the case for how civil rights movements still remain necessary. See "The Long Civil Rights Movement and the Political Uses of the Past," *Journal of American History* 91 (March 2005): 1233–1237.

7. Charles Johnson, "The End of the Black American Narrative," *American Scholar* 77, no. 3 (2008): 34.

8. John Wesley explains that, legally, a defendant has to prove that a law directly harms his or her standing, which descendants of enslaved Africans often find impossible to do. Additionally, statutes of limitation deny the possibility of suing for reparations. See "The Accursed Share: Genealogy, Temporality, and the Problem of Value in Black Reparations Discourse," *Representations* 92, no. 1 (2005): 81–85.

9. Ibid., 83.

10. Ibid., 82.

11. U.S. Congress, "A Concurrent Resolution Apologizing for the Enslavement and Racial Segregation of African Americans," res. 26, 111th Cong. (2009–2010).

12. Ta-Nehisi Coates, "The Case for Reparations," *Atlantic*, May 21, 2014, http://www.theatlantic.com/features/archive/2014/05/the-case-for-reparations/361631/, accessed December 28, 2015; Randall Robinson, *The Debt: What America Owes to Blacks* (New York: Plume, 1991).

13. Angelyn Mitchell, *The Freedom to Remember: Narrative, Slavery, and Gender in Contemporary Black Women's Fiction* (New Brunswick, N.J.: Rutgers University Press, 2002), 2.

14. Michael Awkward, *Philadelphia Freedoms: Black American Trauma, Memory, and Culture after King* (Philadelphia: Temple University Press, 2013), 5–6.

15. Christina Sharpe, *Monstrous Intimacies: Making Post-Slavery Subjects* (Durham, N.C.: Duke University Press, 2010), 3.

16. Charles H. Rowell, "An Interview with Gayl Jones," *Callaloo* 16 (October 1982): 45.

SELECTED BIBLIOGRAPHY

Abraham, Nicolas, and Mária Török. *The Wolf Man's Magic Word: A Cryptonomy*, translated by Nicholas Rand. Minneapolis: University of Minnesota Press, 2005.

Agamben, Giorgio. *Homo Sacer: Sovereign Power and Bare Life*, translated by Daniel Heller-Roazen. Stanford, Calif.: Stanford University Press, 1998.

Aldama, Frederic Luis. "Introduction." In *Multicultural Comics: From Zap to Blue Beetle*, edited by Frederick Luis Aldama, 1–25. Austin: University of Texas Press, 2010.

Alexander, M. Jacqui. *Pedagogies of Crossing: Meditations on Feminism, Sexual Politics, Memory, and the Sacred.* Durham, N.C.: Duke University Press, 2006.

Althusser, Louis. "Ideology and Ideological State Apparatuses." In *Critical Theory Since 1965*, edited by Hazard Adams and Leroy Searle, 238–250. Tallahassee: Florida State University Press, 1992.

———. *Politics and History: Montesquieu, Rousseau, Marx.* London: Verso, 2007.

Araujo, Ana Lucia, ed. *Politics of Memory: Making Slavery Visible in the Public Space.* London: Routledge, 2012.

Awkward, Michael. *Philadelphia Freedoms: Black American Trauma, Memory, and Culture after King.* Philadelphia: Temple University Press, 2013.

Ayittey, George B. N. *Africa Betrayed.* New York: St. Martin's, 1992.

———. *Africa in Chaos.* New York: St. Martin's, 1998.

Badiou, Alain. *Being and Event.* Translated by Oliver Feltham. New York: Continuum, 2007.

Baker, Houston. *Blues, Ideology, and Afro-American Literature: A Vernacular Theory.* Chicago: University of Chicago Press, 1987.

Baker, Kyle. *Nat Turner.* New York: Abrams, 2008.

Bamboozled, directed by Spike Lee. Burbank, Calif.: New Line Cinema, 2000. DVD.

Baraka, Amiri (LeRoi Jones). "An Agony. As Now." In *The Dead Lecturer*, 15–16. New York: Grove, 1964.

———. *The Slave.* In *Dutchman and the Slave*, 39–88. New York: HarperCollins, 1964.

Baron, Zach. "Pharrell Williams on Advanced Style Moves and That Oscar Snub: My Song 'Will Be Here for 10 Years.'" *GQ*, March 25, 2014. http://www.gq.com/story/pharrell -williams-oscar-snub. Accessed April 20, 2014.

Baucom, Ian. *Specters of the Atlantic: Finance Capital, Slavery, and the Philosophy of History.* Durham, N.C.: Duke University Press, 2005.

Berger, John. *Berger on Drawing.* Aghabullogue, Ireland: Occasional Press, 2005.

Berlant, Lauren. *Cruel Optimism.* Durham, N.C.: Duke University Press, 2011.

Bernstein, Robin. "Dances with Things: Material Culture and the Performance of Race." *Social Text 27* 4 (winter 2009): 67–94.

Best, Stephen. "On Failing to Make the Past Present." *Modern Language Quarterly* 73 (September 2012): 453–474.

Best, Stephen, and Saidiya Hartman. "Fugitive Justice." *Representations* 92 (autumn 2005): 1–15.

Bhabha, Homi. *The Location of Culture*. New York: Routledge, 1994.

Billig, Michael. *Laughter and Ridicule: Towards a Social Critique of Humour*. London: Sage, 2005.

Bradley, David. *The Chaneysville Incident*. New York: HarperCollins, 1981.

Brooks, Daphne. *Bodies in Dissent: Spectacular Performances of Race and Freedom, 1850–1910*. Durham, N.C.: Duke University Press, 2006.

Brooks, Gwendolyn. "The Second Sermon on the Warpland." In *In the Mecca*, 54. New York: Harper and Row, 1968.

Brown, Bill. "Thing Theory." In *Things*, edited by Bill Brown, 1–8. Chicago: University of Chicago Press, 2004.

Brown, Wendy. *States of Injury: Power and Freedom in Late Modernity*. Princeton, N.J.: Princeton University Press, 1995.

Brown, William Wells. "A Lecture before the Female Anti-Slavery Society of Salem, Massachusetts (1847)." In *William Wells Brown: Clotel and Other Writings*, edited by William Wells Brown and Ezra Greenspan, 855–872. New York: Library of America, 2014.

Butler, Judith. "Performative Acts and Gender Constitution: An Essay in Phenomenology and Feminist Theory." In *The Performance Studies Reader*, edited by Henry Bial, 154–166. London: Routledge, 2007.

Butler, Octavia. *Kindred*. Boston: Beacon, 1979.

Carpio, Glenda R. *Laughing Fit to Kill: Black Humor in the Fictions of Slavery*. Oxford: Oxford University Press, 2008.

Carr, Robert. *Black Nationalism and the New World*. Durham, N.C.: Duke University Press, 2002.

Carrier, David. *The Aesthetics of Comics*. University Park: Pennsylvania State University Press, 2000.

Caruth, Cathy, ed. *Trauma: Explorations in Memory*. Baltimore: Johns Hopkins University Press, 2000.

———, ed. *Unclaimed Experience: Trauma, Narrative, and History*. Baltimore: Johns Hopkins University Press, 1996.

Catanese, Brandi Wilkins. "'We Must Keep on Writing': The Plays of Aishah Rahman." In *Contemporary African American Women Playwrights*, edited by Philip C. Kolin, 115–131. New York: Routledge, 2007.

Chambers-Letson, Joshua. "Reparative Feminisms, Repairing Feminism: Reparation, Postcolonial Violence, and Feminism." *Women and Performance* 16 (July 2006): 169–189.

Chambliss, Julian. "Black Kirby NOW: An Interview with John Jennings." *Pop Matters*, February 20, 2014. http://www.popmatters.com/feature/179294-black-kirby-now-an -interview-with-john-jennings/. Accessed December 30, 2015.

Chaney, Michael A. "Slave Memory without Words in Kyle Baker's *Nat Turner*." *Callaloo* 36, no. 2 (2013): 279–297.

Chappelle, Dave. *Chappelle's Show*. New York: Comedy Central, 2003–2006. DVD.

———. *Killin' Them Softly*, directed by Stan Lathan. New York: Home Box Office, 2000. DVD.

Cheng, Anne Anlin. "Psychoanalysis without Symptoms." *differences* 20, no. 1 (2009): 87–101.

———. "Shine: On Race, Glamour, and the Modern." *PMLA* 126 (October 2011): 1022–1041.

Chidester, Phil, Shannon Campbell, and Jamel Bell. "'Black Is Blak': *Bamboozled* and the Crisis of a Postmodern Racial Identity." *Howard Journal of Communications* 17 (February 2006): 289.

Cima, Gay. *Performing Anti-Slavery: Activist Women on Antebellum Stages*. Cambridge: Cambridge University Press, 2014.

Coates, Ta-Nehisi. "The Case for Reparations." *Atlantic*, May 21, 2014. http://www .theatlantic.com/magazine/archive/2014/06/the-case-for-reparations/361631/. Accessed December 30, 2015.

Cobb, Jasmine Nichole. "Directed by Himself: Steve McQueen's *12 Years a Slave*." *American Literary History* 26 (summer 2014): 339–346.

Cobb, Jelani. "Tarantino Unchained." *New Yorker*, January 2, 2013. http://www.newyorker .com/culture/culture-desk/tarantino-unchained. Accessed November 3, 2015.

Colbert, Soyica Diggs. "'When I Die, I Won't Stay Dead': The Future of the Human in Suzan-Lori Parks's *The Death of the Last Black Man in the Whole Entire World*." *Boundary 2* 39, no. 3 (2012): 191–220.

Collins, Patricia Hill. *From Black Power to Hip Hop: Racism, Nationalism, and Feminism*. Philadelphia: Temple University Press, 2006.

The Color Purple, directed by Stephen Spielberg. Burbank, Calif.: Warner Bros. Pictures, 1985. DVD.

Connor, Marc. *The Aesthetics of Toni Morrison*. Jackson: University of Mississippi Press, 2000.

Cooper, Anna Julia. "Womanhood a Vital Element in the Regeneration and Progress of a Race." In *A Voice from the South*, 9–47. New York: Oxford University Press, 1998.

Copeland, Huey. *Bound to Appear: Art, Slavery, and the Site of Blackness in Multicultural America*. Chicago: University of Chicago Press, 2013.

Copjec, Joan. *Imagine There's No Woman: Ethics and Sublimation*. Cambridge, Mass.: MIT Press, 2002.

Crouch, Stanley, with Eric Lott, Margo Jefferson, and Michele Wallace. "Minding the Messenger: A Symposium on *Bamboozled*." *Black Renaissance* 3 (summer 2001): 1–14.

Danticat, Edwidge. "Foreword." In *The Infamous Rosalie*, by Evelyne Trouillot, translated by M. A. Salvodon, vii–ix. Lincoln: University of Nebraska Press, 2013.

Dargas, Manohla. "The Blood and Tears, not the Magnolias." *New York Times*, October 17, 2013. http://www.nytimes.com/2013/10/18/movies/12-years-a-slave-holds-nothing -back-in-show-of-suffering.html?pagewanted=all&_r=0. Accessed October 29, 2015.

"Dave Chappelle and Maya Angelou." *Iconoclasts*, directed by Joe Berlinger, episode 6. New York: Sundance Institute, 2006. DVD.

Davis, Colin. "Hauntology, Spectres, and Phantoms." *French Studies* 59 (July 2005): 373–379.

Dent, Gina. "Black Pleasure, Black Joy: An Introduction." In *Black Popular Culture*, edited by Gina Dent, 1–19. New York: New Press, 1998.

Derrida, Jacques. *Of Grammatology*, translated by G. Chakravorty Spivak. Baltimore: Johns Hopkins University Press, 1997.

———. *Specters of Marx*, translated by Peggy Kamuf. New York: Routledge, 1994.

Douglass, Frederick. *Narrative of the Life of Frederick Douglass, an American Slave, Written by Himself*. Boston: Anti-Slavery Office, 1845.

Dubois, Laurent. *Avengers of the New World: The Story of the Haitian Revolution*. Cambridge, Mass.: Harvard University Press, 2004.

Du Bois, W.E.B. *The Souls of Black Folk*. New York: Barnes and Noble Classics, 2003.

———. *Haiti: The Aftershocks of History*. New York: Metropolitan, 2012.

Duden, Barbara. *Disembodying Women: Perspectives on Pregnancy and the Unborn*. Cambridge, Mass.: Harvard University Press, 1993.

Dunbar, Paul Laurence. "Frederick Douglass." In *In Memoriam: Frederick Douglass*, edited by Helen Douglass, 168–169. Philadelphia: Yorston, 1897.

———. *The Collected Poetry of Paul Laurence Dunbar*, edited by Joanne M. Braxton. Charlottesville: University of Virginia Press, 1993.

Edelman, Lee. *No Future: Queer Theory and the Death Drive*. Durham, N.C.: Duke University Press, 2004.

Edkins, Jenny. *Trauma and the Memory of Politics.* Cambridge: Cambridge University Press, 2003.

Edwards, Erica. *Charisma and the Fictions of Black Leadership.* Minneapolis: University of Minnesota Press, 2012.

———. "Tuning in to *Precious:* The Black Women's Empowerment Adaptation and the Interruption of the Absurd." *Black Camera* 4 (winter 2012): 74–95.

Elam, Harry J., Jr., and Michele Elam. "Blood Debt: Reparations in Langston Hughes's *Mulatto.*" *Theater Journal* 61 (March 2009): 85–103.

Ellison, Ralph. "Change the Joke and Slip the Yoke." *Partisan Review* 25, no. 2 (1958): 212–222.

Ernest, John. "(Re)mediated History: *12 Years a Slave.*" *American Literary History* 26, no. 2 (2013): 367–373.

Ethnic Notions, directed by Marlon Riggs. Lancaster, Pa.: California Newsreel, 1987. DVD.

Fanon, Frantz. *Black Skin, White Masks,* translated by Charles Markmann. New York: Grove, 1967.

Farley, Christopher. "Dave Speaks." *Time,* May 14, 2005. http://content.time.com/time/magazine/article/0,9171,1061512,00.html. Accessed December 30, 2015.

Fassin, Didier, and Richard Rechtman. *Empire of Trauma: An Inquiry into the Condition of Victimhood.* Princeton, N.J.: Princeton University Press, 2009.

Fauset, Jessie. "The Gift of Laughter." In *The New Negro,* edited by Alain Locke, 161–167. New York: Boni, 1925.

Felman, Shoshana. *The Juridical Unconscious: Trials and Traumas in the Twentieth Century.* Cambridge, Mass.: Harvard University Press, 2002.

Felman, Shoshana, and Dori Laub. *Testimony: Crises of Witnessing in Literature, Psychoanalysis, and History.* New York: Routledge, 1991.

Fick, Carolyn. *The Making of Haiti: The Saint Domingue Revolution from Below.* Knoxville: University of Tennessee Press, 1990.

Fischer, Sibylle. *Modernity Disavowed: Haiti and the Cultures of Slavery in the Age of Revolution.* Durham, N.C.: Duke University Press, 2004.

Fleetwood, Nicole. *On Racial Icons: Blackness and the Public Imagination.* New Brunswick, N.J.: Rutgers University Press, 2014.

Freud, Sigmund. *Jokes and Their Relation to the Unconscious.* New York: Norton, 1960.

Garraway, Doris. "Memory As Reparation? The Politics of Remembering Slavery in France from Abolition to the Loi Taubira." *International Journal of Francophone Studies* 11, no. 3 (2008): 365–386.

———. *Tree of Liberty: Cultural Legacies of the Haitian Revolution in the Atlantic World.* Charlottesville: University of Virginia Press, 2008.

Garrett, Shawn-Marie. "Return of the Repressed." *Theater* 32 (summer 2002): 26–43.

Gates, Henry Louis, Jr., and Kwame Anthony Appiah, eds.. *Toni Morrison: Critical Perspectives Past and Present.* Princeton, N.J.: Princeton University Press, 2004.

Geggus, David Patrick. "Saint-Domingue on the Eve of the Revolution." In *The World of the Haitian Revolution.* Bloomington: Indiana University Press, 2009.

George, Nelson. *Hip Hop America.* New York: Penguin, 1998.

Gettell, Oliver. "'12 Years a Slave': A Captivating Story of Survival." *Los Angeles Times,* October 18, 2013. http://articles.latimes.com/2013/oct/18/entertainment/la-et-mn-12-years-a-slave-movie-reviews-critics-20131018. Accessed October 29, 2015.

Gilmore, Ruth Wilson. *Golden Gulag: Prisons, Surplus, Crisis, and Opposition in Globalizing California.* Berkeley: University of California Press, 2007.

Golden, Thelma. "Post-Black." In *Freestyle,* edited by Christine Y. Kim and Franklin Sirmans, 14–15. New York: Studio Museum of Harlem, 2001.

Gordon, Devin, and Allison Samuels. "Dave Chappelle: Fears of a Clown," *Newsweek,* May 16, 2005, 60.

Gordon, Lewis R. *Bad Faith and Antiblack Racism*. Atlantic Highlands, N.J.: Humanities Press International, 1995.

Groensteen, Thierry. "The Monstrator, the Recitant, and the Shadow of the Narrator." *European Comic Art* 3, no. 1 (2010): 1–21.

Gueye, Abdoulaye, "Memory at Issue: On Slavery and the Slave Trade among Black French." *Canadian Journal of African Studies* 45, no. 1 (2011): 77–107.

Haggins, Bambi. "In the Wake of 'The Nigger Pixie.'" In *Satire TV: Politics and Comedy in the Post-Network Era*, edited by Jonathan Gray and Jeffrey Jones, 233–251. New York: New York University Press, 2009.

Hall, Jacquelyn Dowd. "The Long Civil Rights Movement and the Political Uses of the Past." *Journal of American History* 91 (March 2005): 1233–1263.

Hall, Stuart. "Cultural Identity and Diaspora." In *Colonial Discourse and Postcolonial Theory: A Reader*, edited by Patrick Williams and Laura Chrisman, 392–403. New York: Columbia University Press, 1994.

———. "New Ethnicities." In *Stuart Hall: Critical Dialogues in Cultural Studies*, edited by David Morley and Kuan-Hsing Chen, 442–451. New York: Routledge, 1996.

———. "What Is This 'Black' in Black Popular Culture?" In *Black Popular Culture*, edited by Gina Dent, 21–33. New York: New Press, 1998.

Hartman, Saidiya. *Lose Your Mother: A Journey along the Atlantic Slave Route*. New York: Farrar, Straus and Giroux, 2007.

———. *Scenes of Subjection: Terror, Slavery, and Self-Making in Nineteenth-Century America*. Oxford: Oxford University Press, 1997.

———. "The Time of Slavery." *South Atlantic Quarterly* 110, no. 4 (2002): 757–777.

Hayden, Robert. "Runagate Runagate." In *Collected Poems*, edited by Robert Hayden and Frederick Glaysher, 59–61. New York: Norton, 2013.

Hayes, Terrance. "The Avocado." In *Lighthead*, 27–28. New York: Penguin, 2010.

Heidegger, Martin. *Being and Time*, translated by Joan Stambaugh. Albany: State University of New York Press, 2010.

———. *Introduction to Metaphysics*, 2nd ed., translated by Gregory Fried and Richard Polt. New Haven, Conn.: Yale University Press, 2014.

Herron, Carolivia. *Thereafter Johnnie*. New York: Vintage, 1991.

Hill, Laban Carrick, and Bryan Collier, *Dave the Potter: Artist, Poet, Slave*. New York: Little, Brown, 2010.

Hirsch, Marianne. "Mourning and Postmemory." In *Graphic Subjects: Critical Essays on Autobiography and Graphic Novels*, edited by Michael A. Chaney, 17–44. Madison: University of Wisconsin Press, 2011.

———. "Surviving Images: Holocaust Photographs and the Work of Postmemory." *Yale Journal of Criticism* 14 (spring 2001): 5–37.

Holland, Sharon. *Raising the Dead*. Durham, N.C.: Duke University Press, 2000.

hooks, bell. "Male Heroes and Female Sex Objects: Sexism in Spike Lee's *Malcolm X*." *Cineaste* 19, no. 4 (1992): 13–15.

Hornaday, Ann. "'12 Years a Slave' Movie Review: A Masterpiece of Form, Content, Emotion, and Performance." *Washington Post*, October 17, 2013. https://www .washingtonpost.com/goingoutguide/movies/12-years-a-slave-movie-review-a -masterpiece-of-form-content-emotion-and-performance/2013/10/16/1b158e76-34e8 -11e3-8a0e-4e2cf80831fc_story.html. Accessed December 30, 2015.

Hurston, Zora Neale. "Characteristics of Negro Expression." In *Within the Circle: An Anthology of African American Literary Criticism from the Harlem Renaissance to the Present*, edited by Angelyn Mitchell, 79–94. Durham, N.C.: Duke University Press, 1994.

Huyssen, Andreas. *Present Pasts: Urban Palimpsests and the Politics of Memory*. Stanford, Calif.: Stanford University Press, 2003.

Iton, Richard. *In Search of the Black Fantastic: Politics and Popular Culture in the Post–Civil Rights Era*. New York: Oxford University Press, 2008.

Jackson, Major. "The Historical Poem." *American Poet* 35 (fall 2008): 3–6.

Jackson, Robert, and Carl Rosberg. *Personal Rule in Black Africa*. Berkeley: University of California Press, 1982.

JanMohammed, Abdul. *The Death-Bound Subject: Richard Wright's Archaeology of Death*. Durham, N.C.: Duke University Press, 2005.

Jarrett, Gene. *Representing the Race: A New Political History of African American Literature*. New York: New York University Press, 2011.

Jenson, Deborah. *Beyond the Slave Narrative: Politics, Sex, and Manuscripts in the Haitian Revolution*. Liverpool: Liverpool University Press, 2011.

Johnson, Charles. "The End of Black American Narrative." *American Scholar* 77, no. 3 (2008): 32–43.

Johnson, Mat, and Warren Pleece. *Incognegro: A Graphic Mystery*. New York: DC Comics, 2008.

Johnson, Walter. "Possible Pasts: Some Speculations on Time, Temporality, and the History of Atlantic Slavery." *Amerikastudien/American Studies* 45, no. 4 (2000): 485–499.

———. *Soul by Soul: Life inside the Antebellum Slave Market*. Cambridge, Mass.: Harvard University Press, 1999.

Jones, Edward P. *The Known World*. New York: Amistad, 2003.

Judy, Ronald. "Fanon's Body of Black Experience." In *Fanon: A Critical Reader*, edited by Lewis Gordon, T. Demean Sharpley-Whiting, and Renee T. White, 53–73. Hoboken, N.J.: Wiley, 1996.

Julien, Isaac. "Black Is, Black Ain't: Notes Toward De-essentializing Blackness." In *Black Popular Culture*, edited by Gina Dent, 255–263. Seattle: Bay Press, 1992.

Kaisary, Philip. *The Haitian Revolution in the Literary Imagination: Radical Horizons, Conservative Constraints*. Charlottesville: University of Virginia, 2014.

Keeling, Kara. "Passing for Human: *Bamboozled* and Digital Humanism." *Women and Performance* 15 (June 2005): 237–250.

Kelly, Robin. "The US v. Trayvon Martin." *Counterpunch*, July 2013. Accessed March 15, 2014. http://www.counterpunch.org/2013/07/15/the-us-v-trayvon-martin/. Accessed October 28, 2014.

Koger, Alicia Kae. "Jazz Form and Jazz Function: An Analysis of *Unfinished Women Cry in No Man's Land While a Bird Dies in a Gilded Cage*." *MELUS* 16, no. 3 (1989–1990): 99–111.

Krefting, Rebecca. *All Joking Aside: American Humor and Its Discontents*. Baltimore: Johns Hopkins University Press, 2014.

Kristeva, Julia. *Powers of Horror: An Essay on Abjection*. Translated by Leon S. Roudiez. New York: Columbia University Press, 1982.

———. "Stabat Mater." in *The Female Body in Western Culture: Contemporary Perspectives*, edited by Susan Rubin Suleiman, translated by Arthur Goldhammer, 99–118. Cambridge, Mass.: Harvard University Press, 1985.

Kunka, Andrew J. "Intertextuality and the Historical Graphic Narrative: Kyle Baker's *Nat Turner* and the Styron Controversy." *College Literature* 38, no. 3 (2011): 168–193.

Lacan, Jacques. *The Seminar of Jacques Lacan: The Four Fundamental Concepts of Psychoanalysis*. New York: Norton, 1998.

La Capra, Dominick. *Writing History, Writing Trauma*. Baltimore: Johns Hopkins University Press, 2000.

Larrier, Renée. "Inheritances: Legacies and Lifelines in Trouillot's *Rosalie l'infâme*." *Dalhousie French Studies* 28 (fall 2009): 135–145.

Laski, Greg. "Falling Back into History: The Uncanny Trauma of Blackface Minstrelsy in Spike Lee's *Bamboozled*." *Callaloo* 33 (fall 2010): 1093–1115.

Leary, Joy. *Post Traumatic Slave Syndrome: America's Legacy of Enduring Injury and Healing*. Portland, Ore.: Uptone, 2005.

Levinas, Emmanuel. *Time and the Other and Other Essays*, translated by Richard A. Cohen. Pittsburgh: Duquesne University Press, 1987.

Levine, Robert S. *Dislocating Race and Nation: Episodes in Nineteenth-Century American Literary Nationalism*. Chapel Hill: University of North Carolina Press, 2008.

Leys, Ruth. *Trauma: A Genealogy*. Chicago: University of Chicago Press, 2000.

Li, Stephanie. "*12 Years a Slave* As Neo-Slave Narrative." *American Literary History* 26, no. 2 (2013): 326–331.

Lin, Maya. "Making the Memorial." *New York Review of Books*, November 2, 2000. http://www.nybooks.com/articles/archives/2000/nov/02/making-the-memorial/. Accessed September 6, 2015.

Lipsitz, George. *The Possessive Investment in Whiteness: How White People Profit from Identity Politics*. Philadelphia: Temple University Press, 2006.

Lipton, James. "Dave Chappelle." *Inside the Actor's Studio*, season 12, episode 11. New York: Actor's Studio, 2006. DVD.

"Lizzie Mae." *Ask a Slave*, directed by Jordan Black. Web series. http://www.askaslave.com/lizzie-mae.html. Accessed December 3, 2015.

Lott, Eric. *Love and Theft: Blackface Minstrelsy and the American Working Class*. Oxford: Oxford University Press, 1993.

Love, Monifa. *Freedom in the Dismal*. Kaneohe, Hawaii: Plover, 1998.

Luckhurst, Roger. *The Trauma Question*. New York: Routledge, 2008.

MacIntyre, Alasdair. *After Virtue: A Study in Moral Theory*. Notre Dame, Ind.: University of Notre Dame Press, 2007.

Madhubuti, Haki (Don L. Lee). "DON'T CRY, SCREAM." In *Don't Cry, Scream*, 27–31. Detroit: Broadside, 1969.

Manovich, Lev. *The Language of New Media*. Cambridge, Mass.: MIT Press, 2001.

Manring, Maurice. *Slave in a Box: The Strange Career of Aunt Jemima*. Charlottesville: University of Virginia Press, 1998.

Martin, Michel. "Toni Morrison on Bondage and a Post-Racial Age." *National Public Radio*, December 10, 2008. http://www.npr.org/templates/story/story.php?storyId=98072491. Accessed September 6, 2015.

Massood, Paula J. "Introduction: We've Gotta Have It—Spike Lee, African American Film, and Cinema Studies." In *The Spike Lee Reader*, edited by Paula J. Massood, xv–xxviii. Philadelphia: Temple University Press, 2008.

Mayfield, Curtis. "We People Who Are Darker Than Blue." In *Curtis*. Chicago: Curtom, 1970. LP.

Maynard, Patrick. *Drawing Distinctions: The Varieties of Graphic Expression*. Ithaca, N.Y.: Cornell University Press, 2005.

Mbembe, Achille. "Necropolitics." *Public Culture* 15, no. 1 (2003): 11–40.

McBride, Dwight. *Impossible Witnesses: Truth, Abolitionism, and Slave Testimony*. New York: New York University Press, 2002.

Mehta, Brinda. *Notions of Identity, Diaspora, and Gender in Caribbean Women's Writing*. New York: Palgrave Macmillan, 2009.

Metzl, Jonathan. *Protest Psychosis: How Schizophrenia Became a Black Disease*. Boston: Beacon, 2010.

Meyer, Eve. "Architecture Where the Desire May Live." Interview with Jacques Derrida. In *Rethinking Architecture: A Reader in Cultural Theory*, edited by Neil Leach, 317–323. London: Routledge, 1997.

Michaels, Walter Benn. *The Shape of the Signifier: 1967 to the End of History*. Princeton, N.J.: Princeton University Press, 2004.

Mitchell, Angelyn. *The Freedom to Remember: Narrative, Slavery, and Gender in Contemporary Black Women's Fiction*. New Brunswick, N.J.: Rutgers University Press, 2002.

Mitchell, W.J.T. "Living Color: Race, Stereotype, and the Animation in Spike Lee's *Bamboozled*." In *What Do Pictures Want? The Lives and Loves of Images*, 294–308. Chicago: University of Chicago Press, 2005.

Mor, Amus. "Poem to the Hip Generation." In *Black Spirits: A Festival of New Black Poets in America*, edited by Woodie King, 134–141. New York: Vintage, 1972.

More Than a Month, directed by Shukree Hassan Tilghman. Arlington, Va.: Public Broadcasting Service, 2009. DVD.

Morgan, Daniel. "Rethinking Bazin: Ontology and Realist Aesthetics," *Critical Inquiry* 32 (spring 2006): 443–481.

Morgan, Lynn, and Meredith Wilson Michael. *Fetal Subjects, Female Positions*. Philadelphia: University of Pennsylvania Press, 1999.

Morris, Susan Booker. "*Bamboozled*: Political Parodic Postmodernism." *West Virginia University Philological Papers* 50 (fall 2003): 67–76.

Morrison, Toni. *Beloved*. New York: Vintage, 2004.

———. *A Mercy*. New York: Vintage, 2008.

———. "The Site of Memory." In *Inventing the Truth: The Art and Craft of Memoir*, edited by William Zinsser and Russell Baker, 2nd ed., 83–102. Boston: Houghton Mifflin, 1995.

Moten, Fred. "The Case of Blackness," *Criticism* 50 (spring 2008): 177–218.

———. *In the Break: The Aesthetics of the Black Radical Tradition*. Minneapolis: University of Minnesota Press, 2003.

Ndounou, Monica. *Shaping the Future of African American Film: Color-Coded Economics and the Story Behind the Numbers*. New Brunswick, N.J.: Rutgers University Press, 2014.

Neal, Mark Anthony. *Soul Babies: Black Popular Culture and the Post-Soul Aesthetic*. New York: Routledge, 2002.

Nietzsche, Friedrich. *The Will to Power*, translated by Walter Kaufman and R. J. Hollingdale. New York: Vintage, 1968.

Northup, Solomon. *Twelve Years a Slave*. Vancouver: Engage Books, 2013.

Nyong'o, Tavia. *The Amalgamation Waltz: Race Performance and the Ruses*. Minneapolis: University of Minnesota Press, 2009.

Olin, Margaret. "Graven Images on Video? The Second Commandment and Jewish Identity." In *Complex Identities: Jewish Consciousness and Modern Art*, edited by Matthew Baigell and Milly Heyd, 34–50. New Brunswick, N.J.: Rutgers University Press, 2000.

Oliver, Melvin, and Robert Shapiro. *Black Wealth, White Wealth: A New Perspective on Racial Inequality*. New York: Routledge, 2006.

Parrott, Russell. "An Oration on the Abolition of the Slave Trade." In *Early Negro Writing, 1760–1837*, edited by Dorothy Porter, 383–390. Baltimore: Black Classic Press, 1995.

Patterson, Orlando. *Slavery and Social Death*. Cambridge, Mass.: Harvard University Press, 1982.

———. "Toward a Future That Has No Past: Reflections on the Fate of Blacks in the Americas." *Public Interest* 27 (spring 1972): 25–62.

Patterson, Robert J. *Exodus Politics: Civil Rights and Leadership in African American Literature and Culture*. Charlottesville: University of Virginia Press, 2013.

Petherbridge, Deanna. *The Primacy of Drawing: Histories and Theories of Practice*. New Haven, Conn.: Yale University Press, 2010.

Piehowski, Victoria. "'Business as Usual': Sex, Race, and Work in Spike Lee's *Bamboozled*." *Frontiers* 33 (November 2012): 1–23.

Podair, Jerald. "'One City, One Standard': The Struggle for Equality in Rudolph Giuliani's New York." In *Civil Rights in New York City: From World War II to the Giuliani Era*, 204–218. New York: Fordham University Press, 2011.

Powell, Kevin. "Heaven Hell Dave Chappelle: The Agonizing Return of the Funniest Man in America." *Esquire*, April 29, 2006. http://www.esquire.com/entertainment/movies/a1122/esq0506chappelle-92/. Accessed December 30, 2015.

Priestley, Brian. *Chasin' the Bird: The Life and Legacy of Charlie Parker*. New York: Oxford University Press, 2006.

Rahman, Aishah. "Unfinished Women." In *Plays by Aishah Rahman*, introduction by Thadious M. Davis, 1–36. New York: Broadway Play Publishing, 1997.

Ramazani, Jahan. *The Hybrid Muse: Postcolonial Poetry in English*. Chicago: University of Chicago Press, 2001.

Rana, Aziz. "Break the Silence." *Asian American Writers Workshop*. http://aaww.org/break-the-silence-vijay-prashad/. Accessed June 25, 2014.

Reed, Adolph, Jr. *The Jesse Jackson Phenomenon*. New Haven, Conn.: Yale University Press, 1986.

Reed, Adolph, Jr., and Kenneth Warren. "Introduction." In *Renewing Black Intellectual History: The Ideological and Material Foundations of African American Thought*, edited by Adolph Reed Jr. and Kenneth Warren, vii–xi. Boulder, Colo.: Paradigm, 2010.

Reinhardt, Catherine. "Slavery and Commemoration: Remembering the French Abolitionary Decree 150 Years Later." In *Memory, Empire, and Postcolonialism: The Legacies of French Colonialism*, edited by Alec Hargreaves, 11–36. Lanham, Md.: Lexington, 2005.

Rieff, David. "In Defense of Afro-Pessimism." *World Policy Journal* 15, no. 4 (1998–1999): 10–22.

Roberts, Dorothy. *Killing the Black Body*. New York: Vintage, 1998.

Robinson, Randall. *The Debt: What America Owes to Blacks*. New York: Plume, 1991.

Rock, Chris. *Chris Rock: Bring the Pain*, directed by Keith Truesdell. New York: Home Box Office, 1996. DVD.

Rogin, Michael. *Blackface, White Noise: Jewish Immigrants in the Hollywood Melting Pot*. Berkeley: University of California Press, 1998.

Rohrbach, Augusta. "'Truth Stronger and Stranger than Fiction': Reexamining William Lloyd Garrison's *Liberator*." *American Literature* 73, no. 4 (2001): 727–757.

Rolinson, Mary G. *Grassroots Garveyism: The Universal Negro Improvement Association in the Rural South, 1920–1927*. Chapel Hill: University of North Carolina Press, 2007.

Rooks, Noliwe M. *White Money/Black Power: The Surprising History of African American Studies and the Crisis of Race and Higher Education*. Boston: Beacon, 2006.

Rothenberg, Paula. *White Privilege: Essential Readings on the Other Side of Racism*. New York: Worth, 2011.

Rowell, Charles H. "An Interview with Gayl Jones." *Callaloo* 16 (October 1982): 32–53.

——. "'The Poet in the Enchanted Shoe Factory': An Interview with Terrance Hayes." *Callaloo* 27 (fall 2004): 1068–1081.

Rushdy, Ashraf H. A. *Neo-Slave Narratives: Studies in the Social Logic of a Literary Form*. Oxford: Oxford University Press, 1999.

——. *Remembering Generations: Race and Family in Contemporary African American Fiction*. Chapel Hill: University of North Carolina Press, 2001.

Russell, Ross. *Bird Lives: The High Life and Hard Times of Charlie (Yardbird) Parker*. New York: Charterhouse, 1973.

Schmidt, Nelly. "Teaching and Commemorating Slavery and Abolition in France." In *Politics of Memory: Making Slavery Visible in the Public Space*, edited by Ana Lucia Araujo, 106–123. New York: Routledge, 2013.

Schneider, Rebecca. "It Seems As If . . . I Am Dead: Zombie Capitalism and Theatrical Labor." *TDR* 56 (winter 2012): 150–162.

Scott, Darieck. *Extravagant Abjection: Blackness, Power, and Sexuality in the African American Literary Imagination.* New York: New York University Press, 2010.

Scott, David. *Conscripts of Modernity: The Tragedy of Colonial Enlightenment.* Durham, N.C.: Duke University Press, 2004.

———. "The Government of Freedom." In *New Caribbean Thought: A Reader*, edited by Brain Meeks and Folke Lindahl, 428–452. Kingston, Jamaica: University of West Indies Press, 2001.

Scott-Heron, Gil. "Comment No. 1." In *Small Talk at 125th and Lenox*. New York: Flying Dutchman/RCA, 1970. LP.

Sepinwall, Alyssa Goldstein. *Haitian History: New Perspectives.* New York: Routledge, 2013.

———. "Happy As a Slave: Review of *Toussaint Louverture.*" *Fiction and Film for French Historians.* http://h-france.net/fffh/maybe-missed/happy-as-a-slave-the-toussaint-louverture-miniseries/. Accessed November 16, 2015.

Sexton, Jared. "People-of-Color-Blindness: Notes on the Afterlife of Slavery," *Social Text* 28 (summer 2010): 31–56.

———. "The Social Life of Social Death: On Afro-Pessimism and Black Optimism." *InTensions* 5 (fall/winter 2011): 1–47.

Shange, Ntozake. "On 'What Is It We Really Harvestin' Here?'" In *In Fact: The Best of Creative Nonfiction*, edited by Lee Gutkind, 109–118. New York: Norton, 2005.

Sharkey, Betsy. "Oscars 2014: For Many, '12 Years a Slave' Is Too Hard to Watch." *Los Angeles Times*, February 27, 2014. http://articles.latimes.com/2014/feb/27/entertainment/la-et-mn-12-years-a-slave-notebook-20140227. Accessed December 9, 2015.

Sharpe, Christina. *Monstrous Intimacies: Making Post-Slavery Subjects.* Durham, N.C.: Duke University Press, 2010.

Shaw, Gwendolyn DuBois. *Seeing the Unspeakable: The Art of Kara Walker.* Durham, N.C.: Duke University Press, 2004.

Sheller, Mimi. *Citizenship from Below: Erotic Agency and Caribbean Freedom.* Durham, N.C.: Duke University Press, 2012.

Shockley, Evie. "Going Overboard: African American Poetic Innovation and the Middle Passage." *Contemporary Literature* 52 (winter 2011): 791–817.

———. *the new black.* Middletown, Conn.: Wesleyan University Press, 2011.

Smith, Caleb. *The Prison and the American Imagination.* New Haven, Conn.: Yale University Press, 2009.

Smith, Valerie. "Black Life in Balance: *12 Years a Slave.*" *American Literary History* 26, no. 2 (2013): 362–366.

Snider, John C. S "Interview: Octavia E. Butler." In *Conversations with Octavia Butler*, edited by Consuela Francis, 213–218. Jackson: University Press of Mississippi, 2010.

Snitow, Ann. "Review of *Beloved* by Toni Morrison." In *Toni Morrison: Critical Perspectives Past and Present*, edited by Henry Louis Gates Jr. and Kwame Anthony Appiah, 26–31. New York: Amistad, 1993.

Spillers, Hortense. *Black, White, and in Color: Essays on American Literature and Culture.* Chicago: University of Chicago Press, 2003.

———. "Changing the Letter: The Yokes, the Jokes of Discourse, or Mrs. Stowe, Mr. Reed." In *Slavery and the Literary Imagination*, edited by Deborah E. McDowell and Arnold Rampersand, 25–61. Baltimore: Johns Hopkins University Press, 1989.

———. "Mama's Baby, Papa's Maybe: An American Grammar Book." *Diacritics* 17 (summer 1987): 64–81.

Sragow, Michael. "Black Like Spike," in *Spike Lee: Interviews,* edited by Cynthia Fuchs, 189–198. Jackson: University Press of Mississippi, 2002.

Stauffer, John. "12 Years between Life and Death." *American Literary History* 26, no. 2 (2013): 317–325.

Stepto, Robert B. *From behind the Veil: A Study of Afro-American Narrative.* Urbana: University of Illinois Press, 1979.

Tate, Greg. "*Bamboozled:* White Supremacy and a Black Way of Being Human." *Cineaste* 26 (March 2001): 15–16.

———. Interview with Mark Sinker. Unpublished transcript, 1991.

Thomas, Bonnie. "Edouard Glissant and the Art of Memory." *Small Axe* 30 (November 2009): 25–36.

Tillet, Salamishah. "'I Got No Comfort in This Life': The Increasing Importance of Patsey in *12 Years a Slave.*" *American Literary History* 26 (summer 2014): 354–361.

———. *Sites of Slavery: Citizenship and Racial Democracy in the Post–Civil Rights Imagination.* Durham, N.C.: Duke University Press, 2012.

Toussaint Louverture, directed by Philippe Niang. Paris: Eloa Prod, 2012. DVD.

Trouillot, Evelyne. *The Infamous Rosalie,* translated by M. A. Salvodon. Lincoln: University of Nebraska Press, 2013.

Trouillot, Michel-Rolph. "The Odd and the Ordinary: Haiti, the Caribbean, and the World," *Cimarron* 2, no. 3 (1990): 3–12.

———. *Silencing the Past: Power and the Production of History.* Boston: Beacon, 1997.

Turan, Kenneth. "McQueen's '12 Years a Slave' Impressive, and Hard to Watch," *Los Angeles Times,* October 17, 2013. http://articles.latimes.com/2013/oct/17/entertainment/la-et -mn-12-years-a-slave-movie-review-20131018. Accessed December 9, 2015.

12 Years a Slave, directed by Steve McQueen. Los Angeles: Fox Searchlight Pictures, 2013. DVD.

"12 Years a Slave—Q&A with Director Steve McQueen and Chiwetel Ejiofor." *National Board of Review.* http://www.nationalboardofreview.org/2013/09/qa-director-steve -mcqueen-chiwetel-ejiofor/. Accessed August 10, 2015.

U.S. Congress. "A Concurrent Resolution Apologizing for the Enslavement and Racial Segregation of African Americans." Res. 26, 111th Cong. (2009–2010).

Vattimo, Gianni. *Nihilism and Emancipation,* translated by William McCuaig. New York: Columbia University Press, 2004.

Walker, David. *David Walker's Appeal to the Coloured Citizens of the World, but in Particular, and very Expressly to those of the United States.* Baltimore: Black Classic Press, 1997.

Walker, Mort. *The Lexicon of Comicana.* Bloomington, Ind.: Comicana Books, 1980.

Wall, Cheryl. *Worrying the Line: Black Women Writers, Lineage, and Literary Tradition.* Chapel Hill: University of North Carolina Press, 2005.

Wallace, Maurice. *Constructing the Black Masculine: Identity and Ideality in African American Men's Literature and Culture, 1775–1995.* Durham, N.C.: Duke University Press, 2002.

Wanzo, Rebecca. "Black Nationalism, Bunrako, and Beyond: Articulating Black Heroism through Cultural Fusion and Comics." In *Multicultural Comics: From Zap to Blue Beetle,* edited by Frederick Luis Aldama, 93–104. Austin: University of Texas Press, 2010.

———. "Wearing Hero-Face: Black Citizens and Melancholic Patriotism in *Truth: Red, White, and Black.*" *Journal of Popular Culture* 42, no. 2 (2009): 339–362.

Warren, Kenneth W. *What Was African American Literature?* Cambridge, Mass.: Harvard University Press, 2011.

Watkins, Mel. *African American Humor: The Best Black Comedy from Slavery to Today*. Chicago: Chicago Review Press, 2002.

Weheliye, Alexander. *Habeas Viscus: Racializing Assemblages, Biopolitics, and Black Feminist Theories of the Human*. Durham, N.C.: Duke University Press, 2014.

Wesley, John. "The Accursed Share: Genealogy, Temporality, and the Problem of Value in Black Reparations Discourse." *Representations* 92, no. 1 (2005): 81–116.

West, Cornel. "Nihilism in Black America." In *Black Popular Culture*, edited by Gina Dent, 37–47. Seattle: Bay Press, 1992.

White, Hayden. "The Metaphysics of Western Historiography." *Taiwan Journal of East African Studies* 1 (June 2004): 1–16.

Whitted, Qiana J. "'And the Negro Thinks in Hieroglyphics': Comics, Visual Metonymy, and the Spectacle of Blackness." *Journal of Graphic Novels and Comics* 5, no. 1 (2014): 79–100.

———. "Of Slaves and Other Swamp Things: Black Southern History As Comic Book Horror." In *Comics and the U.S. South*, edited by Qiana J. Whitted and Brannon Costello, 187–213. Jackson: University Press of Mississippi, 2012.

Wilderson, Frank B., III. *Red, White, and Black: Cinema and the Structure of U.S. Antagonisms*. Durham, N.C.: Duke University Press, 2010.

Williams, Andrea. "Sex, Marriage, and 12 Years a (Single) Slave." *American Literary History* 26, no. 2 (2013): 347–353.

Williams, Raymond. *Marxism and Literature*. Oxford: Oxford University Press, 1977.

Williams-Forson, Psyche. *Building Houses out of Chicken Legs: Black Women, Food, and Power*. Chapel Hill: University of North Carolina Press, 2006.

Winant, Howard. *The New Politics of Race: Globalism, Difference, Justice*. Minneapolis: University of Minnesota Press, 2004.

Winfrey, Oprah. "Chappelle's Story." In *The Oprah Winfrey Show*, directed by Joseph C. Terry. Chicago: Harpo Productions, 2006, http://www.oprah.com/oprahshow/Chappelles -Story. Accessed December 30, 2015.

Winter, Roger. *On Drawing*. New York: Rowman and Littlefield, 2008.

Woodard, Vincent, Justin Joyce, and Dwight McBride. *The Delectable Negro: Human Consumption and Homoeroticism within U.S. Slave Culture*. New York: New York University Press, 2014.

Woolfork, Lisa. *Embodying American Slavery in Contemporary Culture*. Urbana: University of Illinois Press, 2009.

Woubshet, Dagmawi. *The Calendar of Loss*. Baltimore: Johns Hopkins University Press, 2015.

Wynter, Sylvia. "Making of the New Person." In *Black Metamorphosis: New Natives in a New World*, 243–251. Unpublished manuscript in the archives of the Schomburg Center for Research in Black Culture, New York City.

X, Malcolm. "The Race Problem." Speech to the African Students Association and the NAACP campus chapter. Michigan State University, East Lansing, January 23, 1963.

Yenika-Agbaw, Vivian. *Representing Africa in Children's Literature: Old and New Ways of Seeing*. London: Routledge, 2007.

Zagier, Alan Scher. "Along MLK Boulevards in the USA, an Urban Struggle." *USA Today*, January 19, 2014. http://www.usatoday.com/story/news/nation/2014/01/19/mlk -boulevard-urban-struggle /4648519/. Accessed November 3, 2015.

Zimring, Franklin E. *The City That Became Safe: New York's Lessons for Urban Crime and Its Control*. Oxford: Oxford University Press, 2011.

Žižek, Slavoj. *Event: Philosophy in Transit*. New York: Penguin, 2014.

———. "Melancholy and the Act." In *Did Somebody Say Totalitarianism? Five Interventions in the (Mis)use of a Notion*, 141–189. London: Verso, 2001.

NOTES ON CONTRIBUTORS

GERSHUN AVILEZ is an assistant professor in the Department of English and Comparative Literature at the University of North Carolina, Chapel Hill, and has also served as the director of the Program in Sexuality Studies. He is the author of *Radical Aesthetics and Modern Black Nationalism* (2016), and much of his scholarship explores how questions of gender and sexuality inform artistic production

MICHAEL CHANEY is an associate professor of English at Dartmouth College. He is the author of *Fugitive Vision: Slave Image and Black Identity in Antebellum Narrative* (2008) and editor of *Graphic Subjects: Critical Essays on Autobiography and Graphic Novels* (2011). He has published articles in *ESQ: A Journal of the American Renaissance, Callaloo,* and *African American Review* and is currently working on the monograph *Reading Lessons in Seeing: Form and Trope in the Graphic Novel.* Chaney specializes in nineteenth-century American and African American literature and culture, with a focus on race representation, mixed-race identity, and visual culture. Other research and teaching interests include comics and graphic novels, autobiography, and flash fiction.

SOYICA DIGGS COLBERT is an associate professor of African American studies and theater and performance studies at Georgetown University. She is the author of *The African American Theatrical Body: Reception, Performance, and the Stage* (2011) and editor of the "Black Performance" special issue of *African American Review* (2012). Colbert is currently working on her second book, *Black Movements: Performance and Politics.* She has published articles and reviews in *African American Review, Theater Journal, Boundary 2, South Atlantic Quarterly,* and *Theater Topics* and in the collections *Black Performance Theory, Contemporary African American Women Playwrights,* and *August Wilson: Completing the Cycle.*

MARGO NATALIE CRAWFORD is an associate professor of African American literature and the full interdisciplinary spin of global black studies in the Department of English at Cornell University. She is the author of *Dilution Anxiety and the Black Phallus* (2008) and the coeditor of *New Thoughts on the Black Arts Movement* (2006). Her essays appear in numerous books and journals, including *The Cambridge Companion to American Poetry Post-1945, The Trouble with*

Post-Blackness, The Larry Neal Critical Reader, Want to Start a Revolution?, The Modernist Party, Callaloo, American Literature, Black Renaissance Noire, Black Camera, Publishing Blackness, and the exhibition catalog for the 2013 AfriCOBRA exhibit at the DuSable Museum. Her latest book, *Black Post-Blackness: The Black Arts Movement and Twenty-first-Century Black Aesthetics*, is forthcoming.

RÉGINE MICHELLE JEAN-CHARLES is an associate professor of romance languages and literature with a joint appointment in African and African diaspora studies. She is the author of *Conflict Bodies: The Politics of Rape Representation in the Francophone Imaginary* (2014) as well as several articles and book chapters. Her work has been published in *Callaloo, French Forum, Research in African Literatures, Black Camera*, and *American Quarterly*. Jean-Charles's research focuses on Francophone African and Caribbean literatures and cultures, gender studies, feminist theory, African film, African diasporic literatures and cultures, Haitian studies, violence and representation, and human rights in the humanities.

DOUGLAS A. JONES JR. is an assistant professor of English at Rutgers University, New Brunswick. He is the author of *The Captive Stage: Performance and the Proslavery Imagination of the Antebellum North* (2014).

AIDA LEVY-HUSSEN is an assistant professor of English at the University of Wisconsin, Madison, specializing in African American literature, trauma and memory studies, psychoanalysis, and feminist and queer theory. She has published essays in *African American Review* and *South Atlantic Quarterly*, and her monograph, *How to Read African American Literature: Post–Civil Rights Fiction and the Task of Interpretation*, is forthcoming.

BRANDON J. MANNING is an assistant professor of African American studies and gender and sexuality studies in the Interdisciplinary Degree Program at the University of Nevada, Las Vegas. He is currently writing a book about post-soul satire as a site of black masculine self-expression; and his research and teaching areas include African American literature and culture, black feminist thought, queer theory, and popular culture.

ROBERT J. PATTERSON is an associate professor of African American studies and English and director of the African American Studies Program at Georgetown University. He is the author of *Exodus Politics: Civil Rights and Leadership in African American Literature and Culture* (2013), and his work appears in *South Atlantic Quarterly, Black Camera, Religion and Literature*, the *Cambridge Companion to African American Women's Writing*, the *Journal of Feminist Studies in Religion*, and the *Cambridge Companion to Civil Rights Literature*. He also co-guest-edited a special edition of *South Atlantic Quarterly* on "Black Literature, Black Leadership." Extending his scholarly interests in the post–civil rights era, black popular culture, and the politics of race and gender, Patterson has begun work on a second book, *It's Just Another Sad Love Song: R & B Music and the Politics of Race*.

CALVIN WARREN is an assistant professor of American studies at George Washington University. He was awarded a fellowship in Africology from the University of Wisconsin, Milwaukee, and has received research support from the Ford Foundation, the Mellon Foundation, the Bill and Melinda Gates Foundation, and a faculty grant from George Washington University. His research and teaching interests focus on the intersection of contemporary continental theory, Afro-pessimism, ethics, and African American history, limning the relationship between humanism, antiblack violence, and ethics.

INDEX